Return Ticket

The story of SOUTH WALES Transport

Jonathan Isaacs

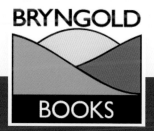

BRYNGOLD BOOKS

Published by Bryngold Books Ltd
100 Brynau Wood, Cimla,
Neath, South Wales SA11 3YQ.

Typesetting, layout, editing and
design by Bryngold Books

Copyright © Bryngold Books 2014
ISBN 978-1-905900-32-9

**Printed and bound in Wales
by Gomer Press**

www.bryngoldbooks.com

About the author

Jonathan Isaacs has always held an interest in buses, but it was a journalistic career spanning more than 30 years that first introduced him to South Wales Transport when he arrived in Swansea to begin a long-term association with the South Wales Evening Post in the mid-1970s.

Whenever he was despatched on an assignment he would jump on a bus — and it would inevitably at the time be operated by the South Wales Transport Company. A keen traveller, Jonathan's leisure time exploits until he passed his driving test also confined him to buses and very often it would be one operated by the same proud company.

He gradually became more acquainted with SWT in the 1970s through his job and that was something that grew further when he was appointed Industrial Correspondent for what became Wales' biggest selling regional daily newspaper.

Jonathan Isaacs

Jonathan's enthusiasm for the South Wales Transport company expanded with each developing news story, the arrival of new vehicles and the gradual metamorphosis in the company's livery. He also got to know many of those who were its driving force through good times and bad. Among them were the managers, trade union leaders, drivers, conductors and even regular passengers.

This helped him gain an in-depth knowledge of the day-to-day life of the company that pioneered the way people in Swansea and the surrounding area moved around at work, rest and play.

Rhondda-born and educated, Jonathan now lives in Swansea. He laments the demise in 1999 of the original, long-serving, legendary South Wales Transport Company and hopes this book will be seen as a fitting salute to the company's existence in what would have been its 100th year.

Itinerary

Foreword

The ease of travel we now enjoy is unprecedented in human experience. Just as the electric light defeated darkness so the train and bus overcame isolation and insularity and widened the meaning of society. All this is shown in this scholarly work by Jonathan Isaacs.

Although the intention was that South Wales Transport should cover the entire area of that same name, almost immediately it was declared that the company should concentrate on Swansea and east Carmarthen bays and their hinterland. To keep it interesting there were a few out of area forays. Consequently, unlike Western Welsh, SWT focussed on a much more tightly defined area, within which there were many frequent services. So, whilst its territory defined South Wales Transport in turn the company did much to create an identifiable area: west South Wales with its hub in Swansea.

As Swansea Corporation never had its own passenger transport operation South Wales took on the role of a major municipal undertaking in 'the hub' and was also a major bus service provider in areas such as Neath, Llanelli and the Swansea Valley, where I spent my formative years. Add in inter-urban, rural and routes into other areas and the romance that was SWT becomes evident. This network meant that I grew up with the company's buses and staff being an ever-present companion, with the Mumbles Train the bonus.

by Professor Garel Rhys
CBE, OBE, FIMI, FIoTA, FLSW, FRSA.

My earliest memories include the feelings of warmth, cosiness and safety travelling on (Swansea) 'Town Service' buses in wartime. I wonder if it was this that made buses so appealing to many of my generation. The SWT buses were so reassuring. They were always there.

This was shown to good effect when we moved to Coedgwilym, Clydach. At times 12 buses an hour passed by on services to Swansea provided by J James, United Welsh and mainly South Wales Transport. This was akin to owning a car.

For many years I would travel to and from school twice a day. I would start with four pennies for the fares and as conductors were very kind I would often end up with some coins at the end of the day. Much later SWT was to play a more important role, taking me to Gwaun Cae Gurwen to see the girl who would become my wife. Finally SWT would transport me to university. Here I became one of the 'elite', a season ticket holder.

All bus companies have distinct personalities, but SWT with its AECs with that classical radiator and grille design was a cut above. With model types such as Regent and Regal they were more than aristocratic. SWT and AEC went together like champagne and strawberries. Indeed, unlike London Transport, SWT had for many years a 100 per cent AEC fleet. This did not kill variety as the company purchased almost every AEC passenger model and often owned oddities like a Crossley-made Bridgemaster or Longwell Green bodied Regal IIIs. This link was two way, as the tough operating conditions experienced by SWT meant that AEC used the company as a test bed with resultant product improvement.

It was testimony to the excellence of SWT maintenance staff that these conditions were dealt with. My uncle was one of the staff at Ravenhill, (to keep a balance another worked for United Welsh). He was part of the pit staff that helped the Swansea Valley Regents to show a clean pair of heels to other double deckers. Yes, those drivers were sporty types and relished competition.

SWT was nothing without its routes and what routes many were. The peerless Mumbles Train (never called a tram) service with its vistas of Swansea Bay, aided by the 77 from Morriston Hospital to Mumbles; the occasional extension of the Brynamman service to the top of the Black Mountains and of course the long, but above all dramatic and scenic 28 to Brecon. A double decker route at that and over the Brecon Beacons . . . fantastic! What was also wonderful was the common use of the Welsh language by staff and passengers. The buses contained the microcosm of the area's culture and society.

As Jonathan Isaacs shows SWT was a company of many superlatives. The gas trailer it made during the war, called the Ravenhill, was judged by London Transport to be uniquely outstanding. The longevity of many of its buses (and trains) meant that SWT was into sustainability long before it was heard of. With its massive preponderance of double deckers it carried far more per bus, if not in total, than Western Welsh and made good use of road (and rail) space.

This book is a fitting testimony to the social and cultural as well as commercial and economic impact of a well-respected bus company. Its intensity of service to the public made it part of so many lives. In the final analysis this book is about people: staff and passengers. The atmosphere of pride, service and contentment within the context of an operating area of much beauty, means that those who read these pages will be better for it.

Tickets, troubles and triumphs

efore the arrival of mass car ownership, if you wanted to get to work, go shopping or set off on a day trip you simply hopped on a bus. Living in or around Swansea that usually meant you were conveyed to your destination by what was often affectionately referred to as 'The Transport' — the South Wales Transport Company to be precise.

The company was formed in February, 1914 and logged its first revenue earning journey in May of the same year with just two vehicles to its name. It was a modest trip of just a few miles, with a handful of local people, but it marked the birth of a passenger carrying legend.

Within a relatively short space of time, the company had grown enormously. More passengers meant more vehicles and with them came the opportunity for route expansion. Like most companies, South Wales Transport had its share of troubles, but it simply changed gear and triumphantly drove itself out of them. And all the while it continued to expand both in terms of its fleet and its geographical territory — some of the most difficult in Britain.

There was a love affair at the centre of all this too. It was sparked by the company's passion for vehicles produced by one of the country's biggest bus builders — AEC. This link began in 1919 and SWT continued to operate AEC engined vehicles until 1986. A product of this long lasting affair was its fondness for one model in particular — the Regent.

The sight and sound of Regents became commonplace wherever South Wales Transport's tentacles reached and they served the company well during its golden years when its annual passenger journeys peaked at 97 million.

But a bus company is not all about buses. The people and politics, the passengers and staff all played a big part in the life of SWT which uniquely owned a railway and at one time also operated trams and trolleybuses.

The route through history ended for South Wales Transport in 1999, 85 years after the company's buses had started to roll. The combination of unsurpassed images, personal anecdotes and reminiscences alongside the history of the company make this book a fitting salute as SWT passes the milestone that marks a century since its inauguration.

The story of South Wales Transport is an important one, not just for the company itself, but also the city of Swansea, in whose development it played such a big part, and also the surrounding towns and villages.

'Courtesy and punctuality are two of the main watchwords of public transport and it should be the aim of everybody to have these words foremost in their mind at all times.'

**Raymond Birch, SWT Chairman
1960-1966**

CHAPTER 1

Pioneering service was a transport milestone

When the first passengers clambered aboard a bus on the outskirts of Swansea one spring day in 1914 they may not have realised it but they were setting off on a journey into the history books. As the vehicle pulled away from the former tram terminus at Ynysforgan on May 2, it put the wheels in motion for a pioneering people mover.

By the time that bus reached its destination, a few miles up the valley at Ynysmeudwy, Pontardawe, the South Wales Transport Company had confirmed that it was serious about making its mark in the growing passenger transport industry. Its early development was slowed by the outbreak of the First World War just weeks later and the four years of hostilities that followed, but by the time it came to the end of the road 85 years later, 'The Transport', as it affectionately became known was one of Britain's longest established bus companies. That, perhaps more than anything else, demonstrated that South Wales Transport was a survivor and for that it owed much to its proud parent, British Electric Traction. Generally referred to as BET, this company grew during the first half of the 20th Century to become one of Britain's largest and most important bus groups giving SWT the strength and resources needed on the difficult journey through the first part of its life.

BET was founded in 1896 by Emile Garcke, a remarkable businessman and entrepreneur. Born in Saxony, Germany, 40 years previously, Garcke's early interests were in banking and mining but over the years he listed among his many talents those of industrialist, author, philosopher and bee keeper. More importantly, as far as SWT was concerned, he was the mastermind behind BET, but it was not with buses in mind that Garcke turned his focus on Swansea during the closing years of the 19th Century. Instead, his sights were set on the town's trams, which at the time were horse drawn. BET had been created with one aim, to convert horse-drawn trams to electricity, and Swansea's were high on his shopping list. But first BET had to wrest control of the system from its original owners, the Swansea Improvements and Tramways Company.

The SITC was registered as a company in 1874 by a group of businessmen who saw the potential offered by the creation of a tramway system in Swansea, which at the time was enjoying a period of enormous growth. They were however, confronted by the problem of its narrow streets which were most unsuitable for trams. So the company — and this was the reason for the word

Driver Bill Harris and conductor Dick Middleditch with a 30hp Milnes-Daimler, one of two taken over by SWT from FL Lewis of Pontardawe in 1914 and used on its first ever route. They were its first double deckers.

Delivered to SWT in 1922, this solid-tyred AEC 403 open top vehicle is about to set off for what would definitely have been a bumpy ride to Mumbles.

improvements in its title — began widening some of the old streets and building other new ones. The first tram line opened on April 12, 1878, and stretched from the town to Morriston. Other sections followed and by the mid-1890s many parts of Swansea were linked by the tramway network. By now however it had become clear to both SITC and Swansea Corporation that horses were not the ideal mode of power. They were incredibly slow. A horse tram took 45 minutes to travel from High Street in the town centre to the terminus at the Duke's Arms in Morriston, a distance of around three miles. Horses also left behind a natural by-product. Anyone who has walked along a country lane shortly after a pair of horses can easily imagine the mess left behind by the 180 equines needed to run Swansea's trams. It might have been fine for gardens and allotments, but not for a growing town centre like Swansea's. Horses also needed to be cared for. They got old and sick and had to be replaced more or less continuously.

So SITC and the corporation agreed that horses should make way for electricity, but fell out over who should run the system. Acts of Parliament were required for such public transport matters and both the company and the council presented their own Bills. To the corporation's fury theirs was rejected on the grounds that it was too speculative a venture for municipal investment. As a result, it was SITC's Act of 1897 that

paved the way for the electrification of Swansea's tramways, but then BET arrived on the scene. It initially offered SITC £54,425 and five shillings for the system, but then changed its mind and instead offered to pay SITC's shareholders £5 for each of their shares. This seemed a good deal to all concerned and BET became the new owner in 1898 by buying the majority of the SITC shares. By 1900 the horses had been made redundant and the town proudly became the first in Wales to boast an electric tramway system.

There was also another transport enterprise in Swansea that BET was keen to get its hands on. This was the steam-powered Mumbles Railway which ran from Rutland Street, around the sweep of Swansea Bay to Mumbles Pier, which had opened in 1898. Mumbles was becoming an increasingly popular seaside destination for day-trippers and holidaymakers, something of which BET was keen to take advantage. The SITC was already negotiating with the railway's owners when BET moved in and in 1899 it was given a lease on the Mumbles Railway and pier for 999 years. This meant that it now had control of public transport over an extensive area of Swansea, from Mumbles across to Morriston.

Just a month after SITC had completed its electrification programme Swansea Corporation announced plans to construct new lines for those parts of the town without access to trams. They also made further unsuccessful attempts to gain control of the SITC system. The council's lines were eventually laid and linked to those run by SITC, so could hardly be run independently. Eventually an agreement was reached

With its destination board indicating SWT's No. 1 route in the Swansea Valley, CY 6531 was a newly delivered AEC 503 Ransomes bodied double decker in 1924. It continued in service until 1932.
Royston Morgan Collection

Chris Taylor Archive

which allowed SITC to lease them from the corporation, but it was a deal that was to prove a headache for South Wales Transport in the years ahead.

While all this was unfolding, BET hadn't forgotten about motor buses which at the dawn of the 20th Century remained simple, basic vehicles. There were already pioneers at work, including the Swansea Motor Omnibus Company which in 1899 began running routes to Sketty and Mumbles. This was the first motor bus service in Wales — another first for Swansea! At one point BET had considered taking over the enterprise, but the proposal never materialised and the company eventually went out of business.

It was clear to BET that motor buses offered huge potential. There were many potential passengers in places like Gower, but laying tram lines across miles of country lanes in the peninsula was impossible. The South Wales valley villages were developing too, as the coal industry grew and these needed to be linked, both with one another and with towns such as Swansea, Neath and Llanelli. But constructing tram lines miles up into the valleys was also out of the question.

The motor bus obviously provided the solution and on February 10, 1914, BET registered the South Wales Transport Company Ltd, as its first such enterprise in Wales. Its first route, from Ynysforgan to Ynysmeudwy, began operation approximately three months later in May following the takeover of FL Lewis, an early bus firm owned by Fred Lewis of Pontardawe. The service, which was soon extended to Ystalyfera used one of Lewis's two Milnes-Daimler double deckers. Like most early double deck vehicles they were open topped, which meant passengers and the two-man crew

suffered in all weathers. Matters were made worse by the fact that these vehicles also had solid tyres which had the bus shuddering over every pothole on roads which at the time were often in appalling condition. Service No. 2 followed just over a month later. This initially ran from Cwmbwrla to Loughor, but was extended to Llanelli on July 11. Both continued for many years, although the first was later extended to run between Swansea and Ystradgynlais. They were followed in August by Service No. 3, between Morriston and Taibach in Port Talbot, and No. 4, which surprisingly, given the fact that SITC was also operating the Mumbles Train, ran from Swansea to Mumbles. At the end of 1914 SWT had 60 employees and owned 26 vehicles which each day ran a total of 1,700 miles and carried 5,550 passengers. This was a tremendous achievement in such a short space of time.

Buses in those days were not only basic, but slow too. The maximum speed allowed was just 12mph. Driver Bill Harris, one of the first to join SWT in 1914, remembered that it was only possible to complete two trips a day between Morriston and Taibach.

"When the lighting on the buses changed from acetylene and paraffin, even candles, to electric light, it caused a sensation," recalled Bill, when he retired from SWT in 1956 at the age of 70. "People lined the route at night to watch the bus pass."

By this time the First World War had begun and Bill was one of the SWT employees who enlisted in 1915 at the same time that 14 of the company's buses were commandeered for military service. Further expansion was hindered as SWT's vehicle allocation was reduced to just 12, although the company did introduce a service between Llanelli and the Royal Ordnance Factory at Pembrey in 1915. This was followed in 1916 by a service from Swansea to Gowerton where the steelworks had been extended to meet war requirements. The young company was also hit by petrol rationing and to help overcome this many vehicles were converted to run on gas supplied by huge bags that were strapped onto the top of vehicles.

Some might consider that South Wales Transport was a rather grand title for a company that had fewer than a handful of routes in the Swansea area, but BET had big plans for its new baby at the start of operations in 1914. It was intended to extend across the whole of South Wales and for the company to become the region's major passenger transport operator.

As early as March 1914 SWT had approached councils in South East Wales for route licences. The reception was less than enthusiastic. The problem was that many councils wanted to run buses themselves and were ideologically opposed to a private enterprise like South Wales Transport operating public service vehicles. The company persevered however and finally, on March 4, 1916, started a service between Merthyr Tydfil and Treharris. But if it had hoped for a warm welcome from Merthyr Tydfil Council because its parent company, BET, had been running the town's trams since 1901, it was quickly disillusioned. The service lasted just seven weeks and was curtailed on April 19, 1916. SWT had a little more luck in Caerphilly, managing to start a service

from the town to Bargoed on August 21, 1915, followed by a second to Senghenydd on May 6, 1916. But then Caerphilly Council announced plans to run its own buses on similar routes and SWT admitted defeat and ended operations on May 19, 1917. The decision would probably have been made easier because controlling bus services in towns like Caerphilly and Merthyr Tydfil from Swansea would hardly have been easy. Roads were in such a poor state that it would have taken hours to get there. So SWT shut its base at Fleur-de-Lys and retired to the slightly less icy embrace of Swansea Corporation.

Its relations with the corporation were better because of the arrangement its sister company SITC had over the running of the town's trams, but they were not ideal. The first routes that SWT chose to operate might at first appear a little unusual. Why did they begin and end at Ynysforgan or Cwmbwrla for example when surely a more logical place would have been the town centre? The answer is that the corporation had no intention of allowing these noisy, uncomfortable and slow motor buses to compete with the town's sleek and efficient trams. Although Swansea Corporation only awarded licences to SWT, it still refused the company permission to run buses alongside the trams. This meant buses could only operate as far as the town's outer tram termini.

It was not until 1921 that Swansea Corporation was finally persuaded to end this stipulation and allow SWT's licensed buses into the town, but even then only on condition that they did not pick up passengers before arriving at or after leaving the tram termini.

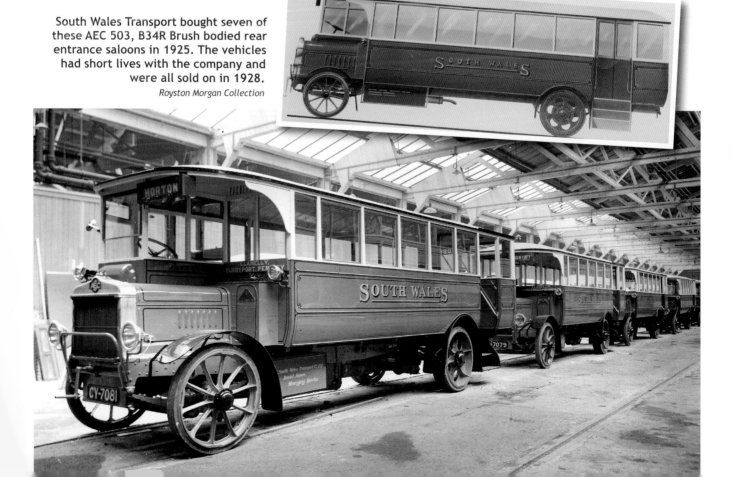

South Wales Transport bought seven of these AEC 503, B34R Brush bodied rear entrance saloons in 1925. The vehicles had short lives with the company and were all sold on in 1928.
Royston Morgan Collection

Percy's first bus had a kick like a mule

WHEN South Wales Transport inspector Percy Pickard retired in December 1959 It was the end of a very special era.

For Percy was one of only two remaining members of staff who had been with the company right from the start in 1914.

The other was Charles Sollis, by then a cleaner at Neath depot, but who had originally been a driver and for a time partnered Percy who had started his life with SWT working as a conductor.

Sadly, Charlie died in 1961 while still working for the company, which broke the final link with the original staff line-up.

When they started, Percy remembered, there were only three services: one from Ynysforgan to Ystalyfera, the second from Cwmbwrla to Loughor, and the third from Morriston to Taibach, Port Talbot which began just after the outbreak of the First World War.

"There were around 60 drivers and conductors at the beginning," said Percy, who fondly recalled the bond of friendship that existed in those days.

During his 45 years with the company he said the number of vehicles grew from about 20 to more than 300. The annual mileage was 60,000 in the early days, but by the time he finished it was 14 million.

Percy even recalled the first bus he took out: "It was CY 1509. It had solid tyres, acetylene lighting and a kick like a mule."

In 1937 he was promoted to inspector and started work on the Mumbles Train in 1944 where he remained until he retired, just a few weeks before it closed.

SWT undoubtedly owed its growth to people like Percy and Charlie who were among the real pioneers of the bus industry.

South Wales Transport inspector, Percy Pickard.

Later this was amended and buses were allowed to carry local passengers, but they had to pay premium fares which were 50 per cent more than those charged on the trams. It meant the local authority was protecting a private company from itself as SWT, which ran the buses, and SITC, which operated the trams, ran side by side with the same managers in charge of both, as subsidiaries of BET.

The end of wartime hostilities in 1918 allowed SWT to begin a period of expansion. By 1923 steady growth and new services within an 18-mile radius of Swansea saw the fleet grow to 55. The company employed 220 men as drivers, conductors and mechanics and in addition there were many office staff and managers. It had become the largest bus operator in South Wales.

In an interview with Commercial Motor magazine in July 1923, SWT's first managing director, David James, pledged the growth would continue. "We shall not stand still, to stand still would be to go back," he declared. "The company's success has been achieved on lines of fair competition, fair service to the public, fair treatment for staff, excellent departmental co-ordination and high departmental efficiency."

Mr James wanted to play it fairly, but unfortunately for SWT this was not the case elsewhere. The 1920s was a time of major competition as new bus operators began to spring up across the Swansea area. They were set up by servicemen looking for work after the war who saw better prospects in transport than a job down the mines. Local businessmen tried their arm at running buses, too, often as a sideline to their mainstay as bakers, butchers or ironmongers. While SWT always behaved properly and sought licences from the councils in whose areas it wanted to run buses, there were plenty of small concerns willing to run unlicensed vehicles and in the 1920s there was nothing in law to stop them. They were prepared to operate a service in any way they could and with any kind of vehicle in order to make a profit.

This was a particular problem in the Swansea Valley as small operators fought their way to bus stops to pick up passengers. Former SWT driver Emrys Jones from Godregraig remembered how he drove a lorry during the day and then in the evening converted it into a bus by fixing a few seats on the back.

"There was no conductor, no ticket machine, and passengers had to tolerate hard seats, solid tyres and open decks," said Emrys, who retired in 1971 after driving buses in the valleys for 45 years.

Passengers wait aboard 1922 AEC 403 bus, CY 5227, for the bumpy trip from Swansea town centre to Mumbles, mid-1970s

Ammanford was another problem. In 1925 no fewer than 16 operators ran in the town and drivers raced to the stops with conductors literally pulling passengers onto their vehicles. People supported individual operators who took to attaching different coloured lights to the front of their vehicles so they could be easily recognised. The firm of J James, for example, had a green light on its buses.

The problem was exacerbated for SWT by the varying attitudes towards licensing held by the local councils. Swansea Corporation only awarded licences to SWT, but Gower Rural District Council refused the company any licences, saying there were already enough operators in its area and they didn't need any more. There was also Swansea Rural Council which covered the area to the north of the town and this allocated licences to virtually anyone who requested one. The result was that competition in its area was intense and there were instances of crews coming to blows as they fought for custom with their vehicles returning to garages battered and scraped.

South Wales Transport might have done its best to rise above the mayhem, but it still had to compete against this unfettered opposition. It faced a further problem in the mid-1920s, fares started to fall as competition rose and this severely dented income. One solution would have been for the company to buy out some of its opponents, but it was reluctant to do this. It believed

that there was little point buying a competitor who could simply set up in business again. It was a policy which was to confront SWT with major problems in the years that followed.

Despite all these difficulties, there is no doubt that the 'Roaring Twenties' was one of the most exciting eras for SWT. The decade saw the company expand from just a small concern with a handful of routes to become the biggest bus operator in South Wales, running a network of services from Pembrey in the west to Margam in the east. The enterprising David James had bigger plans still. New, long distance services were proposed from Swansea and Llanelli to Whitland and Neyland in Pembrokeshire, and to Cardigan and the West Wales holiday resorts. By 1929 SWT buses were running from Swansea, Neath and Llanelli to Aberystwyth and from 1930 to Cardiff, at the time Wales's only city.

Despite its meteoric growth however, all was not well with SWT as the 1920s drew to a close. The intense competition and the company's desire to play it fair were taking their toll. By 1930 it had a monopoly on hardly any routes. It stopped paying dividends to its shareholders in 1928 and in 1931 reported a loss of £3,875, a major sum at the time. The company had encountered its first major crisis. It would not be the last and it was not terminal, but it required firm action from the company that necessitated hard decisions. In retrospect some might appear to be rather surprising.

First garage at Brunswick Street

South Wales Transport's first and also its longest serving garage was at Brunswick Street, Swansea. The company bought the site at the start of its operations in 1914 although it was initially shared with a builders' merchant.

This arrangement ceased after a few years allowing the rapidly developing company to extend the buildings to accommodate the growing number of vehicles it needed for expanding services in Swansea along with Llanelli, Neath and Port Talbot.

Expansion of the fleet was quite rapid after the end of the First World War. In 1919 SWT had 20 buses and just a year later this figure had doubled. Substantial growth followed and by April 1923 SWT had 59 vehicles garaged at the Brunswick Street depot. There were 43 single deck, 26-seaters and eight 54-seat double deckers, all with AEC engines, which would remain the company's favourite power plant for the 50 years that followed. There were also five Leyland 26-seat, single deckers and three charabancs, two Leylands and one Milnes-Daimler, which were used for special outings. The double deckers were all open top and all the buses had solid tyres, poor lighting and harsh springs which made them distinctly uncomfortable for both passengers and the crews that operated them.

One of the 220 SWT employees at the time was cleaner Bob Lewis, who started in 1917. The buses were green then, but after 1920 they were all painted red. Bob said that the company had just 23 buses when he joined. Mainly Belsize and Leyland vehicles, it appears they were not the easiest of machines to operate. "During the winter it could take as many as five men to get a bus started, one to hold the clutch,

one to prime the carburettor and three to swing on the starting handle," he recalled when he retired as a senior fitter in 1967, still at the Brunswick Street depot. Self-starters were not used until the late 1920s or early 1930s and it was as late as the mid-1920s that solid tyres finally gave way to pneumatics.

In 1923 SWT operated 13 routes, all within a radius of 18 miles of the centre of Swansea, and most were from Brunswick Street although the company opened a small garage in Llanelli in 1921 for some of the western routes. At the time it also had plans to establish a garage at Neath to handle its eastern operations. With further expansion in mind SWT took the decision to extend the Brunswick Street depot's large workshop and garage to cater for up to 120 vehicles, which was double the existing capacity of 60 buses.

The depot was a hive of activity. Services operated from early morning until late at night with extra buses on Saturdays when demand was particularly high. All buses were prepared for their duties by the garage staff and a breakdown van with mechanical staff was sent out if a bus broke down near the town centre. Longer distance services, including the Gower routes, were a different matter. Fred Morgan, who retired from SWT as an inspector in 1967, told of how he landed a job with the company as a driver not only on his driving ability, but also through his mechanical knowledge. Bus engines were often anything but reliable in the 1920s and Fred remembered that if a driver wanted to be assured of getting home on a long distance route he had to be prepared to get out of his cab and rectify any fault. "We had to be able to answer about a dozen engineering questions before we got jobs as drivers," he recalled.

SWT did all it could to minimise the possibility of breakdowns. Each bus was taken into the workshop every five weeks for inspection and service and periodical large-scale overhauls were carried out.

Three AEC vehicles at Brunswick Street depot, 1925. Their destination boards indicate the areas the company was focussing on at that time.

Chris Taylor Archive

An open cab, open top, 54-seat AEC 507, CY 8682 at South Wales Transport's Brunswick Street depot, 1925.

The frequency of these depended on the condition and mileage of each vehicle. The Brunswick Street garage handled all the fitting, turning, smithy work, carpentry, glazing and painting work that was needed for the company's growing fleet. It even built new bus bodies for 26-seater single deckers. There was an extensive spare parts and general store and a 10,000 gallon fuel tank, the biggest of its kind laid down in Wales by the Anglo-American Oil Company.

Directing operations at the busy depot, almost from its inception, was a legendary, generally bowler-hatted figure — Fred Lewis. Fred ran his own buses from Ynysforgan to Ystradgynlais until they were taken over by SWT in May 1914. He became SWT manager and engineer, much respected, but with something of a temper it seems. Stories tell of how employees knew the kind of mood he was in from the position of the bowler hat on his head. Flat on top, it was a good day, but pushed to the back of his head, it was a case of look out for fireworks! It seems it wasn't unknown for Fred to hurl his bowler at an employee who had particularly incurred his wrath. He liked things done properly, as did SWT's other managers, who included David James, the managing director; CG Tegetmeier, the chairman and SC Kenwood, traffic superintendent.

Their combined talents meant that SWT had become an impressive operation with an elaborate system of costing and accounts supported by detailed records of the amount of petrol and oil used, vehicle mileage, revenue and working costs.

Dusty roads with lots of potholes

One factor in the life of the burgeoning bus company that would have kept many of its maintenance staff occupied would have been the state of many of the area's roads. The further away from the centre of Swansea routes took buses then very often the worse roads became.

Gower provided the perfect example. Villages miles down narrow country lanes, limestone roads that sent up great clouds of dust in dry, windy weather, why exactly would anyone want to run buses there?

Quite a few did in the early years of the 20th Century, SWT among them. But the company was a little late getting in on the act. By the time it was created, in February 1914, there were already a number of firms trying their hand at running primitive, noisy and uncomfortable buses around the peninsula. So many, in fact, that when SWT applied for licences it was refused by Gower Rural District Council which said there were already enough operators in its area and it didn't want any more. Yet photographs of the period show the buses to be absolutely packed with so many passengers that many were forced to ride on top along with luggage and market produce. One observer at the time described how 'it was not an uncommon sight to see 20 or 30 people perched on top of a bus screaming and shouting with merriment as they ducked to avoid the overhanging branches of roadside trees. They were covered with white dust before reaching the end of the journey, but this only seemed to add to their enjoyment.'

Seeing just how many people were using the services, SWT decided it wanted to join the fun. The drawback was that it didn't have licences and was unlikely to procure any. The only route into this lucrative area, if it wanted to operate in Gower, was to take over an existing operator. The opportunity to do this finally came in 1923 when it bought the 11-vehicle Fairwood Motors Ltd, which ran a service from Swansea to Port Eynon. In 1928 SWT also took over Bishopston and Murton Motors Ltd, which ran a Swansea to Bishopston service with six buses.

One of the first conductors SWT employed on the Port Eynon run after the takeover was Danny Thomas, who spent 15 years on the route. He remembered there were two shifts, the early one began at 6.45am and ended at 7pm while the late duty started at 10.15am and ended at 10.15pm. These early and late shifts meant that a bus stayed overnight in Gower and its crew lodged in Port Eynon. This made them well-known personalities with the villagers and Danny said that before setting off on the run he would collect lists from people and use the bus layover time in Swansea to do their shopping. There was phenomenal demand for the services, particularly at weekends, Danny recalled. It was nothing for 104 passengers to be on board his 34-seat single decker. "If there wasn't room inside, there was plenty on top where the luggage was kept," he said. Later SWT introduced double deckers on its Gower service. They were still packed, but it made the journey a little more bearable. The discomfort of these journeys was often eased by a ritual refreshment stop at The Gower Inn in Parkmill, roughly midway between Port Eynon and Swansea.

Danny said he never lost a passenger at the pub, they were always back on his bus, no matter what their condition. It is likely that the return journey from Swansea would have been the more raucous with the Gower villagers having money in their pockets from selling their produce at the market and no doubt already being reasonably well intoxicated from visiting one or two hostelries in the town. Danny later transferred to Swansea routes and became an inspector in 1948 before retiring in 1960. He considered his 15 years on the Gower route as the happiest though. Later SWT obtained a North Gower service and this threw up some quite different problems. Albert Davies, who retired as an inspector in 1972, spent some time on the Gorseinon to Penclawdd route and remembered occasions when two buses were needed.

"One would have 50 sacks of cockles and the second carried the cockle women on their way to market in Swansea," said Albert, who was always issued with an essential item — a duster to clean

One of the company's early letterheads. *Chris Taylor Archive*

A convoy of SWT Leyland vehicles and their drivers which carried members of Swansea Tripping Club on an excursion to Rhossili, June 6, 1916.
Cindy Arthurs

the bus seats which would get covered in limestone dust blown up from the roads.

Driving and conducting were not the only duties, crews also had to help with luggage, no matter how heavy, recalled Fred Morgan, who retired as an inspector in 1967. His regular route was from Swansea to Llanrhidian.

"I spent the happiest 28 years of my life among the cockle folk of Penclawdd, even though I had to hump cockle baskets weighing about a hundredweight each, on to the roofs of buses," he said.

SWT ran services between Swansea and Gower for 30 years. These were: Route 7, Swansea-Port Eynon, Rhossili; Route 8, Swansea-Llanrhidian and Route 30, Swansea-Bishopston, Pennard. In 1953 it agreed to give them up to United Welsh Services (UWS), a company, which was running competing services in the peninsula. In exchange UWS agreed not to pick up local passengers within the town boundary.

For the next 17 years Gower became the problem of United Welsh with huge demand from visitors to the bays during the summer and few passengers in the winter. Then, when UWS was absorbed by SWT on January 1, 1971, it became SWT's problem once more.

But Gower was just one of many headaches now facing SWT as it took steps to deal with falling passenger numbers and declining revenue. By 1986 there were three main services: Route 14, Swansea-Pennard; Routes 16 & 17, Swansea-North Gower and Route 18, Swansea-South Gower.

The company relied on local authority revenue support to keep them going, as they did for the rest of SWT's existence and for many years after.

Trip on bumpy roads brought a special delivery

Briton Ferry resident Minnie Hall was more than 100 years' old when she told the tale of the day she started giving birth on a South Wales Transport bus.

It was in 1920 and Minnie was on board a No. 3 service from Morriston to Taibach, which before the building of Neath River bridge at Briton Ferry ran through Neath.

Minnie was travelling with her neighbour's young son who had been pleading for ages to be taken for a ride on one of the new motor buses. Although she was heavily pregnant, Minnie agreed to give him the special treat and at first everything was fine, with the lad thrilled by his amazing adventure.

But on the return suddenly things started to go wrong. Minnie put it down to the jolting of the bus. With solid tyres, even at the maximum 12 mph speed limit, passengers felt every bump on the roads which were often in appalling condition.

The jolting was enough to send Minnie into labour, there and then.

"There was pandemonium," she recalled. "The driver and conductor were running round in panic not knowing what to do. Fortunately they were able to get me to a friend's house in Grandison Street, Briton Ferry, and that was where my son was born."

That amazing day remained clearly etched in Minnie's mind for the rest of her life.

And her baby? Well, when Minnie told the tale in 1997 he was a hale and hearty 76-year-old!

A 26-seat, 1926 Saurer saloon with a full complement of passengers heads out of Victoria Road on its way to tackle Mount Pleasant hill on its way to Townhill.
Roy Kneath

Registered as CY 8679 this Saurer vehicle with a Brush B26R body was bought in 1926 specifically for use on the steep Townhill, Swansea, route. *Royston Morgan Collection*

An AEC Regal III pulls in to the bus stop outside St Jude's Church, Terrace Road, 1959 on its long climb up to Townhill. *Colin Riddle*

Hill that was to test the best

Getting up a hill — one particular hill — and down again, created a big headache for SWT in the 1920s and it was one that was to remain for the best part of 50 years.

The Swansea hill in question rose 518ft above sea level and the only way to reach the top was by a 1.5 mile road with steep gradients varying from 1 in 13 to 1 in 5.6.

What made SWT run buses there? Well, at the end of the First World War, Swansea Corporation decided to embark on a major house building project on hilltop sites overlooking the town that resulted in thousands of properties being built on what became Townhill and Mayhill estates. A way had to be found of getting people up to their new homes and that proved to be a formidable task.

It was impossible to extend the electric tramway system up such a steep hill and SWT's buses of the 1920s simply did not have the power. Probably the only thing Mayhill and Townhill have in common with Switzerland are the hills and SWT decided that if buses could run successfully in the Alps,

they would surely be able to cope with the gradients in Swansea. Many experiments and tests were carried out and in 1926 the company bought eight Swiss-built Saurer buses for the route. They had ratchet-type brakes to avoid the possibility of the vehicle rolling backwards on the hill but SWT still had a tough time convincing everyone about their safety, not least Swansea Watch Committee, which looked after transport matters in the town. Eventually it was won over and the company was given the go-ahead to use them on the route, from Swansea Museum, up Mount Pleasant to Townhill every 30 minutes, and every 15 minutes on Saturdays.

Initially people living on the hill wouldn't accept they were safe and refused to use the buses. So SWT had to resort to bribery. "For three days the company carried passengers free in order to allay

any fears they might have had on this alpine journey," recalled one of the first drivers on the Saurers, Charlie Dowdle, in 1956.

Like the other drivers on this route, Charlie received special training both for the Saurers and for getting up and down the hill. His colleague, Alf Maloney, who drove on the route for 16 years, remembered: "At the bottom of Mount Pleasant hill, the ratchet brake had to be brought into action before climbing to Townhill to ensure the bus could not run back when stopping on the hill." Alf, who retired from SWT in 1968 after 44 years with the company, said the drivers had to obey the rule of 'Up in second, down in second.'

"The descent was just as tricky. The ratchet had to be dispensed with, but an engine brake had to be applied by means of a lever in the driver's cabin," he added.

16

The last Mk 1 Leyland National delivered new to SWT in 1980, pulls its way up Mount Pleasant Hill on the Townhill service, May 22, 1982. *Stephen Miles*

The Townhill service started in April 1926 and was extended to Mayhill in 1929 as more houses were built. Another four Saurers arrived in 1930 and in 1933 they were followed by five specially built six-wheeled, 40-seat AEC Renowns, the first in SWT's fleet to have oil engines. They were the result of a year's experimental work carried out by SWT which concluded that an oil-engine vehicle with a pre-selective rather than an orthodox gearbox was best for the Townhill work. The company continued to experiment with different buses on the route and In 1935, five Daimler COG5 vehicles bodied by SWT's favoured bus builder, Weymann, arrived. They had low axle ratios and five-speed gearboxes. Later the same year five revolutionary AEC Q's entered the fleet with 7.7 litre engines mounted just behind the offside front wheel. Thirteen more Renowns with 8.8 litre engines followed in 1939.

The Q's went in 1949, the same year that the first new post-war buses for Townhill arrived in the shape of 18 AEC Regal IIIs with 9.6 litre engines, pre-selective gearboxes and air brakes.

The experiments continued with one of these buses being fitted with progressive braking and another with an 11.3 litre engine in 1952. By 1955 SWT was receiving the highly successful AEC Reliance and the first for Townhill were eight with 44-seat, Park Royal bodies.

It was, of course, essential that only vehicles specially built for Townhill were used on the route and great care had to be taken that others didn't stray on to it. To help engineers and drivers recognise the hill buses, SWT renumbered them into a special series in 1961. The last specially built buses for Townhill came in 1968. They were more AEC Reliances with Willowbrook bodies seating 53 passengers. In 1973,

SWT began to receive the first of what would eventually be 121 Leyland Nationals bought new and some of these were used on the hill. But their more powerful engines meant that special braking and transmission systems were no longer needed.

Few SWT services escaped the minibus revolution in the second half of the 1980s and Townhill was no exception with Mercedes Benz engined vehicles in their two-tone green livery a familiar sight on the hill. They were followed by similarly painted Dennis Darts from 1994, a model that dominated SWT's fleet towards the end of the 1990s. But that never made Townhill an everyday bus route. Even today, it is still an awesome ride!

CHAPTER 2

Expansion brings many different challenges

By 1930 South Wales Transport had established itself as one of the premier public transport providers across a wide area of South West Wales. Passenger numbers were continuing to rise steadily and on its No. 1 route between Swansea and Ystalyfera alone, the company's buses were carrying a staggering 42,000 people a week. Yet despite this, it was entering a decade that would confront it with many different challenges.

Continual expansion throughout the 1920s meant many services had been extended and new ones introduced as the company spread outward from Swansea towards the towns of Ammanford and Llanelli in the west plus Neath and Port Talbot in the east. To cater for this it had set up depots in Neath, Pontardawe and Llanelli.

One of the early challenges presented itself in Swansea, right at the heart of its territory. Here, bus services had been developing alongside those of the electric trams operated by SWT's sister firm, the Swansea Improvements and Tramways Company.

The two had been operated separately, although under common management, but there seemed little point in this system continuing and SWT took over SITC in 1930 running it as a subsidiary. Three years earlier SWT had also taken over the lease on the Mumbles Railway from SITC and by 1929 had replaced its steam-powered locomotives with the electric system that continued until the railway's much mourned closure in January 1960.

South Wales Transport may have operated to the letter of the law, but that was not always the case with other operators. Cut-throat competition from those prepared to do anything to grab extra passengers was hitting the company hard. Fares were slashed and as a result often proved uneconomical. Then came one of the most important pieces of transport legislation of the 20th Century — the Road Traffic Act of 1930. This was intended to bring order to the chaos and benefit respectable companies like SWT. Traffic Commissioners were set up with powers over operators, licences, fares and timetables, something which frightened off much of the competition.

Not all of SWT's competitors were rogues however. Some were well-managed operators and it found itself facing 15 of them across its territory as the decade unfolded. Like SWT, they also benefitted from the demise of the less scrupulous firms. That served to make them stronger and therefore, more of a threat to the company which might have been wise to buy out

Royston Morgan Collection

South Wales Transport bought five of these distinctively-shaped, full-fronted AEC Q buses in 1935. Described at the time as being revolutionary, they had side-mounted engines.

A 1937 AEC Regent heading for Morriston passes a 1939 Leyland TD5 on its way to Brynmill in Wind Street, Swansea, in the early 1950s.

some of its opponents early on in the battle for passengers, but it was slow to do so, unlike Chepstow-based Red and White Services. That company's acquisitions in the 1930s became a major thorn in the side of SWT as the decade ended.

Among SWT's other problems at this time was the fact that its financial position meant that its newest double deckers in 1930 were four year old AEC 507s. In the time since they had been bought, bus design had been revolutionised. Some of its competitors, including the respected, Bishopston-based Swan company, were running newer vehicles and they were proving more appealing to passengers. It was clear to BET that action had to be taken to put SWT back on the right road.

Emile Garcke retired in 1929 and died in 1930, while the innovative managing director David James, one of many who gave their lives to SWT, died just two years later. As a result, the company found itself with a new general manager, the able administrator Percy Roberts Blake. Emile's son, Sidney Garcke, took over as chairman, and together the two took SWT out of the doldrums of the 1930s and lead the company on the road towards its post-war success.

Under the new regime, some directors and staff left, there were cuts in salaries and services were reorganised, but it took until 1937 for the company to restart shareholder dividends. Mr James's bold plans to expand in West Wales were shelved, instead that was left to sister company, Western Welsh, which became part of the BET empire in 1931. For the next 40 years SWT's main operating area was confined to Swansea, west to Llanelli, Ammanford and Carmarthen, and east to Pontardawe, Neath and Port Talbot.

One of the first requirements was the need to modernise the fleet and, in what was a supreme act of confidence, SWT bought 50 new double deckers in 1932, all AEC Regents, the first of the marque for the company which would continue its links with the manufacturer until the last Regent was withdrawn from service in February 1982.

Each year until 1939 SWT took substantial numbers of new buses so that by the start of the Second World War it had one of the most modern bus fleets in the country. It justified this by pointing to the rising number of passengers. By 1939 its 327 buses were carrying 130,000 of them every day. The number of people using buses in South West Wales had risen spectacularly since the 1920s and the social impact was huge. Valley communities were connected to the larger towns and with each other as never before. Previously many miners had been forced to lodge near their pits, now they could stay with their families and travel by bus to work. Day trips for shopping and to the seaside were all made possible and SWT, as the largest company, was having a major impact on people's lives.

A strike in 1935 showed how important the bus had become. It began with the family run firm of J James

Potatoes were a secret weapon on rainy days

A potato was an essential item for bus drivers in the 1920s, recalled Reginald Morgan when he retired from South Wales Transport in Llanelli in 1967.

Reginald started his career with J Bacus, a bus firm that in the 1920s ran every 20 minutes between Llanelli and Burry Port. It was started by Joseph Bacus, who had an ironmonger's shop in Burry Port and it must be said that his vehicles were not of the highest standard. That is where the potato came in.

Reginald remembered the Bacus vehicles as having solid tyres, no self-starters and no windscreen wipers. "In fact it was a luxury to have a windscreen, at all," he recalled.

"That's why a driver would always take a potato with him," said Reginald. "Then, if it rained, he would slice it in half and rub it on the outside of the windscreen."

"This formed a film which temporarily stopped rainwater adhering to the glass and enabled the driver to see through the windscreen."

Bacus shared the Burry Port to Llanelli route with SWT which took over the company in 1935 and with it the driving services of Reginald Morgan.

of Ammanford, whose drivers and conductors wanted pay and conditions parity with SWT crews. They went on strike on August 2, 1935, the company made an offer which failed to match SWT's agreements, and the crews rejected it. So J James brought in men to replace them and the dispute escalated until it affected 21 local bus undertakings including, most unfairly, SWT. The strike, involving 1,600 busmen, began on Sunday August 18 and the effect was dramatic: the following day only six shops in Swansea's bustling High Street opened on time at 9 am. August 20 was market day in Neath, but business was negligible. Summer outings were cancelled resulting in the manager of one Langland Bay hotel commenting that the lack of charabanc trips and cancelled bookings had almost halved their takings. Hospitals and workplaces across Swansea, Neath, Llanelli, Ammanford and Carmarthen were also hit as staff failed to get into work. Miners could also not get to their pits.

So what was SWT paying that the J James crews coveted so intensely? Its drivers were receiving 1s 4d (7.5p) an hour, the conductors 1s 2d (6p) an hour. Time and a quarter was paid for Sunday working; time and three quarters for Bank Holidays. People who worked more than 48 hours a week received overtime, there were eight days annual holiday with pay and SWT provided free uniforms every year.

The strike continued until September 9 when a return to work was agreed. Later the Bus Conciliation Board came up with an extra penny an hour for drivers and conductors, a week's holiday with pay and free

This Brush B40R bodied AEC Renown, Reg No. WN 5815, was one of the first new vehicles with oil engines bought by SWT in 1933. Specifically for the Townhill route it had an 8.8 litre engine, pre-selective gearbox and fluid flywheels. It was withdrawn and scrapped in 1948.

Royston Morgan Collection

This impressive parade of drivers and vehicles at Brunswick Street in the late 1930s includes a number of Dennis Lancets, delivered in 1934 and Leyland Tiger TS7 saloons delivered in 1935 at the far end of the line. *Peter Samuel*

A 1948 Weymann bodied AEC Regent II emerges from Pontardawe depot in the early 1950s.

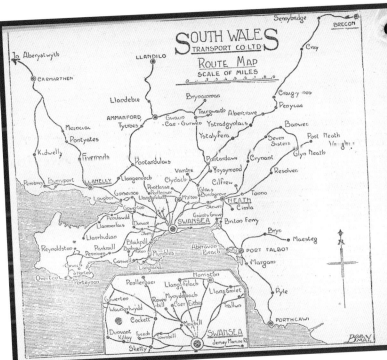

With an additional side mounted destination indicator this Daimler COG5 saloon with Weymann B35F body was another vehicle obtained for work on the Townhill route. WN 7740 was operated from 1935 until withdrawal in 1948 when it was sold to showmen Booth, of Pembrey.
Royston Morgan Collection

21

uniforms issued annually. Understandably perhaps SWT was disappointed by the action of its crews. It had been paying better wages than other operators and unlike them had recognised the importance of good relations with its staff. It was also one of the first bus companies in the country to recognise a trade union — the Transport and General Workers' Union — in 1929. The 25-day stoppage had cost SWT a significant amount of revenue and the company warned staff that it might be unable to continue the pre-strike rate of wages and conditions of employment. It withdrew weekly staff travel vouchers and passes were restricted to the holders.

The company had other meatier matters on its plate as the 1930s unfolded however. Its subsidiary, SITC, was still running trams in Swansea, but it was clear to both SWT and Swansea Corporation that they had outlived their usefulness. The town centre's pre-war streets were narrow, the trams were slow and took up a lot of room, hindering other traffic. In 1933 major roadworks around the King Edward Road and Bryn Road area of the town meant trams could not operate to Brynmill and they were replaced temporarily by SWT buses. These completed the journey in half the time and there were calls to make them permanent. The question was, what should replace the trams and who should run the new services?

SWT obviously wanted its buses to replace the trams which were carrying around 15 million passengers a

Captured on Gower duties during a run to Rhossili, Weymann bodied lowbridge, Leyland TD5, BCY 575, delivered in 1938, is seen after it was renumbered from 75 to 507 in 1939. *Royston Morgan Collection*

Farewell to the trams brought out the crowds

Crowds filled the streets of Swansea on June 29, 1937, to bid an emotional farewell to the town's trams. They had been serving those same people for 59 years, drawn by horses until 1900 when they had become the first in Wales to be powered by electricity.

Swansea's trams ran under a rather complicated arrangement between the Swansea Improvements and Tramways Company and Swansea Corporation which was to create so many problems for SWT when it was decided to close the system in 1935. SITC obtained an Act of Parliament to electrify its lines and by 1900 the deed was done. Initially the company generated its own power, but in 1902 the corporation obtained the Swansea and District Light Railway Order and it built new lines which extended the tramway company's system in 1905. It constructed an electricity generating station which then supplied both its own lines and the SITC system.

The trams ran from Cwmbwrla, Brynhyfryd, Ynystawe and Morriston to Castle Street; from Sketty and Brynmill to High Street railway station; and from St Helen's to High Street station and Port Tennant. By the time the system closed there were 77 cars which were carrying around 15 million passengers a year. It was a sad day when the trams stopped running. The crews, wearing uniforms and white gloves, marched solemnly through the town centre and onlookers thronged the pavements cheering as the last cars passed by, packed to capacity with singing passengers.

Walter Wright was the conductor on the last tram from Sketty and remembered it was almost wrecked as passengers grabbed souvenirs. "Everything removable was taken, even the buttons on my tunic," said Walter who, with his driver, just managed to limp back to the tram depot at the bottom of St Helen's Road where the city's Crown Court now stands.

One little girl especially sad to see the end of the trams was Barbara Cameron whose grandfather, George Christopherson, was a tram driver for 28 years working mostly from Cwmbwrla to Castle Street.

"The crews on the trams worked long hours and for small wages," Barbara recalled in 1997. "If the

Two electric trams pass one another near their terminus at Eversley Road, Sketty, in the mid-1930s.

Crowds line the route of the last two trams ever to run in Swansea on Tuesday, June 29. One of them was driven back to the St Helen's depot, by the town's mayor.
Chris Taylor Archive

Smartly uniformed drivers and conductors, each wearing white gloves, take part in the farewell parade.

car was open in the front they used to get very wet if it was raining, despite having lots of waterproof clothing. I remember how my grandfather would be freezing in the cold weather. I can picture him clasping his arms around his body to try and warm himself up between journeys. No sooner had he succeeded in getting the circulation going again than the tram was ready to go back the way it had come."

The trams were replaced by 74 double deck buses which were legally owned by SITC, although they had the South Wales fleet name on their sides and were included in SWT's fleet numbering system. SITC continued until 1953 when a decision was made to formally close the company. But SWT's link with its trams heritage did not end there. Bus services that had

replaced the trams followed the same routes wherever possible with termini in different parts of the town centre to ease traffic congestion. Tramway replacement bus routes used the former tram route number with the number 7 in front, so the route to Morriston, which had been tram route 1, became bus route 71.

Major changes were made to Swansea city centre routes in 1974 and the old numbers discontinued on April 20. It ended the final link between SWT's bus services and the trams, 37 years after the last trams had run in Swansea.

year. Many however, thought Swansea Corporation, which leased the system to SWT, should run the replacement services, whether it was trolley buses or motor buses. Swansea had its own police force and fire service at this time, so many favoured the creation of its own bus service. Civic pride was also at stake here. Swansea's great rival, Cardiff, had been running its own buses since Christmas Eve 1920, Newport had been running its bus services since 1924 while even tiny Bedwas and Machen Council in south east Wales had its own municipal fleet.

Initial negotiations between SWT and Swansea Corporation went badly. Many years later the town's MP and council leader at the time, Percy Morris, blamed the impasse on SWT's refusal to adequately compensate the council for the assets it would lose with the withdrawal of the system. The corporation put forward plans for its own Bill in November 1935 which would have given the council powers to abandon the trams and substitute them with a municipal bus service. The result of this would have been interesting to see had it gone ahead. SWT would have been in a similar position in Swansea to the one its sister BET company, Western Welsh, found itself in Cardiff and Newport, with the municipal fleets running services within their boundaries and WW running cross-boundary routes. Such a move might have led to a City of Swansea bus company.

The proposed bill also contemplated Swansea Corporation taking over the Mumbles Train and that raises another interesting question. SWT closed the railway in January 1960 claiming

it was losing money and the repair bills were too high. As a private company, it was responsible to its shareholders. But if the council had owned the railway, would it have taken the same decision? Its responsibilities were to the taxpayers who generally didn't want the system closed. The Mumbles Railway might have survived and today there might have been a rapid, 21st Century system whisking passengers between Swansea and Mumbles, easing traffic congestion problems along Mumbles Road.

Eventually SWT and the council did reach agreement. In December 1935 they decided to put forward a joint Bill that would see motor buses replacing the trams. Trolley buses were considered by the council, but Swansea's hills made them unsuitable and they would be more expensive to run. The cost was a high one for SWT, which shows just how important it saw the takeover of the trams to its business, but it was a win, win situation for the council. The Swansea and District Transport Act 1936 was passed which gave the company the right to operate the former tram services within Swansea's area for 21 years, but it had to pay the corporation £5,000 a year or a proportion of its town profits, whichever was the greater. It was usually the share of profits and under the agreement SWT handed

OFFICIAL TIME TABLES
1934 — 19TH MAY UNTIL 16TH SEPT. — 1934

Carrying an English Electric body, AWN 564 was one of a batch of Dennis Lancet 2 vehicles delivered in 1937. Given the fleet number 64 on delivery, this vehicle was renumbered 852 in 1939 and went for scrap on withdrawal in 1949.
Royston Morgan Collection

One of two AEC Rangers WN 5400 was delivered in 1933. The pair were bought for seven and 14 day tours and were fitted with luxury armchairs and folding roofs.
Royston Morgan Collection

over a total of £134,346 between 1943 and 1956. Swansea Corporation was also relieved of what would have been the huge burden of buying buses to replace the trams, training tramway staff to run them, and finding a suitable depot to house the vehicles. SWT did all that. It bought 74 new tram replacement double deck buses in 1937 and 1938 and built a new depot at Ravenhill to house them. It also trained the staff in bus operation and anyone who didn't make the grade was either found an alternative job within the company or given a lump sum to leave. The agreement also included the setting up of a Transport Advisory Committee consisting of three members of the council and three SWT representatives who met quarterly to discuss the town's bus services. This meant that the council had a strong say in how SWT ran its routes in Swansea, but did not have to take any of the financial risks. For those put out at not having a municipal bus service, there was even more. Under the 1936 Act the corporation would have the right to compulsorily purchase SWT's Swansea town services in 1957. It would take 21 years, but they might eventually have their way.

The trams ran for the last time in 1937 and SWT became the dominant bus operator in Swansea though it was not without competition. It had finally started to take over other operators from 1935, including Bacus of Burry Port, Gwendraeth Transport of Pontyates, Willmore Motors of Neath, Treharne Bros of Ponthenri, John Bros of Grovesend and Osborne Services of Neath. Red & White had been quicker off the mark and its acquisitions in the Swansea area included Basset and Sons and Gower Vanguard Motors. In 1938 its companies in Swansea were amalgamated to form United Welsh Services and with 36 double deckers, 76 single deckers and 18 coaches, it was a formidable competitor to SWT which had around 327 vehicles.

The first AEC Regents arrived at SWT in 1932. Among them was WN 4887 which began life with fleet number 287. The Brush bodied 51 seat vehicle was renumbered 321 in 1939, and saw service with local operators in Walsall after it was withdrawn in 1945/46. It was finally scrapped in 1950.
Royston Morgan Collection

Nicknames each told a special personal tale

The company's employees had lots of nicknames, from the bizarre to the downright obscure.

They included Daylight Jack, Dai Chips, Tommy the Lark, Percy Stalecakes, China, Roly Poly, Flash, Guardsman, Margaret Lost Prop, Ditto, Dasher and Dai kill-a-pig.

Most Davids in SWT seem to have been nicknamed Dai and Dai-kill-a-pig's real name was David Thomas who spent 35 years as a conductor on the Swansea Valley routes. But he started life as a butcher and slaughterman, a trade he continued part-time after joining SWT in 1923. Dai retired in 1965 after 42 years with the company.

Tommy the Lark was Tommy Davies, a shunter at Pontardawe depot who originally ran his own bus service, between Clydach and Ystradgynlais, known as Lark Motor Services. He passed his licences to SWT in 1930 and moved to the company as a conductor, becoming a shunter in 1941.

China was Swansea conductor Arthur Evans who used to greet people with the words, "hello, my old china". He joined SWT in 1930 and retired in 1965.

As you might expect, Margaret Lost Prop worked in the lost property department and her real name was Margaret Jones, while Dasher was DW Day who got his nickname because he was only 5ft 3ins tall. Probably shortness was also the reason for Dai Chips while Roly Poly was likely to have had something to do with the man's girth. Percy Stalecakes, well that one is just down to the imagination.

Many of the conductresses taken on by the company got their nicknames from where they lived. Mary Chespey, for example, became Betty Dynevor because she lived in Dynevor Place, Swansea, although it is uncertain why she became Betty.

A Saurer bus descending Mount Pleasant, Swansea, late 1920s, and below a six-wheeled AEC Renown saloon climbing back up, in the 1930s.
Royston Morgan Collection

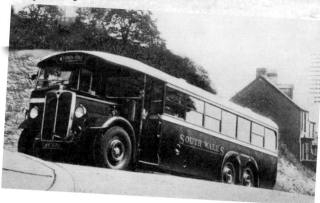

Many of the routes were similar and the two companies were often running in each other's tyre tracks. As the war years beckoned and the need to save fuel became paramount, common sense prevailed and they reached agreement on services, ending cut-throat competition.

By the outbreak of war in 1939, SWT had survived the difficulties of the early years of the decade and triumphed. It ran lucrative town centre routes in Swansea, its passenger numbers were rising annually and it had started a limited tours programme. The war years disrupted all that however and as Luftwaffe bombs rained down on Swansea, the company and its staff were once again challenged to the limits.

This Dennis Lancet was among a batch that consisted of the last new petrol-engined buses bought by SWT . With Weymann B32F bodies they arrived in 1936. WN 8976 originally carried fleet number 376. It was withdrawn in 1940, later passing to the Ministry of Defence.
Royston Morgan Collection

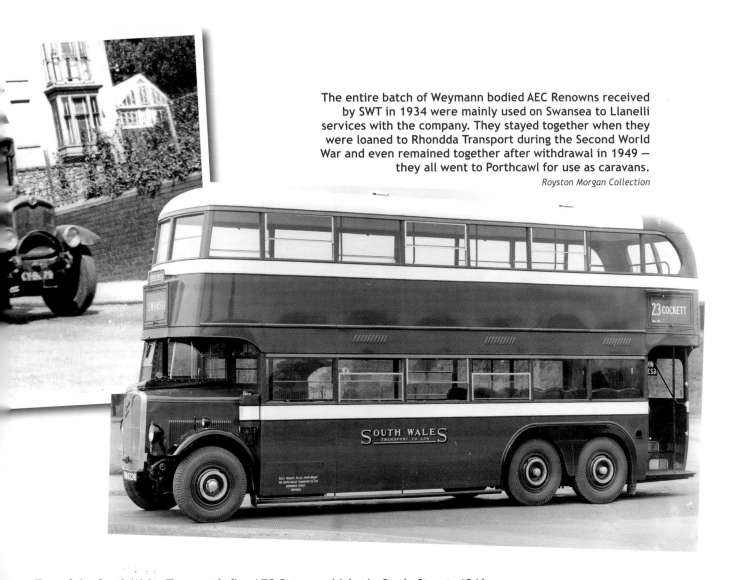

The entire batch of Weymann bodied AEC Renowns received by SWT in 1934 were mainly used on Swansea to Llanelli services with the company. They stayed together when they were loaned to Rhondda Transport during the Second World War and even remained together after withdrawal in 1949 — they all went to Porthcawl for use as caravans.

Royston Morgan Collection

Two of the South Wales Transport's five AEC Q-type vehicles in Castle Street, 1946.

Waiting in Adelaide Street, Swansea, for its next trip to Blaenymaes in the early 1970s, this Regent V was one of the first of its type with forward entrances delivered to SWT in 1958.

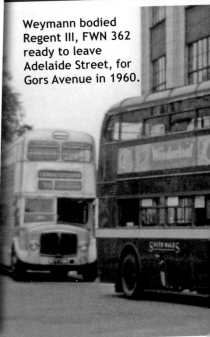

Weymann bodied Regent III, FWN 362 ready to leave Adelaide Street, for Gors Avenue in 1960.

Notorious route

One of South Wales Transport's shortest routes was also regarded as one of its most notorious. The service covered little more than three miles and took just 15 minutes, but was packed with incident and human life, both at its best — and worst.

This was route 79 which for more than 30 years ran from the terminus at The Exchange, in Adelaide

A 1959 Weymann bodied AEC Regent V working the notorious 79 route to Gors Avenue, Swansea in the mid-1960s.

Street, through the town centre to Gors Avenue, which cut through the sprawling Mayhill housing estate. There were five buses an hour in the 1950s and 1960s and they ran from early morning until late at night when most of the problems, or, for some, most of the fun, began. As SWT's staff magazine, Ein Newyddion, put it sardonically: "Gors Avenue may not be every driver or conductor's dream route. Some, indeed, if they do dream of it, break out in a cold sweat."

The route served one of the toughest areas of Swansea and conductors and drivers had to be of a certain character if their lives were not to be made hell on earth by certain passengers. That meant making it clear who was in charge of the bus, making it stick and possessing a rather grim sense of humour. The regular conductors were able to handle themselves and

were well liked by the passengers. Some stayed on the 79 for many years, and enjoyed every turbulent minute of the experience.

They included Bill Pritchard, who retired in 1967. He joined SWT in 1928 and remained for 39 years, 30 of them on the Gors Avenue run.

"It was made possible by a grand bunch of colleagues and passengers, many of whom I knew personally," he said when he handed in his ticket machine for the last time. Passengers got to know the other regular crews as well, including Les Bastyn, Willy James, Bill John and Don Parry.

Regular conductor Dennis Watts recalled: "It was a route full of characters and a community spirit where everyone knew everybody else and always chatted to one other, unlike today's buses where everyone sits in silence."

It was the late buses used by the locals after a night out in Swansea town centre which experienced the main problems, although Dennis said in all his years on the service

Delivered in 1951, AEC Regent III, GWN 93, waits near the former Swansea Sailor's Home for its next turn on the 73 service to Brynhyfryd in 1960.

nicknamed Flagon Alley

he saw little trouble, usually because the passengers were too busy singing! The route served Wind Street, which today is Swansea's nightlife hotspot, but it was also well served by pubs 50 or 60 years ago alongside offices, banks, cafes and hotels. Small and cosy by today's standards, they included establishments such as The Borough Arms, The Cornish Mount, The Adelphi and The Duke, and it was to these hostelries that the 79 route passengers would flock at night.

Their antics on their late night return home were nothing if not unpredictable and the route was often referred to as Flagon Alley.

Closing time then was 10.30pm sharp and there was just 10 minutes drinking-up time to finish that final pint before it was off to the bus stop to catch 'the last Gors.' It left The Exchange at 10.48pm exactly and it was the duty most dreaded by conductors who were not route regulars. It meant struggling to collect fares on a double deck bus packed with inebriated passengers singing, shouting, arguing and occasionally brawling. Some were too intoxicated to do anything at all and Dennis recalled a crew carrying a young soldier

home on leave, from the bus to his home because he was the worse for wear. There were problems in the morning too, involving local children who would pile onto the 79 for Waun Wen and St Joseph's schools. The conductor had less than 10 minutes to collect the fares. It was an almost impossible task, and there were many occasions when, to the youngsters' delight, they got off without paying, to the benefit of the local tuck shop as the children would dart straight in to spend the fare.

TOWN SERVICE No. 79

SWANSEA (Exchange) AND GORS AVENUE

WEEKDAYS

	a.m.	a.m.	a.m.	a.m.	a.m.	a.m.		p.m.	p.m.	p.m.	p.m.	p.m.
NSEA (Exchange) dep	5 48	6 0	6 12	6 24	6 36	6 48	and every 12 mins. until	10 0	10 12	10 24	10 36	10 48
St. (G.W.R. Stn.)	5 52	6 4	6 16	6 28	6 40	6 52		10 4	10 16	10 28	10 40	10 52
S AVENUE .... arr	6 3	6 15	6 27	6 39	6 51	7 3		10 15	10 27	10 39	10 51	11 3

	a.m.	a.m.	a.m.	a.m.	a.m.	a.m.		p.m.	p.m.	p.m.	p.m.	p.m.
S AVENUE ....dep	5 30	5 42	5 54	6 6	6 18	6 30	and every 12 mins. until	9 42	9 54	10 6	10 18	10 30
St. (G.W.R. Stn.)	5 41	5 53	6 5	6 17	6 29	6 41		9 53	10 5	10 17	10 29	10 41
NSEA (Exchange) arr	5 45	5 57	6 9	6 21	6 33	6 45		9 57	10 9	10 21	10 33	10 45

SUNDAYS

	p.m.	p.m.	p.m.	p.m.	p.m.		p.m.	p.m.	p.m.	p.m.	p.m.
NSEA (Exchange) dep	1 36	1 48	2 0	2 12	2 24	and every 12 mins. until	10 0	10 12	10 24	10 36	10 48
St. (GW.R. Stn.)	1 40	1 52	2 4	2 16	2 28		10 4	10 16	10 28	10 40	10 52
S AVENUE .... arr	1 51	2 3	2 15	2 27	2 39		10 15	10 27	10 39	10 51	11 3

	p.m.	p.m.	p.m.	p.m.	p.m.		p.m.	p.m.	p.m.	p.m.	p.m.
S AVENUE .... dep	1 18	1 30	1 42	1 54	2 6	and every 12 mins. until	9 42	9 54	10 6	10 18	10 30
St. (G.W.R. Stn.)	1 29	1 41	1 53	2 5	2 17		9 53	10 5	10 17	10 29	10 41
NSEA (Exchange) arr	1 33	1 45	1 57	2 9	2 21		9 57	10 9	10 21	10 33	10 45

CHAPTER 3

Heroic crews played vital part in the war effort

Swansea played a vital role in Britain's battle to win the Second World War and South Wales Transport was a crucial part of that effort. For three years the German Luftwaffe, unleashed a reign of aerial terror on the area and the company's buses, their drivers and conductors were in the thick of it.

Often under the most difficult of circumstances, defying bombs, death and destruction, staff performed heroically to ensure workers essential to the war effort reached their jobs. Prime Minister Neville Chamberlain announced that Britain was at war with Nazi Germany on September 3, 1939, but the move had been anticipated and Swansea's efforts to protect itself from attack were already under way.

Air raids were expected and SWT staff threw themselves into the task of helping to protect the company's properties and buses. Painter Llew Wallis recalled in 1968 that he and his colleagues were ordered to camouflage buildings, particularly Brunswick Street garage and the depot at Ravenhill, which had only been built in 1937.

"We had to black out windows and lamps on the buildings and paint white lines around the bus bodies and vehicle entrance steps to help passengers pick them out during any blackouts," he said.

Oil was certain to be in short supply and so SWT had to use gas as an alternative in its bid to run a decent level of services. During the First World War the problem had been overcome by strapping huge balloons on top of buses and filling them with town gas. This time the plan was to use producer gas and the company had been experimenting with it before war was declared. By May 1939 SWT was testing a Sentinel 32-seat gas powered saloon. The gas was produced in a trailer towed behind the vehicle using anthracite supplied by Amalgamated Anthracite Collieries, of Swansea. The company put it to work on one of its most testing routes — from the town centre to Caswell Bay — which had lots of stops and a long hill with a gradient of 1 in 6.9 from the beach. The bus performed so well that SWT was contemplating converting more vehicles in the same way, but the outbreak of war forced it to move faster.

Senior fitter at Brunswick Street, Bob Lewis, recalled that most of his time during the war was spent servicing similar coal-fired, gas producing trailers that were attached to many SWT buses. The crews nicknamed them 'fish and chip machines', presumably because of the smell of cooking that they gave off. It was also not

Royston Morgan Collection

A Brush bodied AEC Regent double decker picks up passengers in Wind Street, Swansea, on its way to Brynmill in the mid-1930s. Fleet number 271, WN 4871 was withdrawn from service in 1939.

Two newly delivered Leyland TD5 double deck vehicles ply their trade alongside the market in Oxford Street, Swansea, during late summer, 1938.

unknown for them to leak, as former conductress Margaret Hefferman recalled.

"I remember one day feeling very sickly," she said. "I couldn't understand what was wrong with me until an inspector boarded my bus and, after a few sniffs informed me that we had sprung a leak and gas was wafting through the bus."

The company's war preparations also extended to the Mumbles Railway, which it ran from Swansea to Mumbles Pier. Its 13 tram cars were all housed at the Rutland Street depot and one well-aimed bomb there would have wiped out the service. To avoid this they were kept at various points along the line throughout the war to minimise the risk of total destruction.

With the company prepared for the worst, its staff joined the rest of the town in expecting air raids to quickly follow the declaration of war, but for many months nothing happened. Like the rest of Britain, Swansea was enduring the period that became known as the 'phoney war' and life went on much as before. SWT had drastically reduced its services however and in December 1939 the city's chamber of trade, concerned that fewer buses would mean fewer people in the shops over Christmas, called on the company to run more. This was echoed by the South Wales Miners' Federation which said hundreds of its members in the Amman and

Swansea valleys were being forced to walk many extra miles to get to their workplaces because there were not enough buses.

But then the focus shifted and the Luftwaffe did arrive. In June 1940 France fell and Germany was able to station its aircraft within reach of towns and cities in southern Britain. This included Swansea, one of the country's most important seaports. At 3.30 am on June 27, a golden flare lit the sky above the town and the first bombs fell. Danygraig was hit on this occasion, but over the next three years the terror extended to many other districts. The worst of the raids became known as The Three Nights Blitz which lasted for nearly 14 hours over three nights beginning on Wednesday February 19, 1941, when 230 died, 397 were injured and 7,000 made homeless. The town centre became an uncontrollable inferno and when the smoke cleared was just a mass of fallen rubble. Over three years the air raids resulted in the deaths of 387 Swansea people, while 851 were injured and 802 premises destroyed.

South Wales Transport succeeded in running buses through it all. Miraculously, there were relatively few injuries among the crews which by now included many women. The company's conductors had always been men but with many being called up women were actively recruited for the first time. Margaret Hefferman was among the first to join on September 10, 1940. Together with Kathleen Clarke, Mary Latch, Eileen Bignell and Phyllis Toovey, Margaret was permitted, under the Defence of the Realm Act, 'to act as the conductress of a public service vehicle.' They received

In the winter of 1945 a solitary South Wales Transport AEC Regent double decker crosses the snowy, post-war wasteland that was once the centre of Swansea.

a short period of tuition, for which they were not paid, and the starting rate was 10d, or 4p, an hour.

On September 14, to the amazement of passengers, Margaret took charge of her first bus, the number 12 up to Townhill, with driver Arthur Hearn. She remembered there was a lot of leg pulling with some of the men on her service calling out: 'Hey, there's a girl on this bus!' Other women took up the job over the months and years that followed, some of them very young, others housewives whose husbands had gone to war. The staff magazine, Ein Newyddion, said of them: "They all did a manlike job in a manlike way in conditions which would cause even the best of men to wilt." These days people wince at such sexist language, but it was well meant and well deserved.

"Each and every one of the conductresses who were with us during the war years did a grand job. They kept working with sirens wailing through the night and bombs falling right, left and centre," said Margaret.

It would be easy to write that the drivers and conductresses took out their buses fearlessly, night after night, defying Hitler's bombs. But it would not be true. They were absolutely terrified. Yet despite that they still went out and that makes their courage all the more remarkable.

Sometimes it became too much and after one particularly heavy air raid, conductress Irene Locke went missing. Her colleagues feared the worst. The first they would know if one of them had been killed or injured would be if they failed to turn up for their next shift, and they went into mourning for her. But the following day she was back at work, she had been so traumatised by the raid that she had taken refuge with a family and had to be put to bed. It was not only

mental scars, there were often physical injuries too. Beatrice Francis, who joined as a conductress in July 1941, was badly hurt in one raid that was to claim the life of her driver, William Hicks. Their bus had been out on service when the bombs started to fall and if that happened, there was only one thing to do. Passengers and crews would abandon the vehicle and run off to the nearest communal shelter.

Originally used as a tours coach with a front entrance when new in 1935, WN 7756, fleet number 356 was a Leyland TS7 with a Weymann C28F body. Fitted with an 8.6 litre oil engine it was renumbered 702 in 1939 and the following year was commandeered by the War Department. It was rebuilt in 1948 as shown here with a rear entrance.
Royston Morgan Collection

"Bill stopped the bus and told me and the passengers to go to a nearby shelter," said Beatrice. "I got to the entrance when I noticed Bill wasn't following me. I turned back to look for him and that's all I can remember." The bus had been hit while Bill was still on board. He was killed and the bomb had made a mangled wreck of his vehicle. Beatrice suffered injuries in the blast and was taken to hospital. Despite her ordeal, she returned to conducting and stayed with SWT until May 1957 when she moved to Cardiff with her family.

William Hicks was SWT's only fatality at home during the war. He died a hero, ensuring the safety of his passengers and his conductress.

Margaret Hefferman, who later married and became Margaret Davies, then Margaret Pickard before retiring in 1970, was also nearly killed during a raid. Speaking in 1957, she recalled that she and her driver, Cliff Jenkins, were near the viaduct at Landore when the air raid warning sounded. "Cliff stopped the bus and we went to look for shelter," said Margaret. "There was a pub nearby, but Cliff would not go in, even for

Bus conductor Bernard Phillips and his wife Joyce near the site of the Dragon Hotel in front of the AEC Regal saloon he worked between Morriston and Sketty, 1946.

The bus that eluded Trevor and his mates

Trevor Groocock became a keen bus spotter from the age of seven and remembers many happy hours spent with his mate, Piers Walters, riding on SWT buses or collecting bus numbers.

Trevor now lives in Richmond, Surrey, but for more than 30 years, from 1939, lived in Swansea or Margam, Port Talbot.

"I still have a couple of my notebooks in which I recorded the registration numbers of the buses that I saw on various days in 1945," says Trevor.

"I was able to identify vehicles from the advertisements they carried. One, ACY 11, was an early example of an all-over advertisement for Morriston Star Steam Laundry. I tried to see all the buses over time but one eluded me, BCY 587, fleet number 519, and I never found out why. Piers and I used to go to Llanelli, Neath and Pontardawe, where the garages were located, and we also enjoyed visiting Ravenhill depot.

"In about 1946 there was a yard there which was used to store buses withdrawn from service and it was great fun to play on these. We also spent time at local termini, specifically Sketty and Port Tennant. When buses came to the terminus we would ask the driver if we could change the destination indicator for him. Most were friendly and agreed, as long as we promised to show the correct destination! I used to go on the 74 bus to school and remember in particular a very jovial conductor called Meredith whose favourite saying was: I'm a better man than you, Gunga-din!"

protection. Suddenly we heard the scream of falling bombs. Cliff grabbed me and flung me down. One of the bombs meant for the viaduct fell on the ICI tip, the blast was terrific. Cliff's action saved me from serious injury and peculiarly enough the side of the pub where the passengers had gone for shelter was considerably damaged by the blast.

"It was some hours before the all-clear went and when we eventually reached High Street railway station we were told that all the buses from the Neath Road area, where we were, were being diverted to Ravenhill garage. Two conductors and myself were based at Brunswick Street so we started to walk through the snow and ice. The public library and art gallery were ablaze. When we got to the top of Christina Street one of the conductors, Arnold Demery, slipped on the ice and slid half the length of the street on his back. We rushed to help him, but he just grinned and said, 'St Moritz couldn't be better than this!' Even during the worst raids there was plenty of humour and we were a happy bunch of workmates."

Swansea Docks was thought to be the main target for the Luftwaffe, but Margaret recalled that a large number of bombs seemed to be aimed at SWT's Brunswick Street depot. To aim for the town's transport undertakings would have made perfect sense. Without buses, workers could not get to essential jobs to help the war effort, and not being able to travel would have also affected public morale.

If that was the plan, it failed. Many of SWT's buses were damaged, but services continued, even the vehicle that had been wrecked when William Hicks died was repaired and returned to service the following year. It was fortunate too, that buses had replaced Swansea's trams in 1937. Buses can of course find alternative ways round a hole in the road and are able to continue to run while an inflexible tram can't. On the other hand, the trams ran on electricity and that would have been important in conserving fuel. The Mumbles Railway was also electrically powered and came into its own during the war when SWT was forced to make cutbacks in services due to fuel shortages. It was carrying nearly five million passengers a year by the end of the war so it was fortunate indeed that the bombing raids failed to stop the service.

By 1943 Germany was losing the war and the air raids over Swansea came to an

AEC Regent, ACY 7 — similar to Trevor Groocock's ACY 11 — in Castle Street, late 1940s. *Royston Morgan Collection*

With Swansea Castle ruins behind in 1950, BWN 427 was another of the Leyland TD5s with Weymann bodywork delivered in 1938. Originally fleet number 127, it was renumbered 544 in 1939 and withdrawn in 1953. *Royston Morgan Collection*

end. There was a sting in the tail however. The last raid was on February 16 that year when 32 high explosive bombs and countless incendiaries were dropped on Hafod, St Thomas and Brynmill causing 34 deaths, 110 injuries and severe structural damage. But SWT's war was not yet over for the company was called upon to perform a vitally important part in the push that would help secure an Allied victory.

As the bombing ended, SWT received a top secret call from the Ministry of Labour warning it to mobilise its resources to convey workmen employed on 'a number one priority job.' Preparations were in hand for the D-Day landings in France but the ports of Calais, Cherbourg and Le Havre were heavily defended by the Germans so getting all the vehicles and equipment across as part of the invasion would have to take place on the Normandy coast after the initial troop landings. There were no harbours to do this so the Allies would have to take one with them. The idea of a gigantic floating harbour known as a Mulberry Harbour was born and construction work began in ports and dry docks around the UK. It was the Port of Swansea's job to build two sections and an army of workmen was recruited within 20 miles of Swansea while labour from further afield was billeted at a former military camp a few miles from the docks. It was SWT's job to get them to the construction site and this was to test the company's crews,

A group of SWT inspectors, drivers and conductors in the 1950s.

Unlucky 13 who paid the price for wartime bravery

Thirteen members of staff of the South Wales Transport Company gave their lives during deployment with the armed forces in the Second World War. They were: Stanley Harries, William Hicks, Arthur Jones, Alfred Maslen, William Morgans, and Thomas Morris, drivers; Ieuan Jenkins, Robert Nener and Clifford Williams, conductors; Idris Jones, Donald Nicholas and Thomas Whitworth, clerks, and Arthur Miles, a messenger.

In the First World War a further 12 employees had paid the supreme sacrifice for serving their country. They were George Blewett, Albert Beynon, Charles F Bowden and Robert D Hicks, all conductors; John E Evans, Daniel Hedley, John Hedley and George Noyes, drivers; Daniel Davies, cleaner; Frederick Harvey, painter, Arthur Richards, mechanic and Fred Manning, fireman.

It is likely that those who died in the First World War would have been drawn not just from South Wales Transport, but also the Swansea Improvements & Tramway Company and the Mumbles Railway.

The memorial pictured alongside is a tribute to their bravery and heroism and was proudly displayed in the boardroom at Ravenhill long after the demise of South Wales Transport.

But if these men were the heroes, back home in Swansea there were villains, people described at the time as crooks and spivs only too willing to take advantage of any situation.

Conductress Margaret Hefferman recalled how counterfeit coins were a problem in the blackouts. "Lighting in the buses became dimmer and dimmer until there was a total blackout," she said.

"Some passengers were not slow to take advantage of this to pass counterfeit coins. Halfpennies and farthings were covered with silver paint, some even covered with silver paper."

"Conductresses used to carry small lamps attached to straps on their cash bags to help distinguish coins."

engineers and fitters to the very limits. It was a round-the-clock operation and more than 1,000 men were transported to and from the site every day. In the first seven weeks alone, the buses operated 14,000 miles on this special service. The buses had to travel over the port's roads which inevitably crossed railway lines and this caused major damage to their springs and rear platforms. The number of SWT's engineering staff and fitters was already depleted because many employees were on wartime service. Buses had also suffered in the air raids. Staff were being asked to perform the seemingly impossible. But this was SWT. All the demands were met and the company didn't have to cancel any of its other wartime bus services.

The company's managing director, Percy Blake, praised everyone involved: "Drivers, conductors, mechanical staff and all others concerned did a grand job," he said. It was a bit of an understatement for this was a massive task and it was completed on time. When the sections were towed out of the port they only just managed to clear the lock gates.

But even with this job done, SWT was still having major problems because as the air raids ended, the number of passengers who wanted to use its services began increasing dramatically. In 1944 the company's chairman, John Spencer Wills, said that despite the fact that it could only operate two-thirds of the vehicle miles it ran before the war, passenger numbers had increased by 18 per cent.

Modern fleet proved to be a major asset

At the start of the Second World War, SWT had a large, modern bus fleet and this was to stand it in good stead during the difficult years that followed.

The company had received 74 new vehicles in 1937, 62 of them AEC Regent double deckers to replace Swansea's trams which were withdrawn that year. Another 70 buses arrived in 1938 followed by 50 more in 1939. So at the start of the war in September 1939, the company had more than 180 buses that were no more than two years old. This was to prove a major asset because of the large number of engineering and

garage staff receiving their call up papers which had repercussions on vehicle maintenance for the duration of hostilities. Lack of spare parts was another problem.

At the outbreak of war, 28 buses were commandered by the military and SWT was also in a position to loan 20 vehicles to other operators who were not so well off. These included the eight AEC Renown, six-wheel double deckers which were delivered to the company in 1934 and used mainly on the number 2, Swansea to Llanelly service. They went to SWT's sister company, Rhondda Transport, which was also a British Electric Traction subsidiary. SWT may not have been unhappy to see them go for, impressive as they looked, with their 8.8 litre oil engines, they were fuel thirsty machines. The company received no new buses during wartime, not even what became known as 'utility' buses which most fleets received between 1942 and 1945. These were basic, no frills vehicles which were intended to tide transport companies over until the end of hostilities and normal bus production could resume.

Conductress Margaret Hefferman collects fares from passengers on another busy shift.

When peace was finally declared after six years of hostilities SWT's buses had taken a real hammering and were in urgent need of some tender, loving care which had not been provided due to wartime contingencies and lack of staff. All that would have to be put right in the immediate post-war years, confronting the company with yet another challenge.

An AEC Renown turns from Alexandra Road into High Street, Swansea, 1950.

A Weymann works photograph of the company's B39F body fitted to Dennis Lancet 2, CCY 960, delivered with fleet number 160 in 1939. It was renumbered to 875 soon after and withdrawn in 1949. *Royston Morgan Collection*

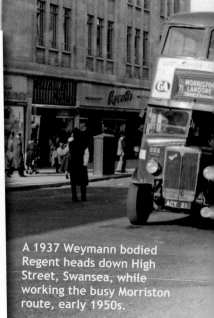

A 1937 Weymann bodied Regent heads down High Street, Swansea, while working the busy Morriston route, early 1950s.

When company's crews

Heroic SWT conductor Tom Bushell saved three buses from destruction in a war time air raid.

Tom, who joined SWT in 1928, was on duty at The Exchange in Adelaide Street, one of SWT's Swansea town centre termini, when an air raid warning sounded. Passengers fled to the nearest communal shelter as incendiary bombs came crashing through the roofs of the buses there. One of these rolled under a bus.

Tom, with the aid of a policeman, dashed to the rescue. They successfully smothered the incendiaries with sand — SWT's buses carried sandbags during the war in case of just such

an attack. The incendiary under the bus proved a little more difficult to deal with, but eventually that too was extinguished. For his brave action, Tom, who became an inspector and retired from SWT in 1963, was commended.

Conductress Margaret Hefferman recalled other incidents of SWT employees saving their vehicles during air raids.

"There was a great deal of unsung heroism among all the staff. Drivers and conductors standing shoulder to shoulder with foremen and clerical staff to deal with

incendiaries when it seemed that the Jerries were intent on eliminating Brunswick Garage. Drivers would always do their best to take buses away from any unexploded bombs," she said.

At the end of the war, many of SWT's conductresses left the company as the men returned home to take up their jobs once more. But some stayed and never again were the buses an all-male affair as they had been in the pre-war years.

Margaret, who married after the war and became Margaret Davies, remained to become a senior conductor with the company, not retiring until 1970.

Irene Locke also stayed with SWT and was one of the organisers of the conductresses' annual outings. She became a renowned charity worker in the 1960s and worked

> **"The Jerries seemed intent on eliminating Brunswick garage."**
> **— Conductress Margaret Hefferman.**

The first of the second batch of AEC Regent vehicles, 12 in total, which arrived at SWT in 1937.

Royston Morgan Collection

became unsung heroes

hard on behalf of the company's pensioners. Unfortunately, she suffered ill health in later life and died at the end of 1970.

Some conductresses found clerical work with the company, among them Margaret Jones who ended up in the company's lost property office. Others left SWT only to return later as conductresses as vacancies arose while a very small number became drivers.

Company fitter 'Dasher' Day came within a hair's breadth of being blown to bits near the company's Brunswick Street, Swansea, garage during the hostilities. A driver in the Royal Engineers, he was with an officer checking for unexploded bombs after a raid and went to the toilet.

"Suddenly there was an almighty explosion," he said. "Manhole covers and debris were flying everywhere. About the only thing I could do was to roll myself into a ball and hope that nothing heavy fell on me."

That call of nature saved Dasher's life. He got away with a scalp wound and bruises, but his officer was killed.

Having started work with SWT as a conductor, he eventually became a fitter's mate at the company's Ravenhill engineering works, retiring in 1968.

Drastic cuts were made to the company's bus services at the start of the war as fuel restrictions hit hard. Passengers were urged to cut out non-essential travel, particularly at peak times. The message didn't always get through however and the company's buses were often grossly over-crowded.

This alarmed Swansea Corporation which in October 1941 urged SWT to run more vehicles. At its meeting that month, the council passed a motion that praised SWT for "the splendid manner in which it had adapted its services to meet conditions during air raids."

But there was a sting in the tail. The council also hit out at the

wartime bus service and called for a fuller service. Councillors said demand for buses from passengers was so high that bus travel "is seriously affecting the people's health as well as their morale."

The problem was particularly serious at the various bus termini around the town centre where would-be passengers sometimes couldn't get on to buses because they were so full, according to the council.

The company felt obliged to point out that it was bound by wartime fuel restrictions which limited the number of services it was allowed to run. The problems would continue until well after the end of the war.

Through thick and thin South Wales Transport always knew that its strength lay in its staff and was determined to look after them in these dark and difficult days. It started a mutual aid scheme which provided help for any of its employees who were bombed out of their homes or suffered damage through enemy action.

CHAPTER 4

Golden age brought battles of a new kind

If ever there was a golden age for South Wales Transport, the 10 years following the end of the Second World War must surely be it. As life slowly returned to normal, the company started buying new buses again including some of the finest AEC Regents ever built.

Weymann was the favoured body builder and for many years hundreds of these magnificent double deckers served the towns and valleys of South West Wales.

Better times saw a revival in demand for tours and during the 1950s the company had one of the country's most successful coaching operations both at home and abroad. Passenger numbers rose to heights not seen before — or since. This was truly the age of the bus. But no golden age is without its problems and that was certainly the case for SWT. There were battles to be fought and difficult decisions to be taken.

As the guns finally fell silent across Europe, the company turned its attention to its buses. At the beginning of the war in 1939 the company had one of the country's most modern fleets but now, six years later, it was in urgent need of renewal. However, as the industry recovered, new buses were in short supply. Just 20 took to the road in 1946, all Regent IIs. A mere one followed in 1947 and only another 20 the following year. It was not until 1949 that larger batches started to arrive to replace vehicles that had taken a real battering during the war years.

There were lots of other problems. By December 1946, wages together with the cost of vehicle parts and tyres had risen dramatically. Even so, SWT announced its immediate plans to restore stage carriage services to the level they had been before the war, and improve them where necessary. Managing director, Percy Blake, reported that the company was already running 90 per cent of the 1939 services and that figure would have been even greater but for the shortage of supplies. By 1948 Mr Blake announced that all SWT's services had returned to their pre-war level and in some cases had been much improved. As Swansea expanded, new routes were introduced, including services to rapidly developing housing estates on the hilly areas around the town, including Penlan.

Just as the company's plans began to come together locally, the spectre of nationalisation began to raise its head and pose a threat to its very existence. State control was the essence of the post-war Labour government. It had been busy with the coal and steel industries and the health service. It also had its eyes set on transport

A conductor stands alongside a 1949 Willowbrook bodied AEC Regal III in Trinity Place, Swansea, late 1950s. The location was one of many used as a terminus by SWT.

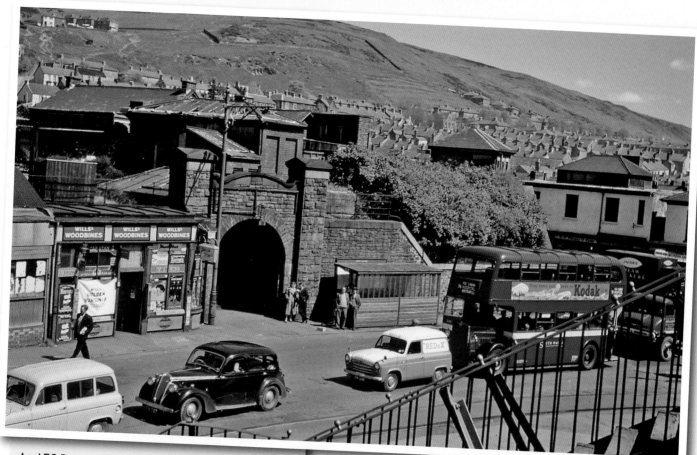

An AEC Regent III alongside St Thomas station on the approach to the River Tawe bridge that was the main link with Swansea's east side, 1958.

and at the beginning of 1948 set up the British Transport Commission taking control of the 'big four' main line railway companies on January 1, that year. Buses were to be next.

At this time SWT's parent company, British Electric Traction, was one of two major UK bus groups in the private sector. The other was Tilling. BET had pledged to fight any attempt by the Government to buy it for the nation, but its battle suffered a major blow in September 1948, when Tilling sold its transport interests to the BTC for what was then the huge sum of £24.8 million. Everyone, even the London Stock Exchange, expected BET to follow suit. Despite the odds, BET won its battle and remained in the private sector. Its size and strength had saved it — and SWT — from an uncertain fate, but it was not yet out of the woods. The Government also intended to create area passenger transport boards to run bus services which, if they had gone ahead, could have sealed the fate of BET's companies in South Wales, including SWT. Luckily, the proposals came at the tail end of the Labour administration and the area boards never materialised.

The company still wasn't safe and secure though. In South Wales there was yet another battle to be fought. By 1950 the Red & White Group, which included the 166-vehicle, Swansea-based United Welsh, had grown to become the largest independent bus company in Britain with around 750 vehicles. Many of its services operated wheel to wheel with BET's buses, including those of SWT. In 1950 it voluntarily sold its bus interests to the state and became part of the nationalised Tilling group. The move caused consternation inside BET. For the first time Tilling now had a firm hold in South Wales with its Red and White and United Welsh subsidiaries. SWT and UWS operated fairly amicably on many similar routes and there was concern over whether this would continue. United Welsh vehicles were strategically placed across SWT's operating area. Its Neath depot, the largest with 56 buses, was nearly twice the size of SWT's in the town. UWS had 52 vehicles at Gorseinon depot, handy for any incursion into Llanelli, and 29 each at Swansea and Clydach depots. There was little doubt that it posed a major threat.

BET acted immediately to protect its interests in the area. In 1950 it bought out the independent J James of Ammanford and followed this up the next year with Thomas Bros and Afan Transport, which ran buses in the Port Talbot and Afan Valley areas. SWT took over Llanelly District Traction which ran trolley buses and buses in Llanelli in 1952 and BET bought the proudly independent N&C Luxury Coaches in 1953. United Welsh got in two for the state side when it acquired seven-vehicle firm, Richmond of Neath, in 1952 and later that year the more sizeable 24-vehicle Swan Motor Company which ran competing services with SWT in Swansea.

It seemed both sides were squaring up to each other and the result could have been bloody, but then

The route that resembled a pub crawl

There were only 12 stops on a SWT bus route used by two sisters, and 10 of them were outside pubs!

Valerie Evans and Jean Blair grew up in the village of Glais in the Swansea Valley and regularly caught the number 29 bus which ran from Swansea to Pontardawe.

"It was 50 years' ago and the bus was always a single decker with a conductor and driver," says Jean, who now lives in Heathfield, Swansea.

"It used to take 35 minutes, today it takes 40 to 45 minutes. There were 12 stops on our return journey from Swansea to Glais: St Mary's Church, Midland Station (The Ship), Foxhole (Maesteg Street), The Rising Sun (Pentrechwyth), The Jersey Arms (Bonymaen), Swansea Vale Works (near The Colliers), The Star at Llansamlet, The Bowens Arms at Birchgrove, The Bridgend Inn at Birchgrove, The Crown at Birchgrove, The Globe at Glais, and The Old Glais."

Valerie, who lives in Glais, said: "The bus was often full and I remember one of the conductors called Albert who would shout out that the bus wouldn't stop until The Rising Sun, when it would be only three-quarters full."

A 1949 AEC Regal III saloon heads along Quay Parade into central Swansea with passengers collected on the 29 route down the Swansea Valley through Glais, Birchgrove and Llansamlet.

everyone saw sense. United Welsh and SWT came to an agreement that was to exist for the following 17 years. UWS would not run local services within Swansea's town boundary in exchange for SWT pulling off its services in Gower. The two companies still ran on many similar routes, but the competition was no longer cut throat. It made perfect sense at a time when bus services were expanding as the number of passengers rose to unprecedented levels. In the 1950s you could walk down long streets and not see a single car. Everyone used buses. When you went to work in the morning and returned home in the evening, you went by bus. Shopping trips into town, visits to friends or relations, trips to the seaside, all were accomplished by boarding a bus.

SWT's annual passenger figures rose during the first half of the decade

An atmospheric view of a 1949 Weymann bodied lowbridge AEC Regent III passing Weaver's Flour Mill, Quay Parade, Swansea, 1958.

to an incredible 97 million in 1954 and 1955. It is a truly amazing figure. SWT's successor company, First Cymru, carried just over 20 million passengers a year in 2013. The decline is even steeper than those figures suggest. For in 1955, SWT had yet to take over J James, United Welsh, Thomas Bros and N&C. It had still to replace Western Welsh, later National Welsh, in Haverfordwest, Carmarthen, Neath and Bridgend. Direct comparisons are difficult, for some routes are now operated by independent bus firms, but at a rough estimate the annual number of bus passenger journeys in the area covered by SWT before it handed over to First Cymru in April 1999, had fallen by 150 million in the 60 years from 1954 to 2014.

Surprisingly despite such prolific passenger numbers in the 1950s as many as one third of SWT's services were running at a financial loss. In those days the company used what was called cross-subsidy to keep them going, in other words the money made by SWT's profitable services propped up the loss-making ones. At the 1952 annual general meeting, company chairman, Raymond Birch, warned that the losses could lead to cutbacks and higher fares, the first increase since the 1930s.

The warning signalled the start of a major battle over fares that would be waged between SWT and local authorities throughout the 1950s and 1960s.

Almost annually SWT would announce plans for higher fares and the councils, particularly Swansea's, would object. The issue would then be decided by the South Wales Traffic Commissioners at inquiries attended by both parties. These hearings didn't last just a few hours. The commissioners usually decided applications by the various bus companies en-bloc and the arguments often took many days, sometimes even weeks.

The councils simply could not understand why SWT needed to raise fares when it was carrying so many passengers. The company blamed rising costs and the Government's tax on fuel. Mr Birch said in May 1952: "I have spent the whole of my business life in road passenger transport, but I cannot recall any period comparable with the past two years when operating expenditure rose at such an alarming rate."

In 1952 SWT reduced its annual mileage by 250,000 compared with the previous year, but costs still escalated by £100,000 and the latest increase in fuel tax added £42,000 to the company's annual costs. The problems continued and SWT joined other BET companies in a major campaign to reduce this tax. Veteran bus man WT James took over as SWT chairman in 1953 and declared at that year's annual meeting: "I cannot help feeling that some local authorities who consistently oppose any increase in our fares would do

43

Passengers wait patiently at Victoria Gardens, Neath in the summer of 1950 for this Willowbrook bodied AEC Regal III saloon to continue on its No. 3 route which took it from Swansea to Margam via Llansamlet.

Cleaners at work at Pontardawe depot, 1959.

Chris Taylor Archive

better to appeal to the Chancellor of the Exchequer to do something about this inequitable tax rather than to appeal to the Minister of Transport against modest and justifiable increases in fares to meet additional costs."

The appeal went unheard and the councils continued to object to SWT's fare increase applications.

The hearings became increasingly acrimonious and at one, in June 1958 lawyer, Mr Alun T Davies, accused it and other BET companies in South Wales of feathering their own nests. It is doubtful that this was the true case. Using SWT's favoured method of measuring expenditure, that is, how each £ was being spent by the company, in 1957 10s 9d (54p) went in wages, 2s 4d (11.5p) on fuel tax and road fund licences, 1s 9d (8p) on materials, 1s 8d (7.5p) on buses and new equipment, 1s (5p) on fuel, 6d (2.5p) on income tax, 6d (2.5p) on building maintenance, 4d (2p) on administration, 4d (2p) on employee benefits, 2d (1p) on publicity, 1d (0.5p) payment to Swansea Council under the 1937 agreement to take over the town's trams, and 7d (3p) on dividends for shareholders. Such figures certainly don't suggest that the company was feathering its own nest.

Four AEC Regents wait for passengers at their terminus alongside St Mary's Church, Swansea in the summer of 1958.

An evocative glimpse of Castle Street, Swansea in 1956 with one of the 1937 Regents and a later Regent III heading for their terminus at The Exchange. *Huw Daniel*

The councils also seemed to fail to appreciate the fact that SWT needed to spend money to update and renew assets, that is, to buy new vehicles. Mr Davies accused the company of 'making no sacrifice' to meet its £87,000 increased costs in 1958 and claimed it wanted to make up for it through the £85,000 it would get it the higher fares were allowed. He also suggested that it had not put forward any programme for economies or increased efficiency.

Each year following the war SWT thought it wise and prudent to spend money on new buses. In 1952, for example, it spent £110,000 on 26 double deckers even though the cost of buses had risen by two-and-a-half times since 1939. In 1955 it bought 20 more double deckers and eight coaches for its extended tours programme at a cost of £120,000. Any firm that doesn't modernise or replace worn out equipment will soon find it has major problems. If SWT hadn't allowed adequately for depreciation its vehicles

would have become uncomfortable and unreliable and as a result, the travelling public would have suffered.

Throughout the 1950s, SWT's fleet was one of the most modern in the country. Most services were run by the maroon double deckers many people remember with affection today. There were Regent IIs and IIIs, most with an open entrance at the back of the bus, and then later Regent Vs with entrance doors at the front which made bus travel safer for passengers. Modern single deck AEC Reliances entered the fleet for more lightly used routes and there were examples of some of the finest coach designs of the period for SWT's growing programme of tours, at home and abroad. But as the good times rolled, there was a spectre haunting everyone who worked for SWT.

Back in 1936 the company had reached agreement with Swansea Corporation which saw it replace the town's

April 28, 1954 brought a visit from the directors of the company including: (front, left to right): WM Dravers, general manager; PG Stone-Clark, director; and WT James, chairman. AE Wilford, accountant and IM Smith, secretary, form the second row while L Parker, chief engineer and EC Hill, traffic manager bring up the rear. *Chris Taylor Archive*

trams with buses. It was agreed that at the end of 21 years the council would have the right to the compulsory purchase of SWT's services within the town's boundaries. In 1956 that moment was becoming perilously close.

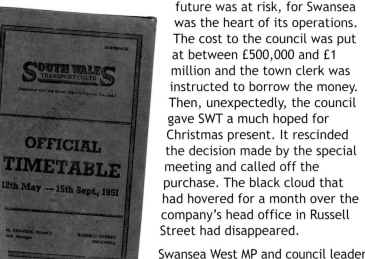

As part of the 1936 agreement, if it decided to go ahead with the purchase the council would have to serve the company with notice between July 1 and December 31. Chairman, Mr W T James, told the company's annual meeting in February 1957 that he was doubtful whether the corporation would "wish to hazard the risks of operating a municipal passenger transport undertaking in today's difficult conditions."

But in November it held a special meeting to discuss it. The decision rocked SWT to the core. By 31 votes to 11, councillors agreed to go-ahead with the purchase.

It was a shattering blow. It meant that SWT would lose one-third of its fleet and its most profitable services. It is not an exaggeration to say that the company's

future was at risk, for Swansea was the heart of its operations. The cost to the council was put at between £500,000 and £1 million and the town clerk was instructed to borrow the money. Then, unexpectedly, the council gave SWT a much hoped for Christmas present. It rescinded the decision made by the special meeting and called off the purchase. The black cloud that had hovered for a month over the company's head office in Russell Street had disappeared.

Swansea West MP and council leader Percy Morris explained the about-turn when he moved a motion in December's council meeting that the town clerk be instructed not to serve a statutory notice on SWT to acquire the undertaking. "I do so with very great reluctance on behalf of the Labour Party of the council," said Mr Morris. "Our colleagues of the Independent Party have made it clear all the way along that they are opposed to municipalisation. It is clear from the report submitted by the town clerk that the Ministry of Transport would agree to us raising the necessary loan, but the policy of the Government and the activities of the Chancellor of the Exchequer make it virtually impossible for the council to do so without imposing an intolerable burden upon the ratepayers of Swansea."

SWT conductresses outside the Glynn Vivian Art Gallery, Alexandra Road, Swansea, all set for their annual day out.

One of SWT's first eight foot wide vehicles, 56 seat Regent III Weymann GWN 82 was new in 1951. Fleet No 370, seen on service in Llanelly, was withdrawn in 1963.

So, as in 1936, cash worries had taken priority over ideology. Mr Morris believed raising a minimum loan would have involved ratepayers in loan charges of £100,000 a year. There would have also been extensive and protracted arbitration and even the possibility of High Court Action. The sighs of relief in Russell Street could be heard all over Swansea.

SWT's general manager, Mr H Weedy, told staff: "By this wise decision we remain one unit and are relieved of any anxiety of our personal future in the general reshuffle which would be bound to follow had the option been taken up. To survive, a company must progress. This company has a fine record of progress over the years but naturally in latter years it has been hampered by the uncertainty of its fate.

"Now, no longer fettered, the outlook for 1957 and the years ahead should be exceedingly bright. Yes, a new chapter is

Upholsterers repairing seats at Ravenhill, 1956.

Tinsmiths and electricians at work in South Wales Transport's busy Ravenhill engineering section, 1956.

beginning for SWT and in this chapter we are the main characters. What is to be written depends on us. Let 1957 be the start of the new era, and when our history is told, may it be said of us, they, too, did their jobs well."

It was rather Churchillian, but well put and Mr Weedy's relief was obvious. Unfortunately he was far too optimistic. For there was yet another, more sinister threat developing that would have major repercussions on SWT. It began in 1956 with the advent of the Suez Crisis when President Nasser of Egypt closed the canal and oil supplies were hit. SWT was forced to cut services, resulting in a massive loss of five million passengers that year.

It was believed at the time to be a one off drop caused by the crisis and that passenger figures would soon be back to the 97 million they had been in 1955. But as the years that followed showed, it was not just a glitch and would prove to be SWT's

A rear platform view of AEC Regent III, FWN 366 (328) outside the Bush Hotel, High Street, Swansea, early 1950s. Both The Bush and the bus are no more.
Peter Nedin

A 1959, Weymann bodied unpainted AEC Regent V takes on passengers at Oystermouth bus station in 1960 before heading towards Newton.

Silver service experiment didn't last

One of the experimental silver double deckers on a summer time trip to Aberavon Beach.

A strange batch of buses turned up in Swansea in 1958. It appeared that someone had forgotten to paint them! In fact, it was quite deliberate. SWT had decided to experiment with buses in an unpainted aluminium finish to see if costs could be reduced. There were six of these 'silver' buses, all Weymann bodied AEC Regent Vs. Two had panels of an aluminium alloy, two of commercial aluminium and two with commercial aluminium but given a coat of varnish. The commercial aluminium ones without varnish proved the best and in 1959 another seven Regent Vs to this specification arrived and the experiment continued until 1966 by which time the buses had become a familiar sight on routes across Swansea. SWT found that in the salt and industrial atmosphere of Swansea, the unpainted vehicles could stand up to the wear and tear and did not suffer more corrosion than their painted sisters. But there were problems. It proved difficult to blend fibreglass with the unpainted panels and if the bus suffered minor body damage the whole panel had to be changed instead of a simple repair using filler and a paint brush. After a seven-year trial SWT decided to abandon the experiment as it found that the unpainted vehicles needed more than normal cleaning to maintain an acceptable appearance. Overall there was little difference in costs between the 'silver' buses and their painted counterparts.

The company's staff magazine, Ein Newyddion, proclaimed: "As it is felt that the painted bus is considerably more attractive, it's back to the redskins for us."

greatest problem for the rest of its existence.

In the meantime, SWT had other, more pressing matters on its mind for it was planning the unthinkable. It wanted to close the Mumbles Railway.

One of SWT's unpainted silver AEC Regent Vs (RCY 350) in Caer Street on its way to the Guildhall, mid-1960s.

An AEC Regal saloon bound for Langland Bay alongside a Regent III all set to convey its passengers to Sketty in Oxford Street, 1950.

Company just grew and grew

From its very earliest beginnings with two Milnes-Daimler double deck vehicles South Wales Transport, despite all the obstacles it had to overcome, made swift progress in the development and growth of its fleet.

By 1952 its buses were a common sight in almost every community. There were 297 vehicles in all, most of them maroon double deckers with a cream stripe running beneath the lower deck windows.

The company had 114 AEC Regent full height double deckers and new legislation had enabled wider vehicles to be built so that 14 of them were 8ft wide instead of the 7ft 6ins allowed previously. This made a surprising difference to their appearance. There were 59 AEC Regent low height double deckers for use on routes with low railway bridges and 15 of these were also 8ft wide. The double deck fleet was completed at the time by 30 Leyland low height buses, all bought before the war. After 1947 SWT only bought AEC products until the advent of the National Bus Company. The single deckers included 39 AEC Regal IIs, 18 AEC Regal IIIs and 13 Renown six-wheelers which were bought for the notoriously steep Townhill route. But pride of the fleet in the early 1950s were the 20 AEC Regal III coaches it

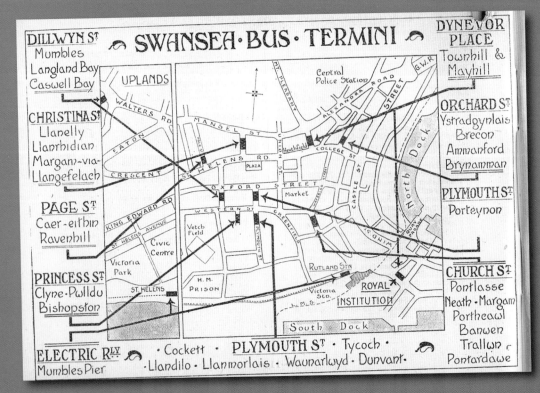

Double deck vehicles entering and leaving Ravenhill depot, 1950.

Some of the vehicles which ferried thousands of workers from a variety of locations to carry out their shifts at the Abbey Works, Port Talbot, 1952.

used on the company's continental and British tours that were growing in popularity. Weymann was again the favoured body builder and all the double deckers had been built by this company and the Regal saloons had mostly been built by Willowbrook while the Regal III coaches had Windover bodies.

The Renowns were bodied by Brush which had also built the 13 double deck trains used on SWT's Mumbles Railway. Each of these carried 106 passengers. At busy times they were coupled in pairs and worked by a driver and four conductors, one for each deck. By this point in its history SWT had five garages, the largest at Ravenhill in Swansea housed 140 vehicles. The company's second biggest depot in Swansea was in Brunswick Street, close to the town centre. This had 85 buses and the site was shared with SWT's head office. The Llanelli depot in Copperworks Road had 41 vehicles, Neath had 33 and Pontardawe was the smallest with 19. Main workshops were housed in a separate building alongside the Ravenhill depot.

SWT was proud of the appearance of its vehicles and each had a wash and brush up inside and out every day. Life was hard for the company's

vehicles as each covered an average of 800 miles every week at this time, the daily fleet mileage total being 35,000. Vehicles were inspected every 5,000 miles while lubricant levels were checked weekly and greasing carried out every three weeks.

Buses bought before the war and those with 7.7 litre engines got a major overhaul at 120,000 miles, but post-war vehicles with the 9.6 litre engine received theirs at 180,000 miles as crankshaft wear was far less than in the smaller engines.

In 1952 SWT operated 68 regular services and five seasonal ones. There were also 14 workmen's services. A year earlier it had carried 82 million passengers.

SWT chief engineer Leslie Parker wanted lighter vehicles so that fuel costs could be cut. He was also urging manufacturers to come up with a low height double decker that had ample head room on the upper deck and single deckers that could carry more than 50 passengers. These things would eventually come to pass, but in 1952 they were only aspirations.

Conductress Rose Davies, complete with all the tools of her daily trade, September 1964.
Chris Taylor Archive

CHAPTER 5

Home and away, SWT's tours were the best

If you wanted to take a holiday abroad by coach from South Wales in the 1950s there was only one company you could take it with — South Wales Transport. It was the only bus operator in South Wales to hold a road service licence for continental tours and during the 1950s and 1960s it gained a countrywide reputation for the quality of the trips that it organised.

The growth in overseas coach tours was phenomenal after the holiday-starved years of the Second World War and the late 1940s. As the 1950s progressed SWT's trips became bigger and better. They went further and further afield — to Switzerland, Austria, Germany, Spain and Portugal. Later there was even a tour to Czechoslovakia, a country which at the time was firmly behind the Iron Curtain.

There was a huge range of tours at home, too. From destinations on the Isle of Skye to Devon and Cornwall, the Isle of Wight, London and the Norfolk Broads. SWT arranged everything, from start to finish, all the traveller had to worry about was being at the collection point on the day of departure.

SWT started running tours as early as 1926. They were ambitious for the time with destinations including Cardigan, Tenby, the Wye Valley, and Llanwrtyd Wells in mid Wales. There were shorter trips to Porthcawl and Gower while the furthest away was Aberystwyth at a cost of 18/- (90p).

In the early 1930s, as coaches started to become more reliable, the company began going further afield with tours to Scotland and North Wales which proved popular. The outbreak of the Second World War curtailed the programme however, and it was not until the late 1940s when wartime emergency powers were being relaxed that the company was able to resume its private hire and day excursions.

At the same time it unveiled a much more ambitious plan — continental tours by coach. The first ran in 1950 and proved enormously popular. Within six years SWT was running 15 separate tours to many parts of Europe which ran throughout the summer holiday season, from May to September. The most expensive in 1956 was a 16-day trip to Madrid and Barcelona at 61 guineas. A guinea was worth £1.05, or 21s in old money, and was a clever way of making the price of something sound less than it actually was. The word also had a hint of aristocracy about it, which is possibly why SWT always quoted its coach tour prices in guineas rather than the more humble pound.

Participants in a tour to Switzerland at Ravenhill on July 21, 1950. Behind them, perhaps about to set off on its first trip is one of three full-fronted Windover bodied AEC Regal IIIs fitted with 28 adjustable reclining seats.

All set for a memorable day's adventure aboard one of the charabancs operated by South Wales Transport in the early 1920s. *Royston Morgan Collection*

Other continental tours included 16 days in Florence, Rome and Pisa for 60 and a half guineas; 14 days on the French Riviera for 53 and a half guineas; 13 days in San Sebastian and the Pyrenees for 46 and a half guineas; 12 days in Belgium, Luxembourg, Germany, Austria, Switzerland and France for 45 and a half guineas; 12 days around the Swiss and Italian lakes for 45 and a half guineas and nine days in Belgium and Holland for 31 and a half guineas.

The British tours included 11 days visiting Scotland and Northern Ireland for 31 guineas; nine days in the Scottish Highlands and Royal Deeside for 27 guineas; seven days touring Devon and Cornwall for 20 guineas and the cheapest tour, four days in North Wales for nine and a half guineas. Another popular three-day trip was to the Blackpool illuminations in September and October at six and a half guineas if you went 'de-luxe', or £3.10s at a 'good class boarding house or hotel.'

Popular though the continental tours were, they may have been perceived as being rather elite. They tended to attract what was termed 'the professional classes.' A miner or steelworker who, if they went on holiday at all, would be more likely to spend it in a caravan in Porthcawl or a guest house on the coast. SWT was aware of this but did not want its coach tours to be seen as exclusive. It regarded the lack of patronage by the working classes as a potential source of new custom

and spent heavily, advertising its tours in local newspapers, on posters and brochures, and even organised film shows in towns and villages all over South Wales.

The tours department produced their own colour film shows and rather than having just one general film for all the trips, each illustrated a particular tour. The films were shot by a courier, also employed by the company, who would be on hand to answer questions during the showing. He — it was invariably a he — would accompany the tour and would be provided with a log book to keep a detailed record of it.

Nothing was left to chance. Tours were planned a year ahead and before a new one was introduced the company would send one of its managers to inspect hotels and restaurants to ensure they met the standard required. Customers could expect the best attention from the time they made their bookings at the company's offices in Russell Street or Plymouth Street, at seven general booking offices in the Swansea area, or through 37 agents in South Wales, to when they stepped off the coach at the end of their tour. Everything was done for them, SWT was authorised by the Bank of England to operate a foreign exchange department, it sorted out passports, issued itineraries. and lists of their fellow passengers. They could expect to be well looked after.

On its British tours, SWT employed what were called driver-couriers, while the continental tours had a driver and a courier. The emphasis was on experience and

Summer holiday brought magical Langland rides

Fond memories of the summer service 40 to Caswell are recalled by Michael Evans, who moved to Walsall in the West Midlands but was born in St Thomas, Swansea.

For two weeks in August every year between the mid 1950s and mid-1960s he returned to Swansea with his parents for their summer holidays and says the thing he looked forward to most was the town's buses. One of his favourite routes was the No. 40 which he and his parents caught in Townhill where they stayed with his grandparents.

"I can still recall the anticipation of seeing that red bus come round the bend as it climbed up Townhill Road," says Michael.

"Loaded up with bucket and spade, cricket bat and ball and picnic, we would clamber upstairs, me hoping, of course, that the front seat would be available for the journey. The route took us across Townhill, past the landmark water tower, down into Sketty, then along the sea-front Mumbles Road where we would often overtake, or be overtaken, by the Mumbles Train. From the square in Oystermouth the bus would climb up to Langland Corner and then make the final steep descent into Caswell Valley and the beach.

"It was a magical journey indeed for a young boy!"

This C32F bodied Dennis Lancet 2, was one of 10 new in 1938 and equipped with five-speed gearboxes, curved glass roof lights and sliding roofs. Delivered in cream and black it wore BET red after refurbishment in1947/48.
Royston Morgan Collection

reliability. The drivers and couriers, who would receive basic foreign language lessons, included members of staff with long, safe driving records and good personal skills. They were middle-aged men who during the winter season would work on SWT's usual services.

They included Walter Pounder who drove on Swansea services during the winter months, then in summer he was employed on continental tours. He started on the Scottish tours after the war and each year for 20 years made eight trips abroad each season, visiting Switzerland and Austria. "The routes were so familiar I could make my own timetable. It gave me the opportunity to see places I would never otherwise have seen," said Walter when he retired in 1972. Keri Evans, who retired in 1969, usually drove double deckers around Penlan and Brynhyfryd, but for 15 seasons he went to Holland, France, Belgium, Switzerland, Germany and Italy.

The tours continued to expand in the 1960s despite the rising popularity of air flights from Cardiff. SWT's attitude was 'if you can't beat them, join them' and it came to an arrangement with air travel companies at Cardiff and Swansea to operate air tours. Holiday travel had become big business and SWT set itself up

A line-up of AEC Regal III Willowbrook coaches resplendant in their ivory and red coaching livery at Ravenhill depot, 1950. Such vehicles formed the mainstay of the South Wales Transport coaching fleet at home and abroad for many years.

This fleet of mixed SWT coaches was used to carry staff of the David Evans department store to Llandrindod Wells, on their annual outing in 1957.

in the travel agency business. In the early 1960s it became an agent for major operators involved in world travel. It meant that the company's Plymouth Street offices were no longer suitable so in 1963 the tours department moved to larger premises in Craddock Street, Swansea.

SWT chairman, Wilfred Dravers, acknowledged the importance of the tours to the company in 1965: "The travel agency and extended tour business is showing encouraging expansion," he said. "Extended tour programmes have become more comprehensive and more ambitious year by year and are enjoying increasing patronage. It is clear that travel from the towns of South Wales by means of a Welsh coach and a Welsh driver to places as far apart as the Scottish Highlands and Czechoslovakia is appealing to an ever widening clientele."

But change was on the way. In 1969 SWT became part of the National Bus Company and that year it produced a joint holiday brochure with United Welsh, also part of NBC and which would be taken over by SWT in 1971. Then in 1972 SWT teamed up with Western Welsh to sell their holiday travel activities jointly. SWT forfeited its own coach livery for National Bus Company livery. Now instead of getting a coach proudly displaying South Wales, or SWT, on its sides, you got an all white one carrying the name, National in red and blue letters.

SWT general manager, Frank Woodworth, argued: "Many of us have felt for some time that the competitive nature of the travel business demands an aggressive and concerted effort and this can surely be best provided on a national basis." But it meant the loyalty to SWT as a local company that had existed previously, and its reputation for high quality tours, were lost and smaller firms were entering the tours field and doing it more cheaply. In April 1972, SWT lost an appeal against a decision by the South Wales Traffic Commissioners to give a licence to J Jenkins of Skewen to operate eight-day extended tours to a number of destinations and three-day tours to London. Jenkins said it could run tours more cheaply than SWT and produced a 1,500 signature petition to show the demand that existed for its trips. Changes were made to the legislation covering tours and excursions and SWT no longer had an exclusive licence to operate tours overseas.

This unusual looking rear entrance coach was SWT's first under-floor engined vehicle which arrived in the fleet in time for the 1953 touring season. *Royston Morgan Collection.*

Lives that were linked by life on 'The Transport'

Peter Samuel's family was connected with SWT right from the earliest days.

His grandfather, Evan Samuel, was one of the company's first drivers, working out of Brunswick Street garage in Swansea in the 1920s. Peter's father, Arthur Samuel, joined The Transport in 1937 when the company operated a parcel delivery service. "I still have his 1939 diary in which he kept a record of his deliveries," says Peter.

"One day he delivered as many as 82 parcels, on another it was 72. He drove an SWT parcels van which he parked outside our home in Hafod. When he came back from the war he started driving the coach tours. He went to Paris more than 100 times and took coaches to Austria, Italy, Switzerland and Norway. During the coaching season, he might return home from one tour on a Saturday and be off on another the following day. I have a colour film of him taken by SWT to advertise the Paris trip, it's a prized keepsake because he died in 1973, shortly after completing a tour." Out of season SWT's coaches would be mothballed and Arthur would drive local services, his regular route was between Swansea and Townhill, up Mount Pleasant Hill.

"He always took a great pride in his appearance and one of his proudest moments was when, with Tommy Webber, he won the prize for best dressed drivers at the British Coach Rally in 1959."

Peter joined SWT at Ravenhill in 1964 as an apprentice electrician. "There were men working there then who had been in the First World War, working 40 or 50 years for SWT wasn't unusual.

"Every type of job was done at the works, upholstery, woodwork, glazing, you name it. There must have been about 70 fitters in the body shop when I joined in 1964."

Peter's time with SWT came to an end in 1970 when he joined Ford's Swansea plant.

"I was being paid £18 a week by The Transport, but at Ford, after overtime and so on, I could earn £55. But I will always remember my links with the company and the people I worked with very fondly."

The rise in air travel during the 1970s also hit coach tours. People began to question why they should spend days on a coach when they could be in the sun within a few hours from their local airport. But SWT did not pull out of the tours and excursions business. In the mid-1980s it was still offering mini-breaks with two to five day tours at home or abroad. There was also a new programme of excursions branded Days Away offering day and half-day tours to places like Alton Towers, the Grand National, London, Bristol Zoo, Devon and Cornwall as well as mystery tours.

But sadly SWT's proud days of leading the way for high class continental and British tours were over.

Pride of the coaching fleet

Pride of the South Wales Transport fleet in 1950 were 20 coaches that the company had bought for its new programme of British and continental tours. To 21st Century eyes they might seem basic and dated. At the time however they were state of the art.

They all appeared in a new red and ivory livery with a Gothic style South Wales fleet name on their side, but apart from that 17 of them appeared little different from SWT's standard single deckers of the time. They were AEC Regal III half-cabs bodied by Windover with open radiator grills and the driver sitting in a cab alongside the engine. The first three arrived in 1949 and caused huge interest for not only did they have some of the most luxurious seating ever seen on one of the company's vehicles, they also had air conditioning and a public address system. Numbered 1001-3, registration numbers FWN 82-84, they were

A wartime view of Arthur Samuel with the Austin Seven van SWT used for parcel deliveries and bill posting.
Peter Samuel

Four of the Weymann bodied Fanfares SWT used on its prestigious continental tours, April 1970. *Royston Morgan Collection*

British & Continental TOURS

South Wales

S·W·T U·W·S

1969

Day, Half-Day and Mystery Coach Tours From Swansea and District, Neath and Gorseinon

followed in 1950 by 14 similar vehicles, 1004-1017, GCY 431-444.

The first three had coach seats for 30, the rest seated 33 and were soon being put to work on SWT's growing programme of British tours. Forget the toilets, hand basins and serveries that come as standard with many of the latest touring coaches. All these 27ft 6ins long and 7ft 6ins wide vehicles — the maximum allowable dimensions at the time — had was luxury seating.

They were followed in 1950 by three more coaches which, although also bodied by Windover, looked very different. Unlike the half-cabs these were 8ft wide and had full-width cabs, although still with open radiator grills. Numbered 1018-1020, GCY 445-447, these were for SWT's new venture into continental tours. This meant that a little extra comfort was needed so these had adjustable reclining seats for 28, although their seating was increased to 30 in 1958. They still lacked toilets however!

Unfortunately for SWT, half-cab coaches were already becoming dated when these vehicles arrived and when it came to coaching it was essential to put on a modern, up-to-date show. So the company made sure it

had the newest available when it ordered its next coaches. These were the first underfloor engined types in the fleet.

They were bodied again by Windover but looked nothing like their predecessors. They were Regal IVs with 35 seats and SWT took four, two in 1953 and two more the following year. One went on display at the 1952 Commercial Motor Show and all four were for the continental tours programme. They have been called striking, which is one way of describing them. Beauty is in the eye of the beholder however and to many eyes they were among the most ugly coach designs of the 1950s with their peculiar car-shape fronts and rear entrances. They may have had all the luxury expected of a coach at that time, but for many, the bodies didn't reflect that.

The first three half-cabs were exported to Spain in 1955 and the rest left between 1955 and 1959 with some seeing further service with SWT's sister BET company, Thomas Bros of Port Talbot. The full-width Regal IIIs went in 1960 and the Regal IVs in 1961 and 1962.

SWT drivers Arthur Samuel and Tommy Webber receiving their awards for being judged the best dressed crew at Brighton Coach Rally in 1959. Below: how the staff magazine saluted winning the best coach award in 1958.
Peter Samuel

Meanwhile SWT had taken batches of some of the finest coaches to grace the roads of the 1950s. The Weymann Fanfare was one of the most successful coaches of the decade and SWT had three batches in 1956 and 1958, all AEC Reliances. They had coach seats for 37 passengers and the company used them widely on its overseas tours, which were growing rapidly at this time. The first three arrived in 1956, numbered 1025-1027, registration numbers MWN 571-573, followed by five more a few months later, 1028-1032, NCY 622-626. The third batch came in 1958, 1033-1037, PWN 64-68, and it was the third of these, 1035, PWN 66, which won a top prize in the 1958 Brighton Coach Rally.

SWT's next coaches were not really coaches at all, although they received the company's coach livery. One, 1038, SWN 997, was entered for the 1959 Brighton Coach Rally. The four, again AEC Reliances with Weymann bodies, had 41 coach seats but were built on bus frames and were dual-purpose vehicles rather than coaches. The idea was that when their days of front-line coaching were over they could be used for bus work, which is what happened in 1963 until they were withdrawn in 1967.

If the Weymann Fanfares were among the best coaches of the 1950s then SWT's next coaches were the best of the following decade. The Harrington Cavalier was regarded as one of the most attractive coach designs of its day and SWT had three batches, all AEC Reliances

with 37 coach seats. The first three arrived in 1960, 1042-1044, VWN 16-18, and were the first new vehicles to carry SWT's arrow-type fleet name, 1043 was also the entrant for the 1960 Brighton Coach Rally. Two more followed in 1961 and another two in 1962.

SWT took two AEC Reliance coaches bodied by Plaxton in both 1966 and 1967 and two more bodied by Duple Northern in 1969 before reverting to Plaxton for four coaches in 1970. All had 44 coach seats. Still conspicuous by its absence on these vehicles was a toilet.

By now the company's days as an independent tour and private hire provider were over. It became part of the National Bus Company in 1969 and soon its coaches were repainted completely in white with National fleet names.

The golden age of coaching for South Wales Transport had reached its final destination.

Company clinches top rally award

The British Coach Rally, later renamed the UK Coach Rally, has been one of the most prestigious events in the transport calendar for nearly 60 years.

In 1958, SWT entered for the first time and won a top prize! There was also a special award for one of its coach drivers, Tommy Webber.

The rally features all the latest and best in coaching and while today's models are years ahead of those of the 1950s, they still offered a style and elegance all of their own. One of the most popular and attractive was the Weymann Fanfare and it was one of a batch delivered in 1958 that took the honours at the coach rally held that year in Brighton. SWT's Fanfares seated 37 passengers and its resplendent 1035, registration PWN 66, in its eye-catching red and ivory livery with Gothic style fleet name, won first prize in the Concours d'Elegance for 36 to 41 seat coaches.

The prize for the best turned out driver at the rally went to Tommy, who was one of SWT's original continental tour drivers. He joined the company in 1944 and was the first to take one of the company's coaches abroad.

Outside the coaching season, like the other drivers, Tommy worked on SWT's stage carriage services and his regular services were the 75 and 76 from Port Tennant to Tycoch or Brynmill.

Fanfare 1035 was immaculate, and had to be, as judging was tough. Points were awarded for exterior and interior condition, cleanliness of the engine, passenger comfort, driving facilities, tools and so on.

The coach was based at SWT's Ravenhill garage and the company said its engineering staff had worked wonders to turn it out in such a superb condition.

"It was team work throughout and that always spells success," said one of SWT's managers at the time. "It speaks volumes for the judgement of our executive officers in knowing a good coach when they see one and building up the fleet accordingly."

The cup for top coach was presented to SWT general manager, H Weedy, by Richard Hearne, a popular character actor of the time who was better known for his role as Mr Pastry. Tommy received a wallet.

Coach 1035 continued working for SWT until 1970 when it was withdrawn. It passed to Williams of Lower Tumble and in 1972 to Jenkins of Penclawdd before being sold for preservation in the autumn of 1974. Sadly that did not happen but it is still possible to get an idea of what this lovely vehicle looked like because one of its sisters has

This Plaxton bodied AEC Reliance joined the coaching fleet in 1970. It was among the last coaches delivered to SWT in the company's coaching livery and soon had the National Bus Company logo fitted to its radiator grill. They were later repainted in all-over NBC white.

Royston Morgan Collection

Rare honour for driver who went further

SWT coach driver Tom Clement received a rare honour in the spring of 1967. He was made an honorary member of Swansea Cricket and Football Club.

Its chairman, David Price, told him: "This is an honour not lightly bestowed."

The award was presented to Tom for services rendered to players and officials at the club when travelling by SWT coach to their away games.

SWT held many contracts with local sports and social clubs and the private hire department took great pains to ensure its coaches met their needs in full.

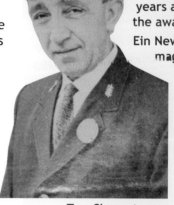

Tom had been in charge of SCFC's transport arrangements for 10 years and SWT was delighted with the award.

Ein Newyddion, SWT's staff magazine, said: "Tom has obviously assisted the club beyond the normal call of duty. We too are proud for it brings to light a record of a long and happy association between ourselves and the club as clients of our private hire department."

Tom Clement

been preserved. This is 1032, registration NCY 626, which can be seen in immaculate condition at Swansea Bus Museum.

Meanwhile, the Severn Bridge opened to traffic on September 8, 1966, and while SWT had no express services using it at the time, it was a major boost for its tours and private hire operations. Construction work on the £16 million bridge had started in 1961 and before it opened traffic had to go via Gloucester. The new bridge saved 50 miles for South Wales traffic with substantial time savings for transport concerns, including SWT.

The first SWT vehicles to cross the bridge were two 1956 Weymann Fanfare coaches. The date was September 9, the day after the bridge opened, and the very first SWT vehicle was Fanfare NCY 624, fleet number 1030, driven by DH Davies. The second was NCY 623, fleet number 1029, driven by D Cadle.

Coaches in the SWT fleet appeared in a rash of different liveries after the company was privatised in 1987. South Wales Transport provided National Express and National Express Rapide services out of South West Wales and 24 of its coaches were in the appropriate colours of white base with red and blue stripes and National Express or Rapide lettering. Coaches used on the local ExpressWest services between Haverfordwest and Bristol carried various liveries while the company had a day tours programme called SWT Days Away, the name appeared as a fleet name on the coaches it used for the trips and the vehicles were painted white with leaf green, poppy red and canary yellow stripes.

An SWT coach used for the company's Days Away tours programme in 1987. *Royston Morgan Collection*

Scientists test coach team to the limit

Many of the world's top scientists were in Swansea in September 1971 and SWT had the task of taking them by coach on a wide-ranging programme of excursions.

It was a herculean effort that needed no fewer than 30 vehicles and tested the company's engineering staff to the limits. The occasion was the British Association for the Advancement of Science conference held at Swansea University attended by around 2,000 people. The conference included travel all over South Wales for association members to pursue their range of scientific interests. There were 85 excursions in total across an area from Cardiff to Pembrokeshire and every route had to be vetted in intricate detail by SWT engineering staff as they included forestry land, farm lanes and places where normally no-one would dream of taking a bus. Many of the excursions were also available for public use and as the company could never be sure how many people would turn up they never knew how many coaches to lay on until the last minute.

SWT tours superintendent, Frank Haines, said at the time: "Many months of planning have gone into this hefty and complex operation. Many of the excursions will be over roads and into parts of Wales not normally used for tour purposes with the result that we have to survey the routes selected."

Amazingly, SWT was able to report at the end of the eight day conference that there had been no mishaps or damage to coaches or property. The company had previously been given the task of looking after VIPs

An ExpressWest service heads over the Severn Bridge on July 27, 1983. The vehicle is a Willowbrook bodied coach delivered in 1982. *Stephen Miles*

from 29 countries across the world in the summer of 1966. It was a mammoth undertaking for the private hire department and the onus was on coach driver, Jack Berry. The visit involved taking top ranking members of agricultural departments from overseas governments on a coach tour of Wales. On board Jack's coach were first secretaries, economic counsellors and attaches, so it was vital that nothing went wrong. He took them to Gower, Carmarthen and Mid Wales.

Mystery trips were a popular treat

Sometimes you never knew where you would end up when you boarded an SWT coach, particularly in the 1950s and 1960s.

This was of course if you had booked to take part in one of the company's highly popular mystery trips. There was the choice of full or half day visits with a destination that could turn out to be anywhere from Carmarthen to Brecon or Porthcawl.

They seemed particularly popular with older people and one interesting anecdote tells of a lady looking forward to her mystery trip from Neath one day in March, 1955.

The trip was booked to leave at 2.30 pm and, as usual, left on time. But at 4.25 pm the lady stormed into SWT's Neath office demanding to know where the bus was for her mystery trip as she had been waiting outside for 15 minutes. She was told the coach had left on time to which she

replied: "Then it's gone early, it's only twenty five past two now."

The clerk replied: "No, madam, it's twenty five past four." Then it dawned on the unfortunate lady. "Oh dear," she said. "We've put the clocks back instead of forward. No wonder we couldn't get the one o'clock news!"

In the 1980s two elderly ladies were not happy about their SWT mystery trip. Instead of the mountains or the sea, they had ended up in Leigh Delamere services on the M4 in Wiltshire. It was hardly what they expected so they complained to the coach driver. "You're not on a mystery trip, we're going to France," he told them in astonishment. They had boarded the wrong coach at Swansea's Quadrant bus station. It was a bank holiday, always the busiest of times for SWT's coaching unit, and on this particular day no fewer than 17 coaches had to be got under way and that took planning, precision and much patience on the part of everyone involved. So it is remarkable that similar incidents did not happen more often.

Reputation that spanned the globe

SWT's tours were renowned far and wide but even tours superintendent Frank Haines was unaware of just how far until he took a call from a woman in Perth.

It happened in February 1975 and the caller said she wanted to book three seats on a trip to the Western Isles and Oban because the tour would coincide with a visit she was making to South Wales. Frank was more than happy to take the booking but could not resist asking why someone from Scotland should come to South Wales and then take a coach tour back home.

"Oh," the caller replied. "I'm not calling from Perth in Scotland, I'm speaking from Perth in Western Australia!"

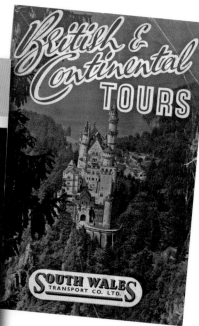

Driver David Beynon with some of the members of Morriston Orpheus Choir near the Berlin Olympic Stadium.

The coach carrying members of Morriston Orpheus Choir negotiates its way through Checkpoint Charlie as it leaves East Berlin behind.

Coach was first

When a South Wales Transport coach made history by conveying a group of Morriston Orpheus choristers to Berlin the assignment had all the ingredients of a Cold War spy story, right down to the fog and sinister border guards. The trip could even have provided an unbeatable plot for a cinema blockbuster.

Back in 1977, when the trip was tackled, Berlin was divided between east and west, but the city was situated in what was then East Germany. This was part of the Soviet bloc and relations between Moscow and the west were as frosty as the air around the city that October.

The choir had been invited to perform at the Berlin Military Tattoo, a huge event attended by thousands of military personnel. SWT held Morriston Orpheus's transport contract and was asked to help when the choir discovered it would be impossible to fly all their members to Berlin. The rest would have to travel there by coach.

It was an expedition SWT drivers David Beynon, from Ravenhill, and Llanelli-based Vic Jones would never forget. They had to travel from Hamelin in what was then West Germany, across the border into East Germany and then through what was known as The Corridor to get to Berlin.

After a briefing from the Military Police in the west, David and Vic set off with their passengers and eventually arrived at the East German border checkpoints. David remembers it clearly as being like the film set of a James Bond movie.

"High floodlight towers with light spilling down through the heavy fog created an eerie atmosphere and did nothing to dispel our apprehension," he said.

It took an hour to check everyone's passport and no-one was allowed to leave the coach while this was done. At last they were allowed through and the journey along the 112-mile corridor began.

"We had been told to drive at a constant 53 mph," said David. "So delicate were relations between the allied nations and the eastern bloc that to have deviated from this speed could have led to problems.

"Taking too long to pass through The Corridor incurred the risk of being charged with spying while taking too short a time could lead to a speeding charge.

"Each checkpoint and junction along the route had been photographed from the air and we had been instructed to memorise the junctions."

Another check awaited at the end of The Corridor and finally a military escort took them to Wavell Barracks, their home in Berlin for three weeks.

"The drive into Berlin was completed in thick fog with visibility down to 40 or 50 yards," said David. "It reinforced the

The history-making coach with the Berlin Wall behind.
David Beynon

at Checkpoint Charlie

impression that somehow this wasn't real, it only happened in spy novels."

The coach was the first civilian coach to pass through Checkpoint Charlie. It was an AEC Reliance coach bodied by Duple and new to SWT in 1973. Its fleet number was 180 and its registration number was TCY 180M. It did not have power steering or semi-automatic gears which made life difficult for the drivers. More importantly for the passengers, it did not have a toilet, not unusual in those days, even for a frontline coach that this was at the time. It was one of the last AEC Reliances in the fleet before it was withdrawn in 1986.

Many years earlier, in 1958, SWT had made another foray into Czechoslovakia which was also in the Eastern bloc. The task was to run a 24-day trip for the Hywel Girls School choir in Llanelli, taking pupils to 18 concerts in various towns across Czechoslovakia. This was the first time coaches from the

UK had travelled there so it was a pioneering trip into unknown territory for SWT.

At 9 pm on Saturday August 9, 1958, two of its AEC Reliance Weymann Fanfares left Llanelli for the long overland trip to Czechoslovakia. "The whole enterprise was in the nature of blazing a trail, but there could be no question of taking any chances," reported SWT's staff newsletter, Ein Newyddion.

As much knowledge as possible was gathered about Czechoslovakia before the trip got under way, but the onus was undoubtedly on SWT's four man team, led by driver Bill Davies and drivers Glyn Harry and Vic Jones. They took a fitter, Ken Symonds, with them in case of any mechanical problems along the way. Finding their way was only one of the problems. There were three changes of costumes for each choir member, whose ages ranged from 11 to 18. The rear seats were taken out of the Fanfares and replaced by steel racks which acted as wardrobes. There was

also personal luggage to be carried and the youngsters had to eat and sleep on the coaches.

Ein Newyddion reported: "They found it easy to sleep on the Fanfares. Indeed, if any proving of the comforts offered by this type of coach were necessary, then this trip was it."

Bill Davies said the coaches were greatly admired in Czechoslovakia. The party returned to Llanelli on September 1, 24 days after leaving the town and completing a journey of 3,300 miles. It had gone without a hitch.

The choir praised the efforts put in by the four SWT men which it said had been an integral part in the smooth running of the trip. It was so pleased, in fact, that three years later it did the same again, this time the trip took in both Czechoslovakia and Romania. There were 72 passengers, 67 of them children aged between 11 and 18 on this 2,613 mile journey.

Chapter 6

Community spirit shone — at work, rest and play

South Wales Transport realised that people were its biggest asset and encouraged efforts to create a happy and stable workforce. It believed passionately that a driver and conductor who took pride in the job and enjoyed their work were much more likely to present a welcoming face to passengers who in turn would probably use the buses more often, so boosting income and profits.

One of SWT's chairmen, Raymond Birch, was once asked if the company should employ a public relations officer. He replied: "We do, two on every bus."

When it ran an on-going pro-active courtesy campaign in the 1950s 'Be polite to passengers' was the company's call to staff.

Its crews became adept at handling passengers. Lots of them stayed with the company for many years, often on just one route, and they virtually became part of the passenger's family. One such employee was Harry Thomas who joined SWT in 1924 and continued in the company's employ until 1968. For 42 years his regular route was from Swansea to Bonymaen and during that time he became known to thousands of passengers as Uncle Harry. When he was in hospital for a time he was overwhelmed with visitors and get well cards.

In March 1956 the headmistress of Oakleigh House School in Swansea wrote to the company to praise its drivers and conductors because "there is hardly a week goes by without me being told of the many incidents of careful attention, courtesy and consideration for the children. I hope you will find the means to tell them of our thankfulness and to let them know their good deeds do not go unnoticed".

Drivers and conductors did not just drive buses and collect fares, they helped passengers whenever they could. In November 1954, Mrs Lilian Wooles of Manselton, Swansea, wrote to SWT after being taken ill on a bus at Cwmbwrla: "The conductor and driver very kindly assisted me to the chemist after seeing that a doctor had been sent for. Will you please convey my sincere thanks to both men for their great kindness as I am afraid I felt too ill to thank them."

In the 1950s the company had one of the best records for the number of long serving employees in the whole of the BET group. Every February SWT held long-service awards and presented certificates to staff with 50, 40 and 25 years' service. It was seen as such an important event that it was held at the same time

A successful snooker team at the Magnet Club, 1954. The club, run by, and for employees of South Wales Transport, spawned many successful sporting teams in its day.

A group of drivers and conductors with an inspector outside Pontardawe depot, all set for their next shift, 1959. *Chris Taylor Archive*

as the annual meeting, and always attended by the chairman and general manager. In 1956, out of more than 1,700 employees, there were 292 who had worked for the company for more than 25 years, 47 for more than 40 years and six for over 50 years.

In 1970 SWT still had conductors and drivers on its books who had spent the first few years of their working lives on the trams. They included Fred George who retired after 54 years service in the spring of 1970. For 48 years Fred worked on the Swansea to Sketty service, first as a tram conductor and later as a bus driver. He started as a 'points boy' on the trams at the age of 13 when his job was to change the points at certain junctions to ensure trams ran the right route.

Working for 'The Transport' was sometimes a family affair and no-one gave more to SWT than the Zeal family of Swansea. Billy Zeal retired in August 1956 after 53 years' service on the Mumbles Train, his brother Frank retired in 1963 after more than 54 years, all but one of them working the Brynmill to Wind Street route, initially on the trams, then the buses. Their father had driven trams for the Swansea Improvements and Tramways Company in the 1890s.

Such long service was by no means unusual. There was no retirement age and staff lived, worked and died in SWT's service. Crews frequently completed more than

40 or 50 years with the company and often passed away just a few years after retirement. They had literally given their lives to SWT. The overwhelming majority were men and it was not until 1958 that the first woman clocked up 25 years' service with SWT. She was Gladys Davies who was in charge of the tours and private hire department at the Plymouth Street office in Swansea where she spent most of her career. Gladys went on to serve 33 years with SWT before she retired in the mid-1960s.

Despite the preponderance of men, there were still romances in SWT. In 1956 conductor Tommy Chivers married conductress Maisie Davies, both worked at Ravenhill garage in Swansea, and just to keep the event in the SWT family their best man was driver John Jones. In 1958 Margaret Thomas, who worked as a clerk in the Ravenhill engineering department, married Terry Smith of the body building shop.

SWT staff felt a strong allegiance to their company too. This was something managers were keen to nurture for it meant employees would do that little bit more to help out in times of need. In the summer of 1955 SWT was hit by serious staff shortages. "Our resources were strained to the limit and day after day, week after week, the staff worked additional duties to cover the heavy shortage," said traffic manager Charles Hill.

Good relations also meant happier staff, a point made by general manager Mr H Weedy in his first message to employees when he took up the job in the early summer of 1955. "It is my wish that the harmonious

Coach convoy for pilgrimage to pantomime

Trips to the pantomime by bus on Boxing Day is one of the favourite memories of Gaynor Harrison whose father, Gwyn Williams, was a coach body builder at SWT's Ravenhill works.

Every year the company's social section, The Magnet Club, organised a visit to the pantomime in Swansea for the staff's children.

"We lived in Pontardawe and I remember in the 1950s SWT laying on dozens of buses from The Cross, in the centre of the town, to take us to the Empire or the Grand to see the annual pantomime," said Gaynor.

"We would be presented with an apple, an orange and a bag of sweets for the show. It was always exciting. The Magnet Club was a wonderful asset, every year the committee would organise a huge flower show at Ravenhill garage. Cricket, football, tennis and other sports were provided. It's such a shame that the club was later disbanded."

Gwilym P Thomas, long-serving secretary of the Magnet Club, and one of its prime movers.

relationships which exist in this company at the present moment between staff and management, and the management and the respective unions, should continue and, if possible, be enhanced, and I shall do all I can in this direction," said Mr Weedy. "I trust that you, too, will do all in your part in helping me to promote the best spirit within the company so that we can say that we 'not only have to go to work' but 'also enjoy going to work'."

Social club was a staff magnet

The idea for a South Wales Transport social club came as bus services and staff numbers began to build up after the Second World War. Employees were asked if they were interested and the response was positive so on December 5, 1947, the first meeting was held and officers elected.

Their first task was to decide what to call it. The obvious choice was the SWT Club but there was already a social club in Swansea with that name, it still exists but is not connected with the company, so a competition was organised and stores superintendent Trevor Toms came up with the clever idea of The Magnet Club. It began in a room at Brunswick Street garage and at first there were just two billiard tables, a dart board and table tennis all looked after by Arthur Parkin who could usually be found snoozing round the cosy stove fire. Later some Nissen huts became available alongside Ravenhill garage and these were converted for the new club.

The Magnet Club was a popular gathering place where many friendships among staff were forged. *Chris Taylor Archive*

THE MAGNET CLUB

The first AGM was held on February 8, 1948, and membership was initially around 900 or just over half the staff. Members each paid contributions of two shillings (10p) a week. Rules were drawn up and the club's first president was SWT's managing director, Percy Blake, who was hugely supportive of the project.

The Magnet Club grew quickly. Depots formed their own sections and raffles, dances, concerts, and whist drives were organised to raise funds. The first major event was The Magnet Club ball held at Swansea's Brangwyn Hall on February 4, 1948. It became an annual affair and one of the highlights of the social year in the town, ranking alongside the Press Ball and Bankers' Ball in importance. There is no doubt that the managers and their wives were the VIPs, at the 1957 ball Ein Newyddion described general manager H Weedy's wife as wearing "a dinner gown of emerald green trimmed with red" while the secretary, DP Drew's wife chose "a gown of midnight blue slipper satin with matching stole." There were magnificent spot prizes. Among them an electric fire, toaster, and a table lamp, for example. These were simpler times after all!.

Each year the club held a horticultural show and for a day buses were evicted from Ravenhill garage and replaced by sweet smelling flowers and market produce. It was claimed to be the largest show of its kind in South Wales. The club organised annual outings for staff and pensioners, there were also regular sports fixtures and Christmas parties.

In 1954 the Magnet Club Male Voice Party was formed and choristers not only performed locally but took part in concerts all over the country. They proudly wore the club's blazer badge with the Latin Motto: Semper Amicina, which means friendship forever.

A group of SWT conductresses and their friends, all set for their annual outing, early 1950s.

Members of the successful women's darts teams at the Magnet Club, 1955. It consisted entirely of conductresses. Inset: Lucy Athernought who won a number of trophies as both a team and singles player. Lucy, a conductress for 25 years, is seen shortly before her retirement in 1978. *Adeline Evans*

There was also a club tie with the Magnet Club design in silver and gold. No one put more effort into the club than its secretary for many years, Gwilym Thomas, whose main job with SWT was chief wages and audit clerk. He was drawing a raffle for the club in Llanelli in May 1963 when he died suddenly. Mr Thomas not only worked for the company, it seemed he lived for it too.

The club held weekly raffles and among the prizes in the early 1950s were 'the latest 14-inch television sets.' Later raffles even included a car, though no-one seems to have seen the irony of a bus company social club raffling the two things that were doing most to hasten the decline of passengers. Big improvements were made to the clubhouse at Ravenhill in 1966, the concert hall was doubled in size, the stage enlarged and there was a new bar.

Unfortunately, all good things come to an end and the Magnet Club is no more. But even today there are thousands of former SWT staff and their families for whom the name still brings back many good memories. They include Adeline Evans of West Cross, Swansea, who remembers going to the children's Christmas parties. Her mother was Lucy Athernought, a conductress with SWT from 1953 until she retired in 1978.

"My mother loved her job on the buses," said Adeline. "As a child I went to the club's Christmas parties. We met Father Christmas and were given presents and had our photos taken. The conductresses had a very good ladies' darts team, my mum was captain for a time. Also in the team were Minnie McQueen and Connie Standen. The men had darts, snooker, football, cricket and tennis teams. There was also a fishing league.

"They were very happy times."

Promoting a team and family spirit

SWT wanted a team and family spirit within the company. After the Second World War, managers supported The Magnet Club, which gave them just that.

At the same time it funded publication of the monthly staff newsletter, Ein Newyddion, the title being Welsh for Our News. During its lifetime there were many different sections at the Magnet Club. Some of the activities they offered or supported were firmly focussed on the summer and outdoor activities and others, more sedate and of the kind that gained popularity during the winter. The aim of the club was to secure membership from 100 per cent of the company's personnel though it is unlikely that this was ever achieved. However, such was the club's popularity that in the staff magazine, Ein Newyddion, published in the spring of 1957 it was suggested that at least 75 per cent of staff were members. If there wasn't a section for any particular interest then the chairman Norman Holt pledged in the same publication that provided it could be shown that there was sufficient interest one would be set up to cater for it. The club fielded a team in a variety of sports both indoor and out, and many of these were feared by opponents for their competitiveness and prowess. Their exploits achieved much significant successes.

Competition aside, many former employees will no doubt remember summertime excursions across the Bristol Channel to Weston-Super-Mare. Often these trips would have meant boarding a paddle steamer for what could be a choppy trip to their destination.

Sadly, the Magnet Club whose proud badge bore the BET logo above a South Wales Transport saloon eventually fell victim to changing times at SWT.

For the 25 years after the end of the Second World War it was a happy, caring company which is why the late 1960s and early 1970s were such a traumatic time all round. It was a period of falling passenger numbers and mounting financial losses and SWT was forced to cut back staff. The general manager at the time, Frank Woodworth,

Inside...

An interior view of the original Magnet Club, complete with its stage.

An external view of the building that once housed SWT's popular Magnet Club.

... and out

spoke of "redundancies arising on a distressing scale in most departments." What followed was a time of sorrowful farewells to staff who had given long and loyal service to the company.

For those who remained, the 1970s were not the same as the happier times of the 1950s and 1960s despite the fact that the original

Blooming lovely . . . a group of women admire some of the flowers on display at Ravenhill depot when buses were replaced with blooms on the day of the annual Magnet Club flower show, 1954. The event was one of the highlights of the club's calendar.

Double success for determined driver Peter

The UK Bus Driver of the Year competition is a major event in the transport calendar and to win it once is a huge achievement.

To win it twice is remarkable but that is the proud boast of Peter Harris, who lifted the trophy in 1988 and again in 1989. SWT driver Peter, based at the Quadrant in Swansea, had won through to the finals every year for the previous five years and just missed out on the title.

In early September 1988 he won the trophy by beating 57 other top drivers from across Britain at the finals in Blackpool. The following year he repeated the achievement.

First Peter had to win through SWT's own heats and then the regional heats before getting his shot at the crown. He faced tough tests of his driving skills, the highway code, safety and his general knowledge of the industry. After SWT's demise Peter continued working at the Quadrant for First Cymru and became a regular driver on the ftr-metro service. On this service drivers are referred to as pilots and conductors as hosts.

Excited children of Neath depot staff with Santa at their annual Christmas party, 1958.

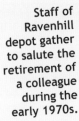

Peter Harris with his trophies.

Magnet Club building was demolished and a new one built. The loyalty felt to a local company which had been so carefully nurtured when SWT was a British Electric Traction company in the private sector was difficult to emulate now that SWT was like any other National Bus Company subsidiary. The buses staff drove, the uniforms they wore, the rules they obeyed were all dictated by managers working far away. The spirit of the company was lost, Ein Newyddion ceased publication in 1972 and a less informative NBC newsletter replaced it. The Magnet Club also eventually became a casualty and closed.

Service cutbacks in the late 1970s and early 1980s also took their toll on morale, although things did improve after 1987 when SWT became an independent company. The importance of good staff and customer relations was realised once more and the company invested in courses highlighting the importance of courtesy to passengers for its drivers.

Staff of Ravenhill depot gather to salute the retirement of a colleague during the early 1970s.

Magnet Club president Mr H Weedy, together with SWT secretary Gwilym P Thomas and Norman Holt, its chairman, surrounded by members and guests at the annual Magnet Club Ball, 1957.

A busman's holiday perhaps. This group of SWT staff was all set for an enjoyable day out in 1949. They went by bus of course!

Members and officials of the successful Magnet Club Cricket team, 1958.

South Wales Transport's route numbers have, of necessity grown, and on occasions been amended. Housing developments around towns and the advent of the Quadrant bus station each brought further route number changes. Using original spellings these were the route numbers in timetable for May 12 — September 15, 1951:

SOUTH WALES

1 Swansea (Trinity Place) — Ystradgynlais

2 Swansea (Christina Street) — Llanelly

3 Swansea (St Mary's Sq) — Margam

3a Neath (Victoria Gardens) — Margam

6 Oystermouth — Newton (Picket Mead)

7 Swansea (Coach Stn) — Porteynon — Rhossily

8 Swansea (Park Street) — Llanrhidian

9 Swansea (Christina Street) — Morriston Cross

10 Swansea (Park Street) — Gowerton via Dunvant

11 & 14 Swansea (Church Street) — Neath — Banwen

12 Swansea (Dynevor Place) — Townhill (Elphin Crescent)

12a Swansea (Dynevor Place) — Mayhill (Hillside)

12b Swansea (Dynevor Place) — Townhill (Gwynedd Avenue)

13 Neath (GWR Station) — Clydach

13a Neath (Victoria Gardens) — Cimla

15 Llanelly — Carmarthen via Kidwelly

16 Llanelly — Llandilo

17 Neath (Victoria Gardens) — Pontneathvaughan

18 Swansea (Trinity Place) Ammanford

18a Swansea (Trinity Place) Brynamman

19 Swansea — Cwmrhydyceirw

20 Aberavon Beach — Maesteg

23 Swansea (Exchange) — Swansea (Castle St) via Penlan and Uplands

24 Swansea (Christina Street) — Porthcawl

25 Ystalyfera — Craig-y-nos Castle

26 Llanelly — Neath

28 Swansea (Trinity Place) — Brecon

29 Swansea (Church Street) — Pontardawe

30 Swansea — Bishopston — Pennard

32 Llanelly — Carmarthen via Pontyates

33 Tycoch — Port Tennant

34 Cilfrew — Giants Grave (Briton Ferry)

36 Swansea (Horton Street) — Llandilo

37 Llanelly — Drefach

38 Swansea (Church Street) — Heol Las

39 Townhill — Jersey Marine Road

40 Morriston — Caswell Bay

42 Swansea (Christina Street) — Margam via Morriston

43 Birchgrove — Briton Ferry

46 Pontardawe — Alltycham

47 Morriston — Velindre

71 Swansea (Exchange) — Cwmrhydyceirw

72 Swansea (Guildhall) — Cwmbwrla

73 Swansea (Exchange) — Brynhyfryd

74 Sketty — Castle Street — Sketty

75 Tycoch — Port Tennant

76 Brynmill — Port Tennant

77 Swansea (Guildhall) — Cwmrhydyceirw

79 Swansea (Exchange) — Gors Avenue

80 Bonymaen Inn — Brynhyfryd via Exchange and Cwmbwrla

83 Swansea (Exchange) — Ravenhill

84 Swansea (Exchange) — Caereithin

85 Swansea (Castle Street) — Caswell Bay

85 Swansea (Castle Street) — Langland Bay

87 Swansea — Penlan (Crwys Terrace)

89 Port Tennant — Pontlasse

90 Penlan — Caswell Bay

91 Cockett Inn — Cefn Coed Hospital

92 Swansea (Castle Street) — West Cross

MUMBLES ELECTRIC RAILWAY

Swansea (Rutland Street) — Mumbles Pier

Neath
Pencaerau
Heol Morfa
Briton Ferry
Port Talbot
Porthcawl
Gorseinon
Morriston
Birchgrove
Resolven
Glynneath
Hirwaun
Min-yr-Awel

Swansea via Neath
Banwen via Neath
Coelbren
Seven Sisters
Crynant
Forest Hill
Fairyland Estate
Neath
Longford
Cimla
Caewathan
Crymlyn Road

Longford
Cimla
Caewathan
Crymlyn Road
Cefn Saeson
dgewood Gardens
sprey Drive
Tonmawr
ntrhydyfen
sternmoor

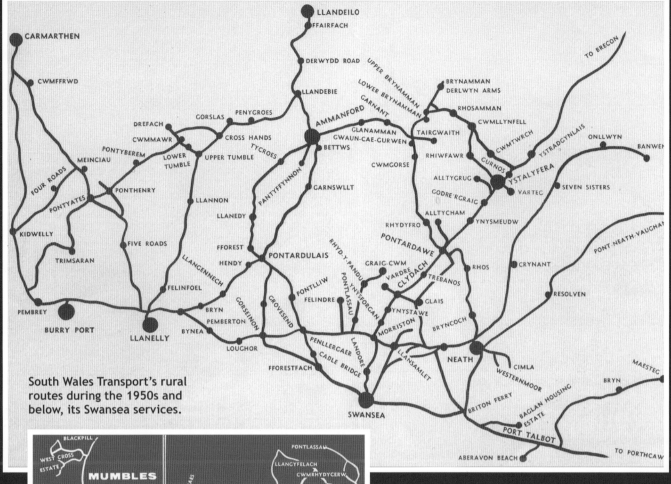

South Wales Transport's rural routes during the 1950s and below, its Swansea services.

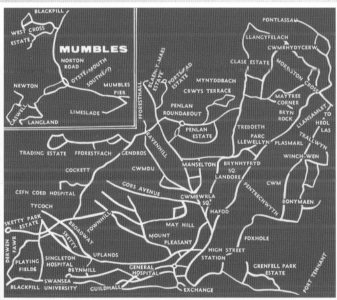

SWT ran only a limited number of bus services in and around Llanelli for 38 years. It was not until it took over Llanelly District Traction in 1952 that it became the major operator in the town. In 1951 Llanelli town services were all prefixed with the letter L when they were taken over by SWT in 1952. Later the practice was stopped but SWT's successor company, First Cymru, reintroduced it for its Llanelli local services. These were Llanelli's town routes in summer 1961. Timetable dated May 20 — September 3, 1961:

L1 Llanelly Station — Loughor Bridge.

L2 Llanelly Station — Felinfoel (Morris Motors)

L3 Llanelly Station — Pwll (Talbot Inn)

L4 Llanelly (Murray Street) — Capel-Dafen (Bush Inn)

L5 Llanelly (Murray Street) — Dimpath — Dafen (Bush Inn)

L6 Llanelly (Palace) — Ty Isaf — Penyfan — Coedcae Road

L7 Penyfan-Hospital — Murray Street — Morfa — Machynis Works

L8 Penyfan — Morfa and Machynis

L9 Furnace (Square) — Town Hall

L10 Furnace (Square) — Town Hall (Square) — Astoria — Machynis (Works)

L11 Penyfan — Felinfoel (Morris Motors)

L12 Morfa (School) — Felinfoel (Morris Motors)

L13 Llanelly Station — Maesarddafen — Penygraig Estate

L14 Llanelly Station — Cefn Caeau—Trallwm Estate

L15 Llanelly Station — Maes Golau Estate

WORKMENS' SERVICES

51 Swansea (Christina Street) — Fforestfach Trading Estate

52 Swansea (St Mary's Sq) — NOR Llandarcy via Bonymaen

52 Swansea (Christina Street) — NOR Llandarcy via Morriston

53 Five Roads — Meinciau — Pembrey (Royal Ordnance Factory)

54 Llanelly — Pembrey (ROF)

54 Kidwelly — Pembrey (ROF)

55 Felinfoel — Pembrey (ROF)

56 Gorseinon — Pembrey (ROF)

57 Mynydd-y-Garreg — Felinfoel (Morris Motors Factory)

59 Gorseinon — Felinfoel (Morris Motors Factory)

60 Ponthenry — Felinfoel (Morris Motors Factory)

61 Sketty Cross — Fforestfach Trading Estate

62 Townhill (Graiglwyd Square) — Graigola Fuel Works (N Shed, Swansea Docks)

62 Gors Avenue — Graigola Fuel Works (N Shed, Swansea Docks)

63 Plasmarl (St Paul's) — Fforestfach Trading Estate

SWT drivers and conductors enjoy a break in the canteen at its Brunswick Street depot, 1953.

Challenges of a

Life on the Transport could certainly be anything but boring whether you were a driver or a conductor. Many people would creak under the strain of some of the weird and wonderful incidents recalled, but for the busmen — and women — it was all in a day's work.

A dip into just a selection of staff memories is ample evidence of what each new tour of duty could bring. Swansea conductor Brian Marks remembered how his bus suddenly became an emergency ambulance and rushed a pregnant woman to hospital.

It happened on a late night bus on the No. 3 route from Cwmrhydyceirw in Morriston to Swansea town centre. Brian's bus stopped at Plasmarl for a plainly anxious young man and a very pregnant woman.

"He asked if I could take his wife to Swansea hospital — quickly," said Brian, who urged the pair to take a taxi instead, but the man insisted on boarding the bus. It was plain that the woman could give birth at any time so Brian had a quick conversation with his driver and they agreed there was only one

thing for it, they would go off-route and convey the couple to hospital.

"I helped her on board and lay her on the back seat making her as comfortable as I could," said Brian. "I knew double deckers were capable of some speed, but that was the fastest journey I ever made in one. We took the shortest route we could across Swansea and screeched to a halt outside the emergency entrance to the old hospital."

They were just in time. The woman was quickly put on a hospital trolley and as it wheeled down the corridor Brian heard a baby's cry. "That was a wonderful moment, just to have been part of bringing that little one safely into the world," he said.

Llanelli driver Percy Thomas was on the town's Penyfan circular service one April day in 1955 when he saved a young girl from drowning. Percy's bus had just arrived at the terminus near Machynys ponds when he spotted a small crowd making frantic efforts to reach the girl, who was aged about 10. She was in the water,

clinging by her finger tips to a pipe hanging just above one of the 18ft deep ponds.

When Percy arrived she was blue in the face and so exhausted that she was only seconds from losing her grip. He did not hesitate.

Percy dashed across the top of the pipe and, hanging on by his legs, reached down and plucked the little girl from the icy water. After seeing she was all right he calmly returned to his bus and continued on his shift.

Staff magazine Ein Newyddion reported: "Percy is to be highly commended for his quick thinking and disregard for his own safety in his singular act of courage."

It was not often that conductors had to act as nursemaids, but it happened to Bob Gilchrist a regular conductor on the 83 and 84 services from Swansea town centre to Ravenhill and Caereithin. They were among SWT's busiest routes and on this particular day Bob had a crowd of passengers on his double deck bus as it made its way up to

The bus wash at SWT's Clarence Terrace garage, during the 1980s.
Roy Kneath

Electrical engineers at Ravenhill depot, 1970s.
Roy Kneath

shift on the Transport!

Ravenhill. Gradually they all got off so that not far from the terminus the vehicle was empty.

Bob, who retired from SWT in 1971, took the opportunity to make the usual check to ensure none of the passengers had left any of their belongings behind. One had, but it was not the kind of item Bob was expecting. As he made his way up the gangway he discovered to his amazement a very young baby lying on one of the seats. There was nothing for it but for Bob to nurse the baby and hope that the mother would be at one of the stops on the return journey into town.

Sure enough, the bus was met by a hysterical mother with a little girl at her side. She sobbed her grateful thanks to Bob, then suddenly turned on the little girl. "You're driving me bloody crackers!" she yelled. "Why didn't you remind me we had the baby with us?"

Everyone on the bus cheered the day Swansea conductor John Hughes suddenly became a rodeo rider. It happened one Sunday afternoon in the late winter of 1969 in the unlikely setting of Mumbles Road.

John's bus was heading towards Mumbles when three horses ran into the road. They had been startled by some children throwing stones and were frantically running round causing danger to themselves and other road users.

John, aged 26, stopped the vehicle and in true cowboy style dashed off towards one of the horses, mounted it and chased the other two. It took 10 minutes, but John caught them and then tethered all three away from the busy road.

Then it was back onto his bus to the cheers of the passengers, all except a man who complained the bus was running late.

Sometimes a simple act of kindness can make a huge difference to a person's whole life and that was certainly true for Dulcie Thomas of Swansea. For the last 20 years of her life Dulcie was bedridden at her home in Midland Terrace, St Thomas, but her family moved her bed so she could look out of the window, her only contact with the outside world.

SWT driver Jack Berry heard of her plight in 1950 and every time his bus passed Dulcie's home he would wave to her. The idea caught on with other crews and for the following 20 years the conductors and drivers on services 3, 38, 114 and 219 took the time to slow down and wave to her when they passed by.

The South Wales Evening Post heard about it and interviewed Dulcie who said: "They are all marvellous people, their kindness brings a ray of sunshine into my life and I look forward so much to seeing them wave to me. It gives me a big thrill."

Dulcie died towards the end of 1970 and her family wrote to SWT to thank the crews for their kindness. They said they wanted everyone to know how much Dulcie and they appreciated the action of the crews stretching over such a long time which had done so much to brighten her life during her long illness.

75

CHAPTER 7

Bosses dined on duck as the Mumbles Railway died

Thousands of people came out on to the streets of Swansea in the summer of 1954 to celebrate a very special event. It was not the Coronation, that was the year before. In fact, this was not a Royal event of any kind, though given the enthusiasm shown by the townspeople those six days from Tuesday June 29 to Sunday, July 4, it might well have been.

Instead, that special event was to commemorate the 150th anniversary of the oldest passenger carrying railway in the world — the Mumbles Railway.

At this time South Wales Transport operated the system and it pulled out all the stops to make the celebrations memorable. On the first day, the three main modes of transport that had been used on the railway, horse, steam and electric, ran together on the line for the first time. Engineering staff at the company's Ravenhill works had built a replica of one of the horse-drawn carriages, and it ran alongside a diesel engine, cleverly resembling a steam train, and one of the existing magnificent electric cars suitably bedecked with anniversary shields showing the dates 1804-1954.

Children were given the day off school, members of Swansea Little Theatre, Mumbles Women's Institute and Mumbles Chamber of Trade, dressed in period costume. Flags and bunting decorated Mumbles seafront and there were band concerts, a photographic exhibition on Mumbles Pier and a celebratory dance organised by the social section of the Magnet Club. Even HC Drayton, powerful head of South Wales Transport's parent company, British Electric Traction, took the time to come to the celebrations.

The company's general manager, Wilfred Dravers, was delighted. He wrote in the staff magazine: "There is no doubt that local people have a great affection for the Mumbles Railway. This was obvious from the large numbers who turned out to witness events on the great day itself and from the many appreciative remarks I have had from different people in the last few weeks.

"It is fair to say that, as a result, our goodwill in Swansea stands high. Long may it continue so!"

Yet within five years, SWT had begun moves to close the railway and by January 1960 it had gone, the rails were rapidly torn up and its huge tramcars scrapped in such haste that pieces of them were left to rust along the trackside. In less than five years the company's commitment to the railway had been replaced by an unhealthy desire to get rid of it at all costs. The enthusiasm of the people of Swansea for the

An electric-powered Mumbles Railway car heads for Mumbles alongside one of the AEC Regent Vs that eventually took over its passenger carrying role in 1960.

Mumbles Railway car No. 3 takes on passengers at Rutland Street, Swansea as it prepares to make the picturesque journey to Mumbles Pier in 1959.

railway hadn't waned, although it was carrying fewer passengers. This was something replicated elsewhere and probably attributable to the growth in car ownership. The Mumbles Railway remained Swansea's favourite passenger carrier and such was the outrage when SWT announced its closure plans that a petition of 14,000 names was drawn up. This was a huge number given the fact that at the time society in general was much less likely to question decisions taken by authority and there were none of the speedy electronic communication methods of the 21st Century.

Despite the widespread battle against the decision, the railway still closed, ending more than 155 years of history dating back to 1804 when the Oystermouth Railway and Tramroad Company began building a line to carry limestone, coal and iron ore from the many quarries and mines that existed in the Mumbles and Clyne Valley to the embryonic port of Swansea. On March 25, 1807, thanks to an enterprising businessman named Benjamin French, passengers were carried on the line for the first time and when it closed on January 5, 1960, it was without doubt the oldest passenger carrying railway in the world.

Horses were the first mode of power on the railway, but in 1826 a road was built between Swansea and Oystermouth and horse buses ran along it. As a result the Mumbles Railway closed to passengers and didn't

carry them again until 1860. Some 17 years later a trial steam engine trip was arranged and this was so successful that the following day, August 17, 1877, this became a regular service. Many legal wrangles over who should run the trains followed and for a time both horse and steam power were used. Finally, on the last day of March 1896, horses gave way to steam entirely and the railway entered its heyday.

The Oystermouth Railway, which in 1879 became a limited company known as the Swansea and Mumbles Railway Company, ran from Swansea to Oystermouth and in 1889 a new company called The Mumbles Railway and Pier Company was set up with the aim of building a pier at Mumbles Head and laying a line from there to connect with the track at Oystermouth. This work was completed in 1898 and that is where the history of the Mumbles Train converges with the history of South Wales Transport.

Back in 1878, SWT's sister company, the Swansea Improvements and Tramways Company, had opened a connecting tram line to the Oystermouth Railway at The Slip in Mumbles Road, but it wanted to do much more than provide feeder trams. It wanted to run the Mumbles Railway as well and in 1899, by now part of the British Electric Traction group, it successfully negotiated an agreement with the other two companies to lease the railway and pier for 999 years.

Given the speed with which SITC electrified Swansea's trams, you might have thought they would have been pretty keen to do the same with the Mumbles Train. There was a feasibility study in 1900 and meetings were held, but that is as far as any proposals went and steam trains continued to run on the line for almost 30 years. The engines were all affectionately known as Puffing Billy, although there were four or five of them in use. They were incredibly slow, travelling at just eight mph, and it took three quarters of an hour to complete the journey. That allowed plenty of time for young girls to pick daisies at stops along the way while the boys would invite the passengers to throw them pennies for turning cartwheels and performing acrobatic feats.

Slow it might have been, but Puffing Billy was amazingly popular and hundreds of passengers would cling like limpets to any hand hold they could find inside and outside the carriages as they slowly made their way from Swansea down to Mumbles and the increasingly popular pier. Bank holidays and summer weekends were the busiest times and a train of around a dozen double deck coaches would carry as many as 1,300 people. The record for one train is reputed to be around 1,800.

These long, slow trains made it difficult to operate the service efficiently so in the late 1920s proposals to electrify the line were resurrected. This didn't happen under SITC though. Instead, on January 1, 1927 the

lease on the line was transferred to SWT. At the time and until the line closed more than 30 years later, the company was the only bus operator in the UK, and possibly the world, to run a railway. It was SWT which put the electric system in motion and within two years, on March 2, 1929 the Mumbles Railway finally switched to electricity for its motive power. What replaced the steam engines were probably the most spectacular tramway-type cars ever produced and it was these that gave the train a new nickname, The Rock 'n' Roll Railway, because of the way they rolled and tilted from side to side as they made their way along the track.

They may have looked like trams, but this was a light railway and these magnificent cars could be coupled together, which they often were at busy times, such was the demand for the service. Built by Brush of Loughborough, a BET associated company, they were easily the biggest electrically driven tramway-type cars used in the UK. They weighed 30 tons and could carry 106 passengers, 58 on the upper deck and 48 downstairs. Initially SWT ordered 11 but as the number of passengers continued to rise it added another two.

Passenger figures rose throughout the 1930s but it was during the war years that the Mumbles Train came into

its own. With petrol rationed and SWT bus services drastically reduced, the number of people travelling on the train increased to just under five million in 1943 compared with just under two million in 1936. The new cars were much faster than the steam trains and could cover the five-and-a-half mile journey in just 19 minutes. This took some doing, particularly as there were nine stops between the Rutland Street depot in Swansea and Mumbles Pier, and the fact that much of the line was single tracked with passing loops.

Summer was a particularly busy time and there were as many as 60 journeys

A Mumbles railway car heading for the pier passes two SWT buses at the Slip, late 1950s.

Crowds throng the Rutland Street terminus of the Mumbles Train, on its last day — January 5, 1960. For most, this was no celebration. It was more like the funeral of an old friend.

each way on weekdays with up to 40,000 people carried on bank holidays. It was fond memories of these pleasure trips to the seaside, the sterling service the train gave during the war years and the efficient way it took people to and from work that all combined to make it so well loved.

No one described more beautifully what the Mumbles Train meant to them than Swansea journalist Paul Chambert, who died in 2013. Paul was brought up in Thistleboon, in west Mumbles, and each morning he would walk the mile or so from his home to catch the train on his way to Dynevor School near the centre of Swansea.

"I boarded the 8.14 am train from Mumbles Pier to Rutland Street every school day and the thrill I had has never left me," he wrote in 1995. "The kids from Sketty and

Morriston went by bus. We travelled on the world's oldest passenger carrying railway. As the red carriages lumbered along the track we would play our games of shove ha'penny in the little leather-covered box in the corner at the top of the stairs, struggling to keep our balance as the train rolled from side to side. Travelling under the footbridge opposite The George pub in Southend was, for some reason, always special and when the sea was rough the waves and spume would hit the windows. It was as though the train was riding the waves. We wondered why the water never shorted the overhead electric cables. No schoolboy could ever travel in a more exciting way and we were lucky enough to experience that twice a day, every day."

The Mumbles Train was dependable. It always ran on time whatever the weather. It was there for you

79

A Mumbles Railway car passes under The Slip pedestrian bridge as it follows the sweep of Swansea Bay towards the pier.

first thing in the morning and took you home late at night, its bright lights making a welcoming sight in the cold and dark. Passengers on those late trains in the 1930s might have travelled with the poet Dylan Thomas, returning home after a night visiting a hostelry in Mumbles. As the train swayed from side to side along the track on its way back to town, Dylan would be composing 'bad poetry,' recalled author and broadcaster Wynford Vaughan-Thomas, who accompanied him on many occasions.

The train was such an important and well-loved part of Swansea life that no-one ever thought there would come a time when it would no longer be there. So when the town learned SWT was proposing to close it because of the cost of repairs, financial losses and declining passenger numbers, it went into shock. Soon this turned to anger and a determination to fight the plans. Much venom was directed at SWT which people in the town said stood for Slow, Wicked, Terrible. The company had previously leased the railway, but bought it outright in 1958 and its closure plan was revealed just a few months later. Protestors suggested that it had all been an underhand trick to get rid of the line.

All that goodwill which Mr Dravers had been so pleased about in 1954 had evaporated. It was left to his successor, Mr H Weedy — who made no secret of the fact that economic facts had to be faced — to defend the move.

"Gradually, over a period of years, the cost of maintaining the railway has risen and the number of passengers decreased," Mr Weedy wrote in Ein Newyddion. He explained that SWT was paying an annual rental of £13,900 for the railway and a decision was taken to buy it for £200,000 in 1958 because it

Mr H Weedy, general manager.

represented economic sense. The lease still had 940 years to run and the purchase price was the equivalent of only 14 years rental which would eventually have totalled £13,066,000. "This meant the travelling public have had a very good deal," said Mr Weedy.

Mr Weedy was surely playing with figures. The Mumbles Railway was certainly a wonderful thing, but it is highly unlikely that it would have continued for another 940 years. In the end, SWT closed the line just two years after buying it so the travelling public didn't get such a good deal. But he was on firmer ground when he revealed the cost of repairs would have been between £300,000 and £350,000. The interest on this sum alone would have been more than £20,000 a year, more than three times the loss made on the line in 1958.

"The railway was inflexible and slow because of Board of Trade restrictions and the need for single line working along much of the route," said Mr Weedy.

People fighting to save the line claimed its closure would cause increased traffic congestion on an already busy Mumbles Road and to this Mr Weedy made no defence. "Will there be congestion? Certainly," he admitted. "We have never denied the difficulties which may arise on such occasions as Whit Monday, August

Bank Holiday and possibly a few other occasions during the height of the summer season."

But he maintained the closure was still to the advantage of the public who would get "an infinitely better service through the buses that would replace it." SWT's plan was to replace the train with 16 diesel buses at a cost of £80,000, plus another £6,000 on road improvements. The closure plan required an Act of Parliament and so the seemingly innocuous sounding South Wales Transport Bill of 1959, which provided for the closure of The Mumbles Railway, went to Parliament for approval. It didn't have an easy passage.

In the debate that followed, Swansea West MP, Percy Morris, warned that: "before parting with this ancient railway, we must be satisfied that it is being replaced by something better." He also launched a cynical broadside at SWT.

"The figure of £300,000 has been mentioned as the sum needed to modernise the railway," said Mr Morris. "If it means all that, I wonder why SWT made the takeover bid. If the railway is in such a decrepit state, why did the company acquire what it would have us believe is akin to a sack of worn out sleepers, broken chairs, bending rails and rusty bolts? There must be more to this than meets the eye."

Mr Morris questioned whether the alternatives to closure had been fully examined and called for an independent expert to be brought in to examine SWT's proposals and an investigation to be carried out into the practicality of retaining and modernising the railway. He spoke for many when he said passengers were unconvinced that buses would provide an equally efficient service.

"They contend that even if extra vehicles are available, road congestion will be so intense that traffic will be brought to a standstill and chaos will prevail at holiday times. It has been suggested that the increase in bus traffic will amount to only one per cent, about 20 additional buses per hour. Such a prospect fills many people with dismay in view of their experience over many years on this very congested road," said Mr Morris.

It was to no avail. On July 29, 1959, the South Wales Transport Act, 1959, became law, sounding the death knell for the Mumbles Railway. Just before midday on Tuesday January 5, 1960, the last train ran. As so often it needed two cars and the ones chosen for the historic final trip were numbers six and seven, both proudly displaying shields proclaiming the railway's lifespan, 1804-1960. The last driver was Frank Dunkin, who had worked on the railway for a remarkable 57 years.

This card accompanied a series of photographs commemorating the 175th anniversary of the Mumbles Railway in 1982.

Dozens of pictures were taken of the final trip and the crowds who gathered to say their farewells were just as numerous as those who had celebrated the 150th anniversary five years previously. But in 1960 it was a wake, not a celebration. They say a camera never lies, but it can certainly mislead and while crowds on the last day were smiling cheerfully for the photographers it is not because they were pleased at the closure. Far from it. And SWT knew that.

It was made even worse by what happened after the final train entered the Rutland Street depot for the last time. Around 125 of the great and the good of the town went off to Swansea's Guildhall for a celebration lunch of smoked salmon with lemon followed by roast stuffed duckling and apple sauce, washed down by fine wines and after-lunch liqueurs. These days it would be termed a public relations disaster. Much more in keeping with the feelings of the town were the group of townspeople who dressed in black, some with widow's weeds, and solemnly boarded one of the final trains with a make believe coffin.

Ein Newyddion put it like this: "Now it's all over. No longer do we hear the familiar toot-toot of its warning hooter; no longer the clackety-clack as it speeds over

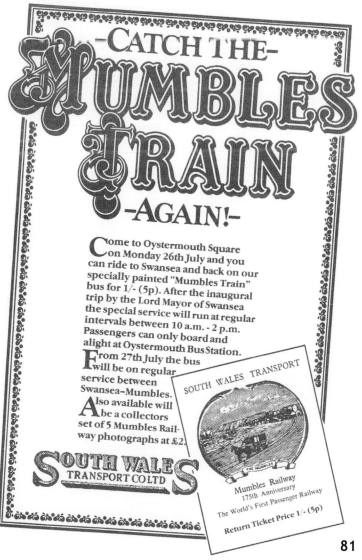

- CATCH THE -
MUMBLES TRAIN
- AGAIN! -

Come to Oystermouth Square on Monday 26th July and you can ride to Swansea and back on our specially painted "Mumbles Train" bus for 1/- (5p). After the inaugural trip by the Lord Mayor of Swansea the special service will run at regular intervals between 10 a.m. - 2 p.m. Passengers can only board and alight at Oystermouth Bus Station.

From 27th July the bus will be on regular service between Swansea–Mumbles. Also available will be a collectors set of 5 Mumbles Railway photographs at £2.

SOUTH WALES TRANSPORT CO. LTD

SOUTH WALES TRANSPORT

Mumbles Railway
175th Anniversary
The World's First Passenger Railway
Return Ticket Price 1/- (5p)

Mammoth paint project took six months to finish

A mammoth repainting project got underway in 1938 which took around six months to complete.

It involved the 13 electric trains on the Mumbles Railway, huge machines weighing 30 tons and seating 106 passengers.

They entered service on March 2, 1929, in a livery that had much more cream than the mainly red style that was to become so familiar in the 1940s and 1950s. SWT decided that the cars on the Mumbles Railway should receive a livery similar to that of its buses and ordered the major repainting project.

One of the painters tasked with the job was Horwood Lewis who remembered that each car had to be repainted inside and out.

"We were allowed 14 days for each one and the job took six months to complete," he recalled.

Horwood started his career with SWT in 1915 when a normal working week was 54 hours and the rate of pay for him was just over 8d per hour.

He injured his right hand during the First World War, but that didn't stop him picking up his paint brushes again for SWT in 1921.

Smartly adorned in its new coat of paint Mumbles Railway car No. 9 heads for Southend.

The 1920s were a busy time for the company's painters. Its buses had been green, but were now being repainted red, the more usual colour for British Electric Traction subsidiary bus companies like SWT.

Horwood retired in 1966 after 51 years painting countless numbers of the vehicles in the smart South Wales Transport fleet.

the rails; no longer shall we have the privilege of doing the rock 'n' roll in a sitting position for the Mumbles Railway has done its last journey."

But the question of whether SWT bought the railway with the sole intention of closing it remained. Speaking at the annual meeting as late as February 1959, just five months before the South Wales Transport Bill of that year to close the railway received Royal Assent, SWT chairman, Mr WT James, insisted: "The company hasn't decided what they are going to do or when they are going to do it."

But in March 1966, Wilfred Dravers gave a rather different story. That year he was president of The Omnibus Society and used part of his presidential address to relate the tale of the demise of the Mumbles Railway. He said that the decline in the number of passengers using the railway had been accelerating and operating costs rising.

"The company made a thorough investigation of the future of the railway and as a result found that the necessary renewals and improvements to the permanent way and rolling stock would require the expenditure of a sum of not less than £350,000," said Mr Dravers.

The fact had to be faced, the Mumbles Railway could not earn its keep and with great reluctance the company decided to close the undertaking and supplant it with a service of buses.

The first thing South Wales Transport had to do was to obtain control of the Swansea and Mumbles Railway Company and the Mumbles Railway and Pier Company, who were the landlords in receipt of a ground rent of £14,247 per annum. After protracted negotiations, a price was finally agreed and the way was then clear for SWT to proceed.

The ground rent figure given by Mr Dravers was slightly higher than that quoted by Mr Weedy, but more importantly the history as related by Mr Dravers clearly shows that SWT had made up its mind to close the railway before it bought it. That is not to say it made the decision lightly or that it did not regret the railway's passing, but it was a private company with responsibility to its shareholders and it couldn't afford to retain a loss-making enterprise. The cost was, as far as SWT was concerned, much too high. But the closure was the single most controversial act the company took in its entire 85-year history.

So why didn't it simply try to give up the lease? The reason was that it wanted to replace the train with its own buses and did not want to see a competitor continue to run the railway. Not that anyone seems to have rushed in to save the train. Any would-be rescuer

One of the last AEC Regent Vs delivered to SWT, this 1966 example is heading along Mumbles Road on its way to Pennard with a packed load, August 1981. Following behind is a Bristol VRT on its way to Mumbles and behind that a MK 2 Leyland National en-route to West Cross. All of them are in National Bus Company poppy red livery.
Stephen Miles

would undoubtedly have been put off by the high cost of repairs, even if SWT had been prepared to let them in. Swansea Corporation was not one of them. Although it initially objected to the closure, after being informed by SWT of the alternative services, it dropped its opposition, no doubt made more amenable by the company's offer to give it the land on which the railway ran free of charge.

As far as SWT was concerned, the closure was inevitable. In the souvenir booklet on the railway titled Over 155 Years of Service, which SWT published in 1960, WT James expressed sadness at the railway's demise.

"But progress does not thrive on sentiment alone," he wrote. "It was to keep step with progress that the changes from horse power to steam and then to electricity were made. Now the electric train is to give place to a more flexible and economic form of transport — the diesel bus. I am confident that the substitution of the bus for the train will be an important step in the improvement of transport in Swansea; indeed, it is planned to give the public even better facilities than they have had in the past."

Shoppers and office workers board the bus that will take them home in Princess Way, Swansea, mid-1960s.

Many in the town disagreed and SWT was forced to continue to fight its corner over the months and years that followed. Its decision continues to cause rancour in Swansea even today. But first there was that immediate accusation to counter: that the buses would not be able to cope with the number of passengers who would be displaced by the axing of the train. SWT maintained passenger numbers were falling rapidly. Compared to the war years, they certainly were. From a peak of just under five million in 1943, the railway was carrying fewer than three million by the mid-1950s. But the war years were wholly exceptional, due to petrol rationing and reduced bus services which inevitably meant more people using the train. A fairer comparison was surely with 1938 when the number of passengers was just under 1.2 million, so the railway was still carrying more people than in the immediate pre-war years. It did not matter: 71-seat Regent V buses on SWT's service 77, from Cwmrhydyceirw to Mumbles Pier, replaced the train. They took 20 minutes to complete the journey from Swansea Market to the pier compared to 22 minutes

taken by the railway from Rutland Street, a rather less convenient stop for the town centre. The buses were strongly defended by the company. Traffic manager, Charles Hill, insisted: "The deed has now been accomplished and buses have taken over with such smoothness and efficiency as to cause many of our severest critics to realise the truth of our statement that the new service would be infinitely better than that which they had experienced on The Mumbles Railway."

SWT new chairman, Raymond Birch, told the company's annual meeting in February 1961 that the buses had "not only proved adequate, but earned the praise of many." He said: "They were at no time during the summer season extended to the limit."

In its souvenir brochure to mark the closure, SWT said: "What of the future? The closure of the railway doesn't mean the end of 155 years of public service. Far from it. That service will still continue with greater ability and efficiency to meet the demands of the traveller in this modern day and age of 1960. The motor bus knows no boundary."

The townspeople were not convinced and over the years there have been many calls to resurrect the railway. Nostalgia has not been the only motive, for as the protestors warned before the railway's closure all those years ago, the road between Swansea and Mumbles has become one of the busiest in Wales, particularly during the summer months. Traffic is gridlocked at peak times. A fast Mumbles Railway would soon sort that out.

So could the railway conceivably return? There are three main obstacles: time, cost and the environment. To rebuild the railway would mean tearing up the

promenade where the train ran and which is now used by countless cyclists and walkers every day. When SWT's successor company, First Cymru, proposed running its tram-like ftr-metro bus on the promenade in 2005, there were howls of opposition. It is hardly likely that laying rail tracks and restricting access to the line with high fencing would be greeted with any greater enthusiasm.

Many Swansea people will only know of the railway from what they have read or the films they have seen and lack of personal experience is always a major problem in bringing something back. But the train is not without its champions. The Mumbles Railway Society was formed in 1975 not only to battle for the train's return, but also to keep its memory alive.

Women staff from Brunswick Street depot are gathered for the photographer after enjoying a Christmas lunch at the Mackworth Hotel, Swansea, 1959.

A 1963 Park Royal bodied AEC Renown travels along a Mumbles Road undergoing widening after the lifting of the Mumbles Railway and the LMS line, December 1972. *Stephen Miles*

Inspector was a real guide to 'The Transport'

SWT crews were real characters in the 1950s and 1960s, recalled Mike Charles, whose uncle, Cyril Seacombe, also uncle of legendary Swansea entertainer Harry Secombe, was an inspector.

Cyril was an invaluable guide for Mike, a young boy with a fascination for buses. "On Saturdays I used to go down to Oystermouth Square and he would tell me about the different types of buses operated by SWT," said Mike, of Thistleboon, Mumbles.

"He always referred to the company as 'The Transport' and he knew which of the buses belonged to Ravenhill or Brunswick depots by looking at the vehicle fleet numbers. Other inspectors had nicknames such as The Bat, Book and Pencil, Twinkletoes and Lighthouse. There were great characters among the drivers, conductors and conductresses too.

"One conductor used to get the driver to stop the bus at Blackpill and would open an upstairs window to pick apples from a tree on the side of the road. Crews had regular routes, they knew their passengers and would often wait if the regulars were not at their stops on time. Conductors were very helpful, aiding people on and off buses. Drivers of on-coming buses used to warn if an inspector was about by flashing their headlights.

"Uncle Cyril used to take me to Ravenhill depot where the buses were maintained and painted," said Mike. "He told me the story of the driver who took a short cut through a newly installed bus wash, activated the water and roller brushes as he walked through and came out the other side soaking wet. I recall all the notices inside the vehicles: 'Have you your ticket? The Road Traffic Act requires the passenger to show the ticket upon demand' and 'Passengers entering or leaving a moving omnibus do so at their own risk'. I can remember the Setright ticket machines used by SWT, and when I was very young the conductor would sometimes give me a ticket roll to take with me when I got off the bus.

"The Sketty Park estate route 74 was one of the first in Swansea to go over to one-man operation and the ticket machine was placed on a stand next to the driver to take fares."

Unfortunately little remains of the railway itself. It closed at a time when attitudes to saving old buses, cars and trains were markedly different to those of today. Shortly after closure a complete Mumbles Railway tram was offered to the Royal Institution of South Wales in Swansea to be kept for posterity but it was rejected by the curator as he felt it had "no historical interest." His attitude was common for the time and that is why there are so few restored SWT buses today and why nothing but the cab section of one of those 13 magnificent tram-like electric cars remains. Part of car number 7, it can still be seen in the tram shed, next to the Waterfront Museum in Swansea Marina, complete with its upper deck 'Do not spit' warning. A replica horse-drawn tram built by SWT's engineering department for the 1954 celebrations is also to be seen there.

In 1960 it looked as if at least one of the cars would be saved when the Middleton Railway Trust of Leeds agreed to buy it. This was car number two which unfortunately was destroyed in an arson attack some years later. What we have to remember the train today is hardly enough and the Mumbles Railway deserves much more. It is a loss that most people today cannot fully appreciate.

Swansea journalist Paul Chambert put it succinctly: "For today's generation, all they know of the Mumbles Train is gleaned from books, paintings and videos. They don't know what they missed!"

Cyril Seacombe, inspector. 1950s.

Heading home from Langland Bay on a sunny day in the mid- 1960s.

Passengers pack into Marshall bodied AEC Reliance 1821, TCY 665 after a day at Aberavon Beach, late 1960s.

Getting people to the seaside was always a seasonal challenge for South Wales Transport.

The problem was the weather. Sunny summer days meant the local bays were packed but when it rained they were deserted. The company had to ensure there were enough buses for the busy times but it inevitably meant crews and vehicles hanging around — just in case.

From SWT's earliest days, services to Mumbles, Langland Bay and

They did like to

Caswell Bay were popular.
In September 1934 Swansea's chief constable told the town's highways committee that one weekend that summer no fewer than 218 buses had brought more than 11,000 visitors to Caswell Bay alone.
One of SWT's first routes was the number 5 from Uplands to Caswell. Fred Ball became a regular conductor on the route in 1925 and he remembered hundreds of

passengers in the bus queues at Caswell. "It was not unknown for it to be late at night before the last passenger was on board," he said. "They were very patient and often started community singing while they waited."

By 1950 service 5 and its singers had gone and SWT ran three services to the bays: the 40 from Morriston to Caswell, the 85 from Swansea Castle Street to Caswell and Langland Bays, and the 90 from Penlan to Caswell Bay, which could be packed out or lightly used, depending on the elements.
There was also SWT's Mumbles Railway with its 106-seater cars. Two coupled together made short work of queues.

But in January 1960 SWT closed the railway and while it was adamant that the replacement buses would cope with demand, even during the hectic summer months, it took an enormous amount of planning.
The bus service was numbered 77 and the crews immediately christened it 77 Sunset Strip after a popular American TV private

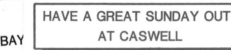

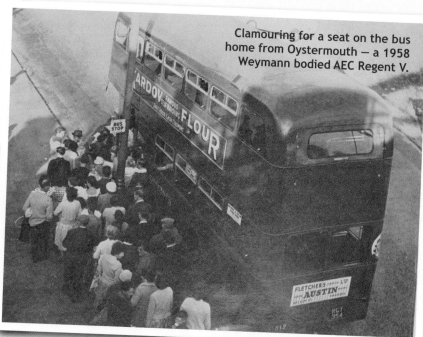

Clamouring for a seat on the bus home from Oystermouth — a 1958 Weymann bodied AEC Regent V.

be beside the seaside!

detective series of the time. Bus conductor Brian Marks recalled it was always busy, on hot summer days.

"The beaches around Mumbles, Limeslade and Bracelet Bays would be packed to capacity," he said. "People relied on buses to get themselves there and back. The trouble was that very often they all wanted to do it at the same time. The control inspector at Mumbles often used to contact our Brunswick Street garage to ask for extra buses. The tannoy in the canteen would burst into life and the required number of crews would tumble out to learn where they were going. Once we had a call to say there were 300 people waiting for us at The Slip. Four extra double deckers were sent down and we cleared the queue in one go. Times like that always revived memories of the Mumbles Train."

The peak return times from the beaches was usually between 5 pm and 6 pm. But if it started to rain at 2 pm, the mass exodus would begin then and SWT had to be ready to deal with the demand.

In 1975 SWT introduced a vintage open-top bus service from Swansea city centre to Limeslade during the summer and augmented this a couple of years later with three more open-top double deckers which ran to Langland and Caswell Bays. While this helped to cope with demand on sunny summer days, not having roofs was a major problem in the rain. It may have been tempting fate but as one of SWT's managers said at the time: "Whenever we start to run our open-toppers the rain starts to come down!" Unfortunately for SWT, once a service is advertised it has to run, no matter what the elements are up to, and often the open-top buses were replaced by closed-top buses with very few passengers. It could be costly and the company had to hope that what it earned during the busy, good weather times more than made up for the quiet, rainy days.

The weather was not the only problem when it came to running buses to Langland and Caswell bays however. Both beaches can only be

accessed via steep hills and this was a nightmare requiring good driving skills. In the 1950s SWT issued the following instructions to crews operating the services:

'First gear must be engaged when ascending and second gear when descending Caswell and Langland hills. Drivers are instructed that when ascending Langland hill and negotiating the bend, buses should keep well to the outside of the corner. Buses standing at the Langland Bay terminus must be properly scotched with the chocks provided and a driver must not leave his cabin until he is satisfied that his vehicle is resting against the chocks. Conductors must ensure immediately that the bus moves away from Langland Bay terminus that the chocks are removed and placed in a box provided alongside the police box. Standing passengers are not to be carried when ascending Langland and Caswell hills. Drivers on these services should check their radiators for water on each occasion they enter Oystermouth Square.'

87

CHAPTER 8

Passengers decline and the going gets tough

S WT entered the Swinging Sixties in much the same manner as it had left the more austere 1950s — facing declining passenger numbers, local authority battles over fares and crippling Government fuel taxation. It would however end the decade as a vastly different company in one of the biggest upheavals witnessed by public transport in England and Wales during the 20th century.

The dawn of the 1960s also brought with it further serious challenges, not least among them a decline in passenger levels though it seems that initially, the significance of this was not fully appreciated by the company. In a way it was a major hangover from the late 1950s and something that would effect the company for the remainder of its life. It was not fully understood at the time just how great an impact the dawn of the private car era would have on buses.

In the summer of 1957, SWT's drivers and conductors joined a national strike in pursuit of a pay claim and its buses were off the road for 10 days from July 20 to July 29. It ended with the Industrial Disputes Tribunal awarding the crews an extra 11 shillings (55p) a week something which cost SWT £65,000 in a full year which meant it had to seek a further fares increase. But the strike also laid bare a much more insidious problem. Traffic manager Charles Hill put his finger on it exactly, although when he commented shortly after the dispute ended he may not have been aware of the full significance of his words.

"In spite of the standstill of our own buses in the area, everybody got to their daily business without much trouble," he declared. "Many found alternative means of transport more convenient, speedier and, in many cases, less expensive, the result being that many of our former patrons will never return, preferring their new found means of conveyance."

Mr Hill's remedy to the problem was, in the light of what was to follow, rather simplistic: "We have got to do all we can to promote friendly relations between our customers and ourselves. We have to demonstrate by the quality of our service that we are worth patronising and trust in our customers to recommend us to other people."

By February the following year, when the number of passengers travelling with SWT had fallen by millions more, general manager Mr H Weedy was acknowledging the scale of the problem, even if his solution of how to win back lost passengers was equally simplistic: "The way to attract them back and solve practically all the

An AEC Regent V tackles a gradient on a narrow, single track country lane while executing the once a day return service to the village of Felindre on the outskirts of Swansea, March 23, 1977. *Stephen Miles*

A 1958 AEC Regent V with Weymann bodywork at Blackpill working the 77 route to Pontlasse, followed by an older, rear entrance version.

Roy Kneath

problems confronting the industry today is quite simple: cheaper fares, luxury buses having all the smooth riding of a motor car and good time-keeping. But to do that in the present circumstances would be nothing short of a miracle," said Mr Weedy.

That miracle was not about to happen and with SWT continuing to seek fare increases to balance its rising costs, cheaper fares were not even on the horizon. Mr Weedy's reference to cars was particularly apt as the rise in private motoring was the main factor in the decline of the bus. From the early 1960s, SWT waged a war against the car that it seemed it could never win.

In 1963 the company's particularly outspoken chairman, Raymond Birch, sounded off about private motoring at that year's annual meeting: "Nobody will deny the right of every citizen of this country to own his own car, or to have an ambition to do so, but is it reasonable that such ownership should confer on the individual the right to occupy for long periods and without payment some of the most valuable space in the centre of towns?" he asked before continuing: "Or at the busiest travelling times to hold up in tedious and extended queues the journeys, to and from work, of the great majority of those travelling, that is to say, bus passengers?"

Mr Birch pointed out: "One bus at peak times carries 50 times the number of people carried by the average private car, and surely that larger number deserves prior consideration."

SWT was finding traffic congestion affected the reliability of its services which, in turn, was resulting in fewer people on its buses. The answer according to Mr Birch was to "Clear the streets of obstruction by parked vehicles, give buses their due priorities in access to town centres, including specially reserved traffic lanes where necessary, relieve them of their dead load of fuel tax, and then the buses can really go to town."

But the decline in passengers continued, not by thousands, but millions every year. At SWT's annual meeting in 1964, Mr Birch announced the company's pre-tax profits had fallen by £47,790 while the number of passengers had dropped by four-and-a-half million, or 5.5 per cent. Some of this was attributed to four unofficial strikes staged by SWT bus crews during the year, which he described as deplorable, but listed the main cause as the growth of private motoring.

"This problem of competition from personal transport is aggravated by growing congestion in the towns which we serve because the ever increasing flood of cars slows down our services and makes them less attractive to passengers, as well as increasing our cost of operation," said Mr Birch.

In 1966 SWT carried only 58 million passengers compared with 91 million in 1956, which was itself a drop of five million on the previous year. It meant that the company had lost a third of its passenger journeys in 10 years and the blame was laid firmly at the door of

89

Worst weather was snow joke for company

The winter of 1962-3 was the coldest for more than 200 years in South Wales with ponds and rivers freezing and 20ft high snowdrifts blocking roads.

It inevitably had a major effect on transport but incredibly SWT managed to keep its buses going for most of the time.

The company's traffic manager, Charles Hill, praised staff for the 'magnificent way the wheels have been kept turning during these last months.'

He added: "The fact that we were able to maintain the majority of our services throughout this bad period was due largely to the skill and dogged determination of our operating staff coupled with the magnificent co-operation received from the engineering staff."

Getting people to work even in bad weather was always a priority for SWT and the company's efforts to beat snow and ice were praised by local employers who would otherwise have seen production hit.

In the winter of 1955, for example, SWT received letters from a number of companies, including the Steel Company of Wales in Port Talbot and Hodges and Son of Fforestfach, Swansea, thanking bus crews for their efforts.

The steel company's personnel superintendent, KDM Dauncey, said: "I am writing on behalf of the company to express our appreciation of the way in which your organisation, especially drivers and conductors, managed to keep services going during the recent spell of severe weather and to get our work people to and from the plant with so little delay."

rising car ownership. Higher fares, of course, did not help and as the company's costs continued to rise, it was forced to go to the South Wales Traffic Commissioners almost annually for permission to increase ticket prices, something which was invariably fiercely opposed by local authorities.

Mr Birch was equally outspoken about this, declaring that he deplored "the unfair tactics adopted by some local authorities in South Wales who appeal habitually to abuse their rights of objection to our applications to the traffic commissioners and deliberately use the machinery of the Road Traffic Act to obstruct and delay in every possible way the introduction of reasonable increases in fares."

Mr Birch said SWT was a commercial undertaking and it had to be kept in a healthy condition in its efforts to reduce rising costs. Wages were rising and the company was having to pay out more in fuel tax. It has to be said that usually SWT got its way over fares, but that cut little ice with the local authorities who continued to object through the 1960s and 1970s until the traffic commissioners eventually lost the right to determine fares under the new liberalised transport regime introduced by Margaret Thatcher's Government in the 1980s. For their part, the South Wales councils said that by objecting, they could vary or limit the increases and delay their implementation, which benefitted the travelling public. They also believed that SWT could make greater operational economies to which Mr Birch replied that had it not been for the "continuous ingenuity, skill and contrived economies developed by the company's departments the people of Swansea would be paying much higher fares and getting less frequent and less convenient services."

SWT pointed out that its fares would not be as high if the Government reduced the tax on fuel which had started at 9d (4.5p) in 1950 and had risen to 2s/6d (12.5p) by the end of 1958, costing the company £176,000 a year. By 1966 this had risen to £250,000 a year which saw the company's costs rising spectacularly. A new sick pay scheme for staff was introduced in February followed by a 40-hour week in April. Costs rose during the year by £145,000 and SWT's new chairman, Wilfred Dravers, who had been the company's general manager in the first half of the 1950s, warned they were in a predicament.

"The loss of passengers is severe," he told the annual meeting in

An SWT Regent III battles through the snow of January 1963, the worst to hit Swansea and elsewhere for more than 25 years.

A row of retired AEC Regent Vs await their fate at the former United Welsh depot, Gorseinon, 1980. *Royston Morgan Collection*

February 1967. "It is not merely a question of cutting mileage. We have also got to cut our costs per mile. With a fall of over one third of our passengers, it seems to me common sense that we should, in those cases that are appropriate, transfer more services to one-man operation." Mr Dravers said other bus companies were already doing this and warned: "We in this company lag behind, and we can't afford to, because loss of traffic, loss of revenue and rising costs are overtaking us."

Unfortunately for the company's finances, very few services would be converted and these were over routes where there were few passengers. SWT was also continuing to take into its fleet double deck buses that could not be used for one-person operation, the last AEC Regents didn't arrive until 1967. By May that year SWT had just 12 driver only routes, although by this time more were being planned.

In the meantime another idea to cut costs had emerged and that entailed closer integration with SWT's arch rival, United Welsh

Services. The 1953 agreement between the two companies had ended much cut-throat competition but they still operated on similar routes, particularly in the Neath and Swansea valleys. It was a considerable waste in the miles operated, vehicles and manpower, so in December 1964 they decided to investigate ways of

running their services more efficiently. It took until April 1967, but that month saw SWT, a private company and part of British Electric Traction, start to run services in conjunction with state-owned United Welsh. The Swansea Valley was chosen as a pilot scheme and the companies agreed to provide a pool of vehicles to run the services. The size of the companies determined the number of buses each ran on the routes and the savings in mileage each made. It meant a reduction of 150,000 miles a year, with SWT operating 100,000 fewer miles and UWS 50,000. Passengers now saw fewer buses but they enjoyed complete inter-availability of tickets and the pilot scheme was such a success that in the autumn of that year it was extended to the Neath area. It was proposed to introduce it in other areas as well and that would have seen the eventual saving of around 100 buses. In 1964 SWT had 360 buses and this would have dropped to 300 while the size of the UWS fleet would have fallen in the same period from 194 to 150.

By now however, more revolutionary changes on a national scale were being planned and they would radically alter the bus industry in England and Wales. It wasn't only SWT that was having problems and Harold Wilson's Labour government thought it knew the way to resolve the country's transport woes: create passenger transport authorities and take over BET. One of the most gifted politicians of the 20th century was put in charge as Minister of Transport — Barbara Castle, a flame-haired, diminutive woman nicknamed Labour's Red Queen. Best remembered for introducing the breathalyser and seat belts in cars, she also changed forever the way bus services were run, and SWT was at the forefront of those changes in South West Wales.

The story goes that in May 1967 Mrs Castle called in BET's chairman, J Spencer Wills, and told him that unless he sold his bus interests to the Government she would take steps in the Transport Act she planned the following year to force him to do so. The story may, or may not, be true, although it certainly has a ring of truth about it. What is a fact is that the following November, BET sold out to the state sector and SWT suddenly, for the first time in its life, found itself a nationalised bus company without the parent which had cared and nurtured it for more than 55 years. Why did BET sell out when 20 years' previously, it was prepared to fight to the last mudguard to remain in the private sector? The £35 million the Government offered to the group for its bus interests was certainly a factor and was more than it probably would have got if it had been purchased compulsorily. BET also realised that it was facing a Transport Minister determined to push forward with her plans, unlike in the late 1940s when Atlee's Labour Government was trying to nationalise the bus industry at the tail end of its administration.

Also, by 1967 buses were no longer the cash cows they once were and the problems were becoming more serious each year. BET had also become involved in other fields, including television, printing and publishing, plant hire, laundry and linen rental, it even had a controlling interest in Wembley Stadium. The group had to protect these other interests and concluded that would be best done by getting rid of its bus companies — including SWT. So a deal was struck and announced on November 22. It came as a surprise to many, not least people working within BET which in the months before had been running advertisements on its buses in South Wales warning of the perils of nationalisation. Only the month before SWT had joined other bus companies in South Wales in forming a group to fight against the proposed PTAs.

That summer SWT's new general manager, JH 'Jim' Gilbert had made quite clear what he thought: "We are given no justification for this upheaval other than a vague claim that the present organisation of the industry is wrong and that there is insufficient co-ordination, neither of which makes much sense. It would seem obvious that the transport industry and the public it serves could receive very much more benefit if left to get on with its job and if the minister would devote herself to assisting in some of the problems like traffic congestion which beset the industry at the moment."

But the Transport Act of 1968 which provided for the setting up of the National Bus Company was passed and SWT became a subsidiary of the world's biggest single bus operator with 21,000 vehicles and 81,000 staff. The new organisation started trading on January 1, 1969 and BET's former South Wales companies, SWT, Western Welsh, Rhondda Transport, Thomas Bros of Port Talbot and Neath & Cardiff Luxury Coaches, began the year facing the great unknown — the prospect of operating as state-owned companies. For a while, nothing appeared to happen. N&C continued running its chocolate brown and red coaches between Swansea and Cardiff, Thomas Bros still operated turquoise and cream single deckers around Port Talbot and SWT still had its large fleet of AEC Regent Vs, although it had started painting them in a brighter red livery.

There was, of course, plenty going on behind the scenes as managers jostled for positions within the new set up. But many began to think that life for SWT and the other former BET companies in South Wales might not be that different in the nationalised sector. There were certainly many who did not want to see radical change, even those high up the ladder. They included Bernard Griffiths, who became SWT chairman in July 1968.

Despite the destination, new Park Royal bodied AEC Renown 1241 is heading for Winch Wen as it picks up passengers in Castle Street, Swansea, in 1963.

Speaking at Western Welsh's annual long-service dinner in February 1969, he cautioned against NBC being regarded as "one large nationalised undertaking."

Mr Griffiths said: "There is a tremendous value in company names, company livery and company loyalty, and loyalty is something which cannot be bought or obtained by statute. I believe, and I hope, as far as nationalisation is concerned under the Transport Act, the companies will remain with the same names as they have now, with the same management and run in the same way."

The words were hardly out of Mr Griffiths's mouth than all of what he had warned against came about. On Tuesday November 17, 1970, trade unions and other staff representatives from four companies, SWT, United Welsh, N&C and Thomas Bros were called to a meeting with Frank Woodworth who had taken over as SWT manager in February 1968. It was the most momentous meeting between management and staff in the history of the four companies.

At the meeting Mr Woodworth announced that UWS, N&C and Thomas Bros would be transferred to SWT's formal ownership and become part of an enlarged SWT from January 1, 1971. He revealed

Roy Hutchins was a one time private bus operator in the Swansea Valley, but sold out to SWT after the 1926 General Strike. "Part of the deal was that I had a job for life in any department," said Roy. "I decided to be a driver and from then until I retired in 1971, must have driven over two million miles."

that N&C's Briton Ferry depot and garage, which had opened only seven years previously, would close as would SWT's Neath depot in Eastland Road, on March 1, 1971. In future all major office functions for the four companies would be handled at SWT's head office in Russell Street, Swansea, while vehicles in the four fleets would be renumbered into one system and carry a single identity — that of South Wales.

Manager Frank Woodworth

Mr Woodworth explained why the companies couldn't retain their identities as Mr Griffiths had hoped fewer than two years previously. "Co-ordination, which has been the companies' by-word in recent years," he said, " has shown its own measure of success in cutting out wasteful duplication and producing necessary economies. Although initially we thought it might be practicable to continue under the separate names, the degree of integration that has become necessary and possible has made the adoption of one name inevitable."

The new company had a fleet of 539 buses, including 257 double deckers, 219 single deckers and 63 coaches. SWT was now larger than it had ever been and operating more

An AEC Renown working the No. 80 service to Cefn Road, Bonymaen, waits for the green light at the traffic light junction between Princess Way and Caer Street, Swansea, in the early 1970s. The vehicle is seen in the livery used by SWT from 1968 until 1972 when the company began painting its vehicles in NBC poppy red.

services over a much wider area. But its deep-rooted problems had not gone away. As the early 1970s unfolded they would be described as disastrous years for the company which was in a state of crisis. Its survival was at stake yet again.

Havoc and stress of traffic jams

Traffic congestion is the bane of any bus company. It plays havoc with timetables, causes stress among drivers who have to make up journey time.

The same congestion also infuriates passengers who find themselves waiting in the cold and rain for a bus they cannot be sure will eventually turn up.

For SWT, it was always a major problem, right from the earliest days.

Soon after the First World War there was traffic congestion in Swansea town centre and it was to remain a problem for the rest of SWT's existence. The problem in the 1920s was not the number of cars, there were very few at this time. It was the narrowness of the streets, the trams, which were slow and took up so much room on the roads, and the numerous bus operators plying for trade around Swansea.

The lack of a central bus station was a headache that would remain for more than 50 years. Back in 1923, there were so many firms running buses in the town centre that the highways committee fixed 'standing places' for buses in seven streets and limited the

A number of buses including two SWT single deck vehicles tackle a congested Station Road, Port Talbot in 1958. The opening of the M4 seven years later eased this daily scene.

number of buses at each stand. Even then there was so little room that the council had to turn down operators who wanted licences to run buses into town.

Over the years there were a number of bus station schemes which did not materialise. One of the earliest, and most ambitious, was in 1924 when the council proposed a bus station on the site of Swansea market. If it had gone ahead it would have cost, for the time, a colossal £110,000, and would have been the largest bus station in the country. It didn't and buses continued to park at places all over central Swansea which caused major administration problems for SWT and confusion for passengers, who had to hunt for their bus stops.

Then in December 1938 a new bus station was announced for Singleton Street. It had waiting rooms, parcels and inquiry offices, refreshment rooms and shops. The ground floor had a 'grand façade' for passengers. It was felt that abolishing street termini in favour of a central bus station would ease traffic congestion in the town.

The new bus station eventually opened in May 1940, but there was a major problem. It wasn't large enough and Swansea's biggest bus operator, SWT, was forced to continue using street termini, a situation that would remain until 1978 when the long-awaited Quadrant bus station finally opened. It meant that for many years SWT's town services left from different termini. Some routes departed from the Guildhall, others from Castle Street, Orchard Street, Alexandra Road, Christina Street and what was known as The Exchange in Adelaide Street. Rural services left from the streets around St Mary's Church and this was the only place in the entire SWT network where crews from all the company's depots met up. It was a logistical headache for SWT which had to have inspectors or regulators at the termini to ensure the network ran smoothly.

By the late 1950s traffic congestion was beginning to hit SWT's services in a big way. Once again, it was not so much the number of cars, although the figure was rising. It was the lack of traffic controls and the narrowness of the roads. In 1960 you could bring your car into Swansea town centre and park virtually anywhere you liked. Parking restrictions were years away as were dual carriageways and bus lanes. SWT chairman WT James told the company's annual meeting in 1960: "The congestion disrupts our schedules and annoys our passengers, thereby damaging our goodwill. Moreover, many of our shorter distance passengers find it quicker to walk than wait for a bus."

There was another major traffic bottleneck — Port Talbot town centre, which according to Mr James was the biggest problem. He described it as simply

The secret they didn't reveal to new drivers

One secret that no-one lets you in on when you first start driving double deck buses is the difference a full standing load of passengers has on the handling characteristics of the vehicle.

One-time employee David Beynon, discovered that difference the hard way. "No matter how gently you turned the steering wheel the weight of the passengers caused the bus to lean in the opposite direction and that could often bring problems of its own," he recalls.

David who scooped the West Glamorgan Driver of the Year award in 1975 recalled that nowhere did this manifest itself more than when pulling up at the bus stop outside the Cwmfelin Social Club, Cwmbwrla.

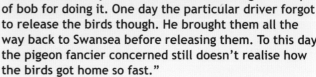
David Beynon

"The approach to the roundabout is on a hill so you automatically begin to brake as you are turning the wheel to the right to negotiate the roundabout and at the same time the bus would start to lean to the left to counter the movement and the floor of the driver's cab would tilt and jam the brake pedal.

"I remember the first time it happened to me on service 84 from Blaenymaes into town at around 8.20am one morning. At first I didn't understand what was happening. When I did I started stamping on the brake pedal to free it. As the bus leaned the other way it freed itself and I was able to pull the bus to a halt safely just past the bus stop.

"That was the first week I had been driving for SWT and it was one lesson that I never forgot.

"The old boys used to tell tales of buses used on the Brecon route. These double deck vehicles were AEC Regent IIIs with Weymann lowbridge bodywork and the first to have doors fitted to the rear platform.

"On market days it was not unusual to find a farmer holding a couple of sheep in the cubby hole under the stairway. They also put baskets of racing pigeons on the bus up to Brecon to be released at the terminus which at the time was at Bishop's Meadow.

"That was all very well. The driver used to get a couple of bob for doing it. One day the particular driver forgot to release the birds though. He brought them all the way back to Swansea before releasing them. To this day the pigeon fancier concerned still doesn't realise how the birds got home so fast."

appalling. SWT did not become Port Talbot's main bus operator until 1971, but before that it ran services through the town from Swansea and Neath to Margam and Porthcawl. The problem was that the main Swansea to Cardiff road, the A48, snaked through the town on a route dating back to horse and carts. For more than miles the average speed was 18 mph. It was often much slower because a railway line cut across the main A48 road in the town centre and when the level crossing gates closed traffic ground to a halt. The problem was even worse after the steelworks opened, so in 1953 a by-pass was announced for the town, although it was not until 1966 that it finally opened. This was the 4.5 mile motorway route that runs over Port Talbot on 45ft high concrete stilts. SWT's staff magazine, Ein Newyddion, said of the long awaited opening: "It was as if someone had waved a magic wand and all traffic problems had been solved overnight. After many years of weekday traffic congestion, every day now seems like a Saturday in Port Talbot."

It was a different matter in Swansea however, even though the council introduced limited parking controls in the town centre for the first time on April 25, 1966. They were welcomed by SWT's new chairman, Wilfred Danvers, because they helped improve traffic flow, although he pointed out they had displaced traffic to other streets. He backed a Ministry of Transport report — Roads in England and Wales — which advocated restraints on cars, especially for commuting; waiting, loading and unloading restrictions for vehicles, especially during peak hours, in towns and cities; and bus only lanes and streets. All these would later come about, but not fast enough for SWT.

A sticker designed to promote Park 'n' Ride service in 1973.

As car ownership continued to rise and traffic congestion worsened during the 1960s, Swansea Council initiated a roads survey in 1969. SWT general manager Frank Woodworth said the company would play a prominent role: "We shall strongly press the case for priority consideration of the needs of the bus, its drivers and its passengers because we know that the bus is the most economical vehicle in terms of road space and cost," he said. "We don't seek wholesale banning of cars from town and city centres but we believe further restrictions of parking and delivery of goods in daytime are necessary. This is common sense."

More on-street parking restrictions followed, but shopping development schemes in Swansea city centre, Llanelli, Neath and Port Talbot, came with additional car parks which meant even more vehicles and traffic congestion worsened, despite road improvements. Motorists were not prepared to forsake their new found freedom to hop on SWT's less convenient buses so councils came under pressure from shop owners who were concerned that making it more difficult and expensive for cars to park in town and city centres would hit business. SWT found it increasingly difficult to maintain bus schedules, passenger numbers dropped and it was forced to put up fares, which in turn led to fewer people using the buses. It was self-perpetuating. But there were advances. In 1980 a new £40,000 scheme was devised which it was hoped might be a solution in Swansea city centre. It involved fitting electronic transponders to SWT's buses to give them priority at traffic lights. Vehicles were fitted with a unit which, when they approached traffic lights, activated an electrical loop of wire in the road. This speeded up and changed the phasing of the lights to give buses priority. Called the Selective Detective Scheme, it became the subject of a film, The Bus Signals Go, made by the Department of the Environment with help from the Welsh Office and West Glamorgan County Council. The DoT said: "It has resulted in little delay to ordinary traffic and faster bus journey

A mix of AEC Regents at Llanelli depot, early 1960s.

One of the last batch of Regent Vs delivered in 1966, heads into Swansea city centre, liveried in NBC poppy red April, 1980.

One of SWT's former front line coaches plays its part in the early days of Swansea's Park 'n' Ride service at Landore, December 18, 1976. *Stephen Miles*

times." The county council was pleased because it cost less than bus only lanes and other bus priority schemes and didn't physically change or affect the environment.

Park and Ride was another concept for helping reduce traffic congestion in city and town centres. It involved people leaving their cars at out-of-town car parks and making the rest of the journey into the shopping centre by bus. Swansea's first was introduced at Christmas in 1973 after a car park was created by bulldozing some

tips opposite what was at the time the Morfa Stadium in Landore, about two miles to the north of the city centre, near the Liberty Stadium. It has since become a permanent park 'n' ride site. Those bus only lanes Mr Danvers was keen to see back in 1966 were a reality by the end of 1994. A segregated bus-only road, with a distinctive green surface, was built that year to speed up buses on their way in and out of the Quadrant bus station. There was also a short section to help with congestion just outside the city centre in Dyfatty.

Two AEC Bridgemasters pass one another in Fabian Street, St Thomas, 1961. Construction of the Fabian Way dual carriageway erased much of this scene.

People cheered at arrival of their first bus

It isn't often that people run out of their homes shouting and cheering at the sight of a bus, but that's exactly what happened to learner bus driver Peter Parker in 1963.

"During my training, which was mainly in AEC Regent ACY 29, we'd follow a variety of routes around Swansea. On this particular occasion we went over the Tawe bridge heading for St Thomas," said Peter.

"We went up to the top where buses normally turned right and the instructor told me to do the complete opposite and turn left. I thought I'd better tell him that we didn't normally turn left to which he replied that I should do as I was told! We headed towards where a new road had been cut into the hillside to carry traffic to the Grenfell Park estate.

"The instructor got out of the bus and called me up slowly checking as I went that there was plenty of clearance between the double decker and any electricity cables that spanned the road.

"The vehicle cleared all of them and eventually we reached the new turning point. That's when people came out to see what was going on. They were delighted that they were to get a bus service. It was almost as though they hadn't seen a bus before."

Peter wasn't the first member of his family to work for South Wales Transport. His father Stuart, was also a driver although he had finished before Peter climbed behind the wheel.

"He started in the early 1950s," said Peter. "Like me he worked out of Brunswick Street depot. Like me he found there was an excellent spirit of cameraderie there. Everyone knew everyone and you were all mates then."

At one point in his 47 year driving career, Peter worked for N&C and recalls those years with an even greater fondness. "There really was an excellent feeling of comradeship there. We were all sad when the depot closed in 1971. It was the end of an era."

But the traffic congestion problem never went away. "City Choked by Traffic: SWT Forced to Reshape its Services" was just one of the many headlines in the South Wales Evening Post in the early 1990s. SWT was forced to spend an extra £120,000 a year on three minibuses on city bus routes because this was the only way buses could keep to time. The company's managing director, Alan Kreppel, said: "All bus services are being choked at certain times of day by ever increasing traffic. They just cannot keep to long standing schedules. It is time for a determined, co-ordinated approach before cars choke off the city centre to all but those willing to waste time and money queuing up for unacceptably long periods."

SWT never resolved its battle with the private motorist. It would become one of the problems for its successor company, First Cymru, when it took over in April 1999.

Delays — blame it on the elephants!

There were many reasons why SWT sometimes failed to run a service but only once was it because of a herd of elephants.

The occasion was the visit to Swansea in the autumn of 1965 of Billy Smart's circus. In those days, unlike today, performing animals were an accepted part of the big top entertainment and elephants, tigers, lions and horses were all included in the show.

The elephants that stopped the SWT service running were being transported through Llanelli and the procession caused major traffic jams.

Bus services were hit and one conductor presented a waybill saying they were unable to run the 3.15 pm service from Llanelli railway station to Felinfoel "because of a herd of elephants."

Peter Parker and, below, AEC Regent ACY 29.

Just to show there were no hard feelings, SWT later came to the circus's rescue after it set up on the Recreation Ground in Swansea's Mumbles Road. A number of SWT buses had taken hundreds of children to see the show when suddenly a strong wind blew up which threatened the big top. It looked as if the performance might have to be cancelled, disappointing the

youngsters. But the crews came to the rescue and parked their buses around the tent to act as a giant mobile windbreak enabling the show to go on!

Stirring moment on cultural duty

Despite the aggravation of congestion, SWT did its best to cope with any task it was set. Not least among these was when the National Eisteddfod, the premier annual cultural event in Wales, was held within its territory.

In August 1962 it was located in Llanelli and the company had the role of transporting thousands of people to the festival. As a result, every two minutes a bus left Llanelli railway station for the showground.

The company said there were no complaints of anyone being left behind.

An atmospheric night-time view of an AEC Regent V approaching the junction of Oxford Street and Union Street, Swansea, as it heads to Mumbles pier on a typical cold, wet winter's evening, mid-1960s. *Huw Daniel*

"Well done, our drivers!" said a spokesperson for SWT.

Amazingly, what must have been one of the most stirring moments of the event was on an SWT bus as it made its way to the Eisteddfod ground. A local newspaper reporter summed it up: "Suddenly a roar came from the upper deck, enough to lift the roof off. It was all the passengers breaking into a spontaneous performance of Calon Lan!"

Electricians employed at SWT Ravenhill, 1970s.
Roy Kneath

The Swansea to Brecon route took in many valley villages as this Leyland TD5 shows, late 1940s.
Royston Morgan Collection

Perils of a long run over

For many years the company's longest route was that from Swansea to Brecon. It was also the most scenic and, during the winter, often one of the most difficult.

Numbered 28, it began in the late 1920s and continued for nearly 60 years before SWT lost it to an independent operator in the huge upheaval of local bus services that occurred in the mid-1980s.

Unlike any other SWT service the route started in the busy centre of Swansea and headed through the heavily industrialised Lower Swansea Valley to Morriston, made its way through the valley's mining communities to Ystradgynlais, where it became rural in nature, before the hard slog up the Brecon Beacons above Craig-y-Nos, and then down the other side, serving isolated agricultural villages on the way. Nearly 50 miles and some hours later the service terminated in the market town of Brecon.

For more than a third of the journey, the No. 28 wouldn't meet any other SWT service and was one of the few of the company's routes to break out of the operating area. Joyce Jenkins was six when she remembered first travelling on the route. It always brought back special memories because her father Alfred Bowen, known to everyone as AB Bowen, was an SWT inspector and a regular on the 28.

"The journey was nothing like it is today," Joyce recalled in 1997. "It took a lot longer. That's not surprising for the roads were bumpy and often narrow. But it was a great adventure for me. I remember the farms along the route and how my dad used to have to get off one bus going up and wait for another coming back so that he could check the fares. The farmers got to know him and often when they saw him they would give him a rabbit or a chicken for the pot. These days such a thing would probably be frowned upon."

Her dad retired in 1952 by which time the 28 had become a two-hourly service and took two hours 25 minutes from Swansea to Brecon.

Like most SWT routes, it was operated by double deckers and with open rear entrances must have been very cold for passengers and conductors, especially on the mountain tops. There were five journeys each way on weekdays and three on Sundays. The first journey left Swansea at 6.25am to get to Brecon before 9am. The last bus left Brecon as late as 9.13 pm and that could cause real problems, particularly in winter time. The service was scheduled to get to Swansea by 11.40 pm, but its actual arrival was often later and this often meant an anxious wait at Ravenhill garage.

It was not only at night that the mountain weather caused difficulties. Mist could descend at any time and often a driver would have to open his cabin window and peer out into the gloom with visibility down to a few yards. By the time he descended the Beacons his eyes would be red and watering. Snow and ice were the main problems and one day the 3.13 pm service from Brecon was very late. In the 1950s and 1960s, before

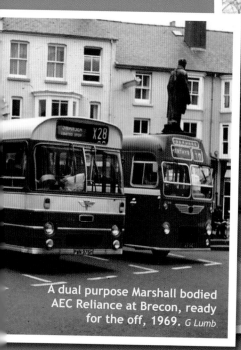

A dual purpose Marshall bodied AEC Reliance at Brecon, ready for the off, 1969. *G Lumb*

A 1959 Park Royal bodied AEC Reliance at St Mary's Church, Swansea before setting off on the long trek to Brecon.

the hills and far away

the days of mobile phones and radios, if a bus was long overdue there was only one thing to do. You had to go and look for it. So on this particular winter's day inspector Dai Gealy and driver Bobby Vaughan jumped into an inspection car. As they started to climb into the Beacons they met people walking towards them, passengers from the bus which they said had become stuck in a snow drift a mile and a half further up. Dai and Bobby found it difficult to believe because where they were it was dry and clear. They continued along the road until suddenly they were hit by a tremendous blizzard which had caused snowdrifts on the road. They saw the bus but only its front was visible, the rest was covered in snow right up to the upper deck windows.

Even in ideal weather conditions, the 28 was hardly a fast service so in 1967 SWT decided to introduce faster journeys between Swansea and Brecon which it numbered X28 and ran limited stop between Swansea and Abercrave, the journey speeded up to take 105 minutes.

It was a first for the company which at this time didn't have express journeys. One person, or one-man operation as it was known then, was also only just being introduced and SWT converted two of its 1956 AEC Reliance Weymann Fanfares, 1029 and 1030, registration numbers NCY 623 and NCY 624, so that the X28 could run with the driver taking fares. They were coming to the end of their working lives with SWT and were later replaced by newer dual purpose single deckers.

Unfortunately the X28 wasn't a success and early in the 1970s it was withdrawn and the 28 service renumbered to 118. Later a 117 service with minor route variations in the upper Swansea Valley was added. Like many other SWT routes during the 1970s the Swansea to Brecon service became single deck and one-person operated, although as the decade ended double deckers returned. A fast, limited stop service was also re-introduced on Saturdays. The end came as far as SWT was concerned

with the deregulation of local bus services in the mid-1980s. After that point companies had to register the services they wanted to run commercially and as SWT couldn't hope to make money on such a route so it didn't register it. When it was put out to tender by the local authorities it was won by Silverline, an independent bus firm based in Merthyr Tydfil, and renumbered 63.

SWT's Swansea to Brecon route was a pioneering service in every sense. For nearly 60 years it provided a vital link for isolated communities in one of the most difficult of bus operating areas. SWT never regained the route.

Brecon here we come!

Colin Scott

Web expands as takeovers swallow the competition

Takeovers began early for South Wales Transport. The first came in May, 1914, the same month that the company began operating. This was the acquisition of FL Lewis of Pontardawe which gave the company its first double deckers, two open-top Milnes-Daimlers, for the inaugural service from Ynysforgan to Ynysmeudwy in the Swansea Valley.

At about the same time SWT took over a horse bus business run by Moses Lee and his son James without licences between Swansea town centre and Mumbles. Then in 1915 the business of TE and J Evans of Fforestfach was acquired. It had operated three vehicles between the town, Fforestfach and Gorseinon.

There were few takeovers in the 1920s, a time of intense competition in the rapidly growing bus industry. Firms ran more or less as they liked and SWT took the view that there was little point in buying out operators who could start up again the next day. It decided that internal growth was the way forward. Two firms that were acquired however gave the company its first routes into Gower: Fairwood Motors, with 11 vehicles and a route from Swansea to Port Eynon, was taken over in May 1923 while The Bishopston and Murton Motors business followed in July 1928. It had six buses and ran from Swansea to Bishopston. In December 1927 SWT acquired the four vehicles of A Thomas (MMT Services) of Tirydail in Ammanford and this gave the company a route in a completely new area, from Ammanford to Llandeilo.

That was it until 1935 when SWT engaged in a further flurry of takeover activity as it sought to lessen the intense competition it was then fighting. In May 1935 JM Bacus, which competed with SWT on routes in the Llanelli area, was bought out, quickly followed the same month by Gwendraeth Transport of Pontyates which also ran buses from Llanelli. SWT then turned its attention to Neath and in November 1935 acquired Willmore Motors with a service from Neath to Briton Ferry, Aberavon and Margam. The company focussed again on Llanelli in July 1936 when Treharne Brothers of Ponthenri with its route from the village to Llanelli was acquired and the same month John Brothers of Grovesend with 11 vehicles was taken over. It ran from Neath to Llanelli and operated an express service from Llanelli to Porthcawl.

The intricate web of linking services in SWT's operating area was developing nicely and in June 1937, the same year the company took over Swansea's trams, T Davies (Osborne Services) of Neath was bought with routes from

A 1958 Weymann bodied Leyland Tiger Cub which came into the fleet when the company took over Thomas Bros. of Port Talbot in 1971. It was withdrawn just two years later.

A 1954 Leyland Titan, which began life with J James of Ammanford and transferred to SWT in 1962 when that company was taken over.

Birchgrove to Briton Ferry and Neath to Banwen. The last pre-war takeover came in September 1938 when, jointly with the fast growing Red and White Group, Gorseinon and District Omnibus Services Ltd was acquired.

It was not until March 1952 that SWT took over another public transport firm and this was on a much larger scale than any of the others. It would make it the dominant operator in Llanelli which would become second only in importance to Swansea for the company. Llanelly District Traction had 27 trolleybuses, all double deck, operating across the town and 15 motor buses, all single deck, linking parts of Llanelli not accessible by the trolleybuses. The company had been part of the Balfour Beatty electricity supply group and when this was nationalised in 1948 the South Wales Electricity Board took over. Running public transport was not its primary purpose and it sold out to SWT, a rare example at the time of a nationalised undertaking becoming part of a private group. It was a shrewd investment by SWT as Llanelli was a growing town.
The trolleybuses carried just under eight million passengers in 1951 and the motor buses around 2.7 million. The trolleys lasted only a few months and the system was abandoned by SWT in favour of motor buses.

There would not be another takeover for 10 years. By 1962 bus passenger figures were dropping fast and it was clear that economies were urgently needed.

J James of Ammanford had become part of the British Electric Traction group, and a sister company to SWT, in 1950. Their services ran side-by-side and in 1962 it was decided that SWT would take over the James company. Angus James, son of the firm's founder, retired and the J James name started to disappear from its buses to be replaced by South Wales. Many felt that it was a sad day for public transport in Ammanford. J James had been the town's first bus operator and ran 21 services to Neath, Swansea, Llanelli, Burry Port, Lampeter and Aberystwyth. With the company came 35 Leyland vehicles which caused some difficulties as SWT's fleet at this time was all AEC.

Even so, there was no attempt to swap vehicles with other BET concerns. Three Leyland Leopards ordered by James and delivered in 1963 were taken into stock and the 13 Leyland Atlanteans that the company was operating stayed for another eight years under SWT ownership, not leaving the fleet until 1970 when they were transferred to City of Oxford Motor Services in exchange for nine of its AEC Regent Vs. The James Atlanteans included the first of its type to enter passenger service, this was 1227, RTH 637, which began operating in the Ammanford area in 1958.

The need for economies was the main cause of the biggest bus upheaval of the 20th Century in South Wales and at the end of it SWT was a vastly different company. The National Bus Company was formed in 1969 and SWT assumed control of three important bus firms in its operating area: United Welsh Services, Thomas Bros of Port Talbot, and N&C Luxury Coaches.

In January 1971 it took them over completely and they were merged into a larger SWT undertaking with around 569 vehicles.

United Welsh had grown to become a major competitor to SWT in Swansea and Neath. Originally part of the Red and White Group, it had become a nationalised company in 1950 when Red and White sold out to the state run Tilling bus group. So the vast majority of its buses were of Bristol/ECW manufacture, other than a very small number of Duple bodied Bedford coaches. SWT took over 149 UWS buses in 1971 and these were a mixture of elderly Bristol LS and MW single deckers, rear and front entrance Lodekka double deck vehicles, and some newer RELLs. The company operated in a similar area to UWS although it now regained the Gower services it had handed over to United Welsh in 1953.

Thomas Bros had become a BET company in 1951. It operated in Port Talbot and in the Afan Valley and had 49 vehicles at the time of the takeover. They were a mixture of BET-style AECs and Leylands, but in an unusual turquoise and cream livery. SWT had started to paint them in its new lighter red livery when it took control of the company, although they retained Thomas Bros fleet names until the actual takeover in 1971 when SWT became Port Talbot's main bus provider.

N&C was one of the more unusual BET fleets. It ran two express services from Swansea to Cardiff and had 32 coaches painted in an attractive chocolate brown and red livery. By the start of 1971 SWT and Western Welsh had carved up the fleet between them, 26 coaches becoming part of SWT, the rest going to WW. They were all AECs with bodies by a range of coachbuilders. The oldest were 1958 vehicles bodied by Weymann, the newest, two Plaxton vehicles that were actually ordered by SWT and so their gearboxes and body styles were to the company's standards. SWT had become a different company again by the time of the next takeover. It was the late 1980s and NBC was no more, now SWT was an independent concern.

In January 1988 the business of AE and FR Brewer of Caerau, near Maesteg, with a mixed bag of 34 vehicles, was acquired. This was a family run concern dating back to 1921 whose members wanted to retire. It was actually bought by United Welsh Services, not the old company, but one with the same name that had been revived when the managers bought out SWT during the privatisation of NBC in 1987. Even so, the managers

Five of the Atlanteans operated by J James of Ammanford on parade after being re-signed with the South Wales fleet name in the mid-1960s. Alongside is one of the Oxford AEC Regent Vs for which they were exchanged.

were the same and the vehicles taken over carried 'On hire to South Wales Transport' labels for a time. There were many exchanges of vehicles between the two fleets and in July 1988 the business of Llynfi Motor Services, also of Maesteg, and its Port Talbot to Maesteg service, was also taken over and extended to Swansea.

There was one more takeover in 1988: in December the Swansea operations of JD Cleverley Ltd of Cwmbran, which ran under the Capitol Coaches name, were acquired. Capitol had taken over Morris Bros. of Swansea, a well-known coach and private hire firm running in a distinctive two-tone blue livery, in May 1984. It operated a competing service with SWT in Swansea called the City Triangle.

The final takeover by SWT came at midnight on January 5, 1996, when it bought the local bus services in the Amman and Swansea valleys of D Coaches, which it ran under the well-established name of Rees & Williams. Vehicles included some minibuses and early examples of the Dennis Dart.

Luxury and speed with the N&C

Despite the decades that have passed since it was absorbed by SWT, people still have fond memories of N&C Luxury Coaches.

Many will wistfully recall how its vehicles — in their distinctive chocolate brown and dark red livery — whisked them rapidly and efficiently between Swansea and Cardiff, so quickly that they earned the nickname of Brown Bombers.

The N&C company was unique. It only ever had an average of 32 vehicles on its books and even after it was

taken over by SWT's parent company, British Electric Traction, in 1953 it still operated to all intents and purposes as an independent company. The takeover may have made N&C a sister company to SWT, but there was no love lost between the two. N&C's legendary managing director, Colonel and later Sir Godfrey Llewellyn, accused SWT of being jealous of his company's success — and he had a point. At the beginning of the 1930s, shortly after N&C was set up, they fought a battle to run an express service between Swansea and Cardiff, one that SWT expected to win. It had the support of Cardiff and Swansea councils for its service, which was run jointly with Western Welsh. Swansea's town clerk said this was a 'more satisfactory arrangement' than the one proposed by N&C. In those days local authorities issued bus companies with licences

With a freshly coated brown panel where the N&C monogram used to be and the South Wales fleet name and number, 232 BWN, Harrington Cavalier C51F still had its original red and brown livery when seen at Bridgend in 1970. *Colin Scott*

Two N&C vehicles at Cardiff bus station in the summer of 1969, one having just arrived from Swansea, the other about to head back there. *Colin Scott*

for their services and in March 1931, Swansea and Cardiff both refused an application by N&C, but the company still managed to launch their service because Neath and Port Talbot councils both gave it licences, although at the beginning it could only run between Neath and Cardiff.

The Road Traffic Act of 1930 changed everything. In 1932 traffic commissioners took over responsibility

A Brewers coach engaged in Continental contract operations for Leger Travel, in the mid-1980s. This was in the post-SWT era when the Brewers name was revived.
Royston Morgan Collection

for issuing bus companies with licences and N&C won the right to operate between Swansea and Cardiff. Western Welsh retired from the battle to run a service from Cardiff to Carmarthen which paralleled N&C as far as Neath. SWT persevered, but it soon became clear that passengers preferred the newcomer and it withdrew to lick its wounds. It would be nearly 40 years before SWT ran again between Swansea and Cardiff.

From 1933 N&C reigned supreme on the 48-mile Swansea to Cardiff express route which, in the days before the Neath River bridge was built at Briton Ferry, had to run through Neath. The journey was time-tabled to take two hours and even in those traffic free days, that meant the coaches had no time to waste. The service was tremendously popular and that probably had something to do with the cheapness of the fare. Sir Godfrey's ethos was to get the maximum number of passengers on to the service by charging the lowest possible price and for more than 20 years the return fare from Swansea to Cardiff was just 4s 6d, or 23p, and 3s, or 15p, between Bridgend and Swansea.

But if the fares were cheap, the operation certainly wasn't. N&C was run to military precision by its managing director, Sir Godfrey, who, whenever anyone wrote of him, bestowed on him his full title, so it was always Col Sir Godfrey Llewellyn Bart, CB, CBE, MC, TD, DL, JP. The general manager was JJ Newbury, who became a captain in the Home Guard during the war and he was assisted by Colonel John Lloyd. If you look

Back down to earth after a life of luxury

John Hughes, of Taibach, Port Talbot, won't forget the day he began driving for the N&C Luxury Coach Company behind the wheel of a Duple Commander bound for Cardiff.

"Everything was going fine until I pulled out of the bus station in Bridgend and had the misfortune to scrape the side of a parked car," said John. "What a way to start my new job I thought."

"After that most of the thousands of miles I drove between Swansea and Cardiff were without incident, thank goodness."

"There was a pride within the N&C company and people seemed to respond to this. Coaches were always well kept and clean. Everyone who worked for the company felt sad at the final closure of our depot at Briton Ferry on January 9, 1971.

"Along with about half the driving staff I was transferred to the former United Welsh garage at Clarence Terrace, Swansea. Suddenly, from driving smart luxury coaches I found myself coming back down to earth and getting behind the wheel of Bristol Lodekkas.

"Often I worked the route to Rhossili in Gower, but there wasn't much chance to admire the scenery.

"After less than a year I transferred to the former Thomas Bros depot at Port Talbot. This company had also been absorbed by SWT. That was something of a culture shock too as now, for the first time I found myself driving a one-man operated vehicle. It was different, but I just got on with things.

"I was driving Leyland Tiger Cubs then. These vehicles were quite a bit older than some of the others I had driven. They still had crash gearboxes similar to the Bristols, but like everyone else you just got used to that.

"Although there was a lot of change going on in the bus industry at that time, most people locally rose above the stress and worry and we all seemed to get on with one another in our new locations and often new jobs."

John certainly settled. He stayed in his driving job at Port Talbot for a further 31 years and in that time worked most of the routes in the area.

John Hughes — fond memories of driving for N&C Luxury Coaches.

at photographs of N&C staff taken in the 1930s it is impossible not to be struck by how immaculate they always looked. Even the sternest of sergeant majors would have found it difficult to fault their appearance and drivers and conductors remembered being inspected by Captain Newbury before beginning their shifts to ensure they reached the company's exacting standards.

This was also reflected in the company's vehicles. You never saw a scruffy, down-at-heel N&C coach, nor one that needed cleaning. The number of garage staff employed for such a small number of vehicles was amazing. In 1963, the company moved from its base in James Street, Neath to modern premises alongside the A48 at Briton Ferry, where each morning a team of seven cleaners gave each vehicle a wash and brush up before it went on service. Garage foreman Norman Dewitt also had charge of three fitters and two apprentices, two panel beater/body repairmen, a coach painter, trimmer and electrician, the storeman and two night watchmen.

The coaches also looked the part, no matter their age or whether they had been bought new or second hand. The livery on each was applied so that it fitted the lines of each vehicle. They included some of the most highly regarded buses of the 1950s and 1960s. There were Weymann Fanfares of 1958 and Harringtons in 1960, 1962 and 1963, machines similar to those SWT was using on its continental tours.

For the first 20 years N&C went from strength to strength, then the problems began. The cost of running buses rose after the war, wages had increased by 120 per cent, vehicle parts by 200 per cent, while the cost of tyres went up by a staggering 300 per cent. But N&C continued to charge the same fares as in 1933 and in the 12 months ending March 1953 it recorded a trading loss of £10,946, a significant sum in those days, and for the first time it was forced to seek a fares increase. At the fares inquiry, the chairman, HJ Thom, was surprised. "The impression we had was that this service was a little gold mine. Is this no longer the case?" he asked. Mr Thom was told by Mr Llewellyn Jones, representing N&C, that it was not and the company was allowed its increase. But the problems were quickly resolved for when N&C put in another fares increase application in 1955 it was refused because 'very substantial' gross dividends of 22.7 per cent were paid to shareholders in 1954 which showed the company was in a healthy financial state.

By now N&C was part of BET and had a new chairman, veteran busman WT James, who was also SWT's chairman. It seemed to make little difference, Sir Godfrey continued as managing director running the company in its own unique way and Captain Newbury stayed as general manager, not retiring until 1964. There was expansion in 1955 when the Neath River bridge was opened at Briton Ferry. N&C started running a faster service between Swansea and Cardiff across the bridge, which received the route number 10. This shaved six miles and 15 minutes off the original route, which continued as route number 7.

When it was taken over by SWT and Western Welsh in 1971 a furious Sir Godfrey described the company as having been destroyed and "delivered into the hands of South Wales Transport and Western Welsh: killed, as some of the staff claimed, by nationalisation and mourned by all." He said the loss of the company's identity was a tragedy and in a dig at SWT added it was "perhaps satisfying to companies who for years had appeared to be jealous of our success and cast envious eyes upon us."

So SWT returned to the route it had abandoned nearly 40 years previously and changes were made. The number 10 variant was renumbered 252 and was extended to Llanelli. It became a joint operation with Western Welsh, with SWT providing three vehicles, two from its Clarence Terrace depot in Swansea and one from Llanelli, and WW two buses from its depot in Penarth Road, Cardiff. The limited stop journey was scheduled to take 135 minutes so the drivers could not afford to hang around, particularly at peak times.

N&C's original route, the number 7, was discontinued and Western Welsh's service from Carmarthen to Cardiff became 251 and timed on an even headway with the 252 from Port Talbot. When SWT took over WW's Neath Abbey depot in 1972, it gained most of the workings on the 251 and the route, which at 74 miles had been Western Welsh's longest stage carriage service, now became SWT's longest route. But the days of those wonderful coaches in their distinctive brown and red livery were over. Both WW and SWT used single deck buses with coach seats on the services although SWT did continue to run some of the 252s with former N&C vehicles it had taken over. By now the tradition of adapting liveries to suit the body style was over, it was poppy red below the windows and white above and the lovely winged motif that had

graced the sides of N&C's coaches was no more. The practice of displaying the names of places served along the route above the coach windows was also ended.

New coaches returned to the 252 in the second half of the 1970s. SWT and Western Welsh both ran Leyland Leopards, although SWT painted its vehicles in poppy red and white, while WW used National all-white livery. In 1980 SWT and what had become National Welsh started a new motorway service between Swansea and Cardiff and coaches were transferred to it away from the 252 which at the same time became the X1. Through passengers were encouraged to use the new service while the X1 was intended as a fast inter-urban service for people travelling between Swansea and Port Talbot or Bridgend, and Bridgend and Cardiff on the A48. Many still preferred the longer X1 route however. "The motorway bus is too fast," one elderly passenger said. There were timetable changes in quick succession but eventually it settled down to run hourly between Swansea and

A United Welsh conductor steps aboard a 1948 ECW bodied, Albion Venturer at Neath Abbey depot, 1950.

Cardiff, with two SWT vehicles from Clarence Terrace depot and two NW buses from its Cardiff depot. Coaches were still used but lots of journeys saw Leyland Nationals with coach seats on NW journeys and at busy times both companies used double deckers, initially Bristol VRTs and later Leyland Olympians. It was the first time double deckers had been used on the through journey. N&C had bought two Crossley double deckers in 1946 to run on the service at busy times and reduce the need for duplication. They were even painted in N&C livery but it was a case of counting your chickens as the all-powerful traffic commissioners refused the company permission to use them.

In 1981 National Welsh closed its Penarth Road depot in Cardiff and transferred its share of the X1 to Barry depot while SWT continued to operate it from Swansea using a mixture of Bristol VRTs and coaches. Then it occurred to someone at NW that the service did not run anywhere near Barry but travelled through Bridgend bus station, so the route was transferred to Bridgend depot. But in 1986, bus services were deregulated, NBC companies privatised and SWT and NW decided to split the route. SWT would run a new X1 on a limited stop basis between Swansea and Bridgend, with an X2 variant serving Pyle, while the Bridgend to Cardiff section was operated by NW as part of its Porthcawl to Cardiff service which became, confusingly, another X2. It was the end of the historic route that had run for more than 55 years. Sir Godfrey had blamed nationalisation for the demise of his company in 1971, now, ironically, it was privatisation that had led to the demise of the route. Sir Godfrey died in 1986 in his nineties and would surely have been outraged at the way events had turned out.

But it was not the end. After SWT took over sole running of the X1 it used bus-seated Leyland Nationals

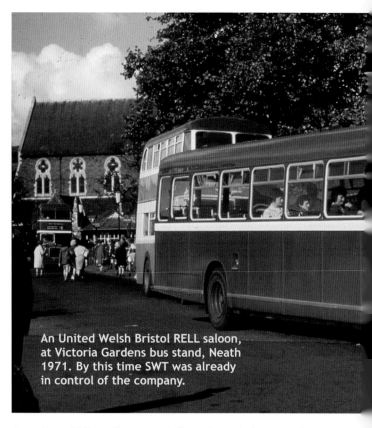

An United Welsh Bristol RELL saloon, at Victoria Gardens bus stand, Neath 1971. By this time SWT was already in control of the company.

from Port Talbot depot and then the minibus revolution arrived and not even such a historic route could escape, although SWT had the grace to use coach-seated examples. More changes followed. In 1990, SWT was taken over by Badgerline and its Port Talbot depot joined an expanded Brewers company that reinstated the through service from Swansea to Cardiff. It even bought coaches for the service, although these were elderly vehicles transferred from SWT's sister Badgerline companies, Thamesway and Eastern National. They did not last long and were replaced by another bus that was becoming standard in the 1990s — the Dennis Dart. These had coach seats for 40 passengers, but were not really suitable for such a fast inter-urban service.

In 1995 Badgerline merged with GRT of Aberdeen to form First Bus which decreed that SWT and Brewers should merge into a larger SWT undertaking which was eventually renamed First Cymru. The X1 was truncated again to run from Swansea to Bridgend augmented by alternate journeys from Neath. Col Sir Godfrey Llewellyn Bart, CB, CBE, MC, TD, DL, JP, would be unlikely to be pleased with the legacy, for First Cymru ran the route with elderly Dennis Darts before a fleet of new vehicles was introduced. With just 31 seats passengers often had to stand, something N&C would never have tolerated. They compared poorly to the magnificent brown and red coaches that made every journey on N&C an adventure.

An United Welsh Bristol Lodekka shortly before the company came under the control of SWT in 1970.
Stephen Miles

United Welsh was biggest takeover

United Welsh was the largest bus company to be taken over by SWT. When it was absorbed on January 1, 1971, it had 154 vehicles.

All of them, apart from four Bedford VAM70 coaches, were of Bristol manufacture. This was because it had been state-controlled since 1950, unlike SWT which had been part of the private BET group until it sold out to became a member of the National Bus Company in 1969.

Only state-run bus companies had been allowed to take Bristols and it meant SWT's fleet after 1971 included vehicle types the company had never previously operated. The Bristols were made up of 78 double deckers, all Lodekkas, dating from 1958 to 1965, while the single deckers included LS, MW, and RELL vehicles. They operated on many similar routes to SWT, apart from Gower, where UWS had a near monopoly, while SWT had exclusive local pick-ups in the city centre.

Before the Second World War, UWS, or more accurately, the companies that were to become United Welsh in 1938, had seemed a real threat to SWT. At this time they were also in the private sector, part of Red & White Services Ltd which had been busy buying up local companies across South Wales since its formation on January 1, 1930. Until 1938 companies bought in the Swansea area had been operating separately and details of how they all came together are a little complicated.

Religious regime of the Sunday safety checks

The absorbtion of companies in 1971 inevitably brought with it concerns for staff often faced with a job move and changes in working practice.

Roy Wilcox, of Neath, was no stranger to such changes. He began his apprenticeship with N&C Luxury Coaches at their James Street, Neath, garage, in 1943 aged just 14. He stayed for 10 years before landing a job with SWT at its nearby Eastland Road depot in the town.

"I had almost grown up with N&C and wondered if I'd made the right move," recalled Roy. "Many considered N&C to be the best in the business and there's no denying that all the employees shared a pride in the company, but the working conditions for garage staff certainly weren't very good. They were much better at SWT, as were the wages too.

"Standards of workmanship were high in both garages although SWT led the way when it came to vehicle safety checks.

"Every Sunday morning all of the garage's 41 vehicles, mainly double deckers, would be driven over a pit by a small group of drivers. Each would be examined for any broken springs, worn brake liners, prop shafts or exhaust systems.

"Neath was the only SWT garage during the 1950s and 60s to conduct this weekly, Sunday morning check. Something of an innovation, it was later adopted universally in all SWT garages.

"We mainly dealt with maintenance at Eastland Road. Major work was referred to Ravenhill. There was never any cutting of corners. One difference between N&C and SWT concerned engine and transmission work. N&C fitters would strip defective units themselves, replace parts and then rebuild them. At Eastland Road such units would be replaced with reconditioned units from Ravenhill which allowed a quicker turn around of vehicles."

Change beckoned again for Roy when SWT closed its Eastland Road depot and he was transferred to the former United Welsh garage at Neath Abbey.

"Some of the happiest days of my working life were spent at Eastland Road," said Roy.

"I managed to hang on there for a while as I had the responsibility of overseeing the closure. I'll never forget shutting the door behind me and turning the key in the lock for the last time. That was a sad moment indeed."

In 1933 Eclipse Saloon Services Ltd of Clydach, with 17 single deckers and seven double deckers, was taken over and in 1934 Eclipse acquired Harris & Co and Lewis Bros. In 1938, Eclipse merged with Neath Omnibus Ltd. Red & White took over Roderick's Service of Dunvant in 1934 and followed this up the same year with Enterprize Motor Services of Gorseinon. In 1935 D Bassett & Sons of Gorseinon was bought and merged with Enterprize and the new company, with 26 vehicles, became known as Bassett-Enterprize. In 1938 it purchased Gorseinon & District Bus Company. Gower Vanguard Motors Ltd was one of the first motor bus operators in Gower. Its origins can be traced back to brothers George and Rowland Taylor of Llangennith who had run horse-drawn coaches since the 1890s. In 1910 they introduced small Dennis motor buses on the route from Llangennith and Rhossili to Swansea. By the mid-1930s, Gower Vanguard was operating 14 vehicles and was taken over by Red & White in 1936. The following year Red & White took over Blue Bird Services of Skewen which later bought Windsor Services of Briton Ferry.

In 1937 it was decided to create Red & White United Transport Ltd to take a controlling interest in Red & White Services and the Swansea area companies, which in 1938 were amalgamated to form United Welsh Services with 36 double deckers, 76 single deckers and 18 coaches. UWS was now a major force in the Swansea and Neath areas. It had 475 employees and carried more than 1,000,000 passengers a month. In 1940 it opened a new head office and bus station in Singleton Street, Swansea.

Red & White voluntarily sold its bus interests to the state in 1950 by which time UWS had four depots, in Swansea, Neath Abbey, Gorseinon and Clydach, with 166 vehicles. It was carrying more than 25 million passengers a year and employed more than 700. UWS now became an independent company within the state-run Tilling group and could have chosen to compete strongly with SWT, but instead the two wisely decided to co-operate and although they ran on many similar routes, there was no cut-throat competition. There were two further UWS takeovers after nationalisation, both in 1952. They were that of Richmond of Neath, with two double deckers, two single deckers and three coaches, and the larger Swan Motor Company of Swansea which had 21 double deckers and three coaches in a distinctive yellow livery. It had run jointly with SWT on the Swansea-Bishopston-Pennard route for many years and was a much respected and well loved local bus company.

UWS disappeared in 1971 but the name was resurrected in 1987 as the holding company that oversaw the privatisation of SWT. David Bending, who led the successful management bid to purchase SWT from the National Bus Company, had started his career as a conductor with UWS and wanted to revive the historic name. In December 1988, United Welsh Coaches was formed when the Swansea operations of the J Cleverley coaching firm were taken over and the name appeared for a while on coaches employed on school, contract and private hire work.

Thomas Bros. had an unusual livery

For 20 years from 1951 the Thomas Bros. company ran buses in the Port Talbot area in an unusual turquoise and cream livery.

The firm was part of British Electric Traction which made it a sister company to SWT. Its buses were the usual BET types, but that colour scheme certainly made them stand out.

The company's origins dated back to pre-war days when Port Talbot, despite being a relatively small town, had been a hive of bus competition. At one time there were no fewer than 20 to 25 competing firms, 13 of them had raced for passengers on one route alone, from the town up the Afan Valley to Pontrhydyfen. In 1933 most of the competitors came together to form Thomas Bros and in June 1951 BET took it over along with Davies Brothers, Thomas & James and Lewis & Jones to form a new Thomas Bros (Port Talbot) company. There was also a closely allied company called Afan Transport.

The purchase was a shrewd one, for Port Talbot was a growing town in the 1950s as steel production

A former United Welsh Bristol SUL4A liveried for SWT coach tours, June 1971. Royston Morgan *Collection*

A Marshall bodied AEC Reliance dating from 1967 operated by Thomas Bros of Port Talbot, 1971.

Short bodied AEC Regent OD 7497, new to Devon General in 1934, passed to Thomas Bros in 1961 and was used on the Aberavon seafront service. Behind it are some of the vehicle types absorbed by SWT and eventually repainted in the company's red livery.

soared. The Steel Company of Wales had built the Abbey Works, the largest continuous steel strip mill in the world, and this was providing employment for many thousands who needed to get to work by bus. By the time of the BET takeover, Thomas Bros was carrying just under 6,000,000 passengers a year, in 49 vehicles which operated from Margam in the east to Baglan in the west and up the Afan Valley. There were many low railway bridges in the new company's operating area and double deckers were banned from large parts of Port Talbot. Even so, Thomas Bros had seven, five ex-City of Oxford Regent IIs, similar to SWT's, one Leyland and one Daimler, all operating on the Aberavon to Tonmawr service. New vehicles started to arrive shortly after the takeover, all standard BET types. But whereas SWT went for the AEC Reliance in the 1950s, Thomas Bros chose Leyland Tiger Cubs and these were still in the fleet in 1971 when it was absorbed by SWT.

By this time the 49-strong fleet, comprising 39 single deckers with bus seats, four with high backed seats, and six coaches, was a mix of Leylands and Reliances.

They sported bodywork by Weymann, Park Royal, Marshall, Harrington and Duple Northern. In addition it had three rare Leyland Panther Cub rear-engined buses bodied, unusually for a BET fleet, by Strachans. SWT took control of Thomas Bros in 1969 and that unique livery started being phased out in favour of SWT's new, light red and cream livery. The buses still had Thomas Bros fleet names, but this practice went too when SWT absorbed the company on January 1, 1971 and buses received the generic South Wales name.

Another sad loss was the open-top service Thomas Bros had provided all through the 1960s along Aberavon seafront, but which was discontinued by SWT. The vehicles, double deckers, were painted in the firm's coach livery of cream and light blue and were given names — The Afan Belle, The Margam Belle and The Sandfields Belle.

Bristol VRT 932 heading for Langland Bay on July 24, 1982, snapped from the top deck of Bristol KSW 500. Stephen Miles

South Wales Transport made sunny summer's day excursions to local beaches an even more exciting experience in the late 1970s when it went topless!

Topless times

The company ran five open top double decker buses in that decade and the one that followed, with the first of these arriving in a rather unexpected manner in 1974. This vehicle was to become one of the company's best known and most loved vehicles, even though it was already 21 years old when it arrived at the company.

It was Bristol KSW5G, registration number WNO 484, which had started life as an ordinary service bus with Eastern National in 1953. Later the company converted it to an open top vehicle and operated it along the Southend and Clacton seafronts until an unfortunate incident in 1974 when it ran out of control and smashed into a house. Its days looked numbered and Eastern National sold it to SWT as a source of spare parts. However the clever engineers at Ravenhill looked at it and said: "We can do something with this!" They repaired it using parts from United Welsh Bristol K tow bus, HWN 399, and by 1975 it was reborn in immaculate, roadworthy condition once more.

SWT numbered it 500, painted it in National Bus Company poppy red livery and put it to work that summer on a new open top service from the city centre along Mumbles Road to Limeslade Bay. Two years later it was joined by three more open

toppers which enabled SWT to add another two summer time routes, to Caswell and Langland bays. Unlike 500, they had detachable roofs which could be refitted out of season so they ran on service all year round. They were Bristol VRTs, numbered 930, 931 and 932, and were delivered new in the second batch of 90 similar buses that entered service with SWT between 1977 and 1980. They were the only three with convertible roofs and the company painted them and 500 all over white with a red stripe above the lower deck windows. It named 500 Madam Adelina Patti, 930 Dylan Thomas, 931 Sir Harry Secombe and 932 John H Vivian, and gave them all the brand name Skyrider.

Then in 1984 SWT further extended its open top fleet when it bought a Daimler Fleetline double decker from London Transport whose roof above the upstairs window was also detachable. Built in 1975, it was registered KUC 220P and SWT numbered it 864 and also painted it in Skyrider livery. The company

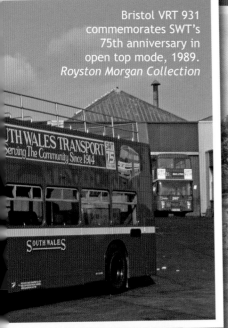

Bristol VRT 931 commemorates SWT's 75th anniversary in open top mode, 1989. *Royston Morgan Collection*

Bristol VRT 931 in Skyrider livery and named, Sir Harry Secombe, August 1985. *Stephen Miles*

on the bay run

named this vehicle William Gammon in memory of a former Mumbles lifeboat coxswain.

SWT later cut back on its open top services and in 1990, 931 was sold to its sister company, Badgerline, for use on the Bath City Tour. In 2003 it went to Western National at Penzance for the Penwith Tour and entered preservation in 2007.

Two of these fine vehicles are now back on their home stomping ground, thanks to Swansea Bus Museum, which is restoring them. It was planned to put 931 in the company's colours to mark the 100th anniversary of the founding of SWT. It was also the vehicle chosen by SWT to commemorate the company's 75th anniversary in 1989 when it was restored in the former maroon and cream band livery.

There seems plenty of life left in the KSW5G, which is also now based at Swansea Bus Museum. It remains one of the most popular vehicles at rallies. There can be few vehicles with such a chequered history.

It was nearly written off a second time when it collided with a lamp-post, but once again SWT engineers came to the rescue and got it back on the road. It is a bus that has taken people to the seaside in summer, has been bedecked with lights and decorations at Christmas time, and been used by many wedding parties.

It was painted blue and silver to celebrate the Queen's Silver Jubilee in 1977 and has appeared at various times in poppy red, red and white, and green and white liveries.

It was the open top bus used to welcome home Gorseinon boxer Colin Jones after his world welterweight bout with Milton McCrory in Las Vegas in 1982 and it even became a TV star when it appeared on the title sequence of the BBC's Russ Abbott comedy show during the autumn of 1990.

Here's to its next 60 years!

Open toppers come in handy at other times too as this shot of 500 taking part in a celebration parade shows.

113

CHAPTER 10

Company's huge losses spark fight for survival

The National Bus Company's first annual report in 1970 described the previous 12 months as 'not an easy year for the bus industry.' At SWT the language was a good deal stronger: 'fight for survival', 'serious plight' and 'threat to our very existence' are among some of the stronger expressions that spilled out of company mouths at the time.

SWT suffered a huge loss of £365,000 in 1970 and for the following two or three years drastic action was needed in a bid to bring its finances back into line. It came at great cost to the number of people employed by the company and the services it operated.

Being part of NBC didn't help, the Government expected the state owned bus sector to pay its way and there were no mass hand outs from taxpayers. On January 1, 1971, SWT absorbed United Welsh Services, N&C Luxury Coaches and Thomas Bros of Port Talbot. General manager of the new larger company, Frank Woodworth, warned they had entered what he described as 'a period of acute crisis for the company.'

"This has been largely brought about by three factors: our failure to win back passengers who left us for various reasons in 1970; the severe increase in costs; and importantly the refusal of 75 per cent of our recent applications to increase fares."

The drop in passengers that had started in 1956 was continuing and in 1970 SWT's costs rose by £344,300, mostly caused by a national pay award amounting to £260,000 which, of course, was beyond the company's control.

The South Wales Traffic Commissioners had also rejected most of its applications for higher fares to offset the increases, a decision which the company appealed against to the Department of the Environment and won. As ever it was the local authorities which had objected to higher fares, claiming that the company should cut costs through increased economies and efficiency as well as increasing ticket prices and on this occasion the traffic commissioners had largely sided with them. They pointed out that it was SWT's third proposed increase in 16 months and said it had already been clearly indicated that there was serious concern about SWT's financial control and efficiency.

The local authorities had expressed concern about the effect the higher fares would have on passengers, particularly pensioners. But when he granted the appeal, the Environment Secretary said SWT should not be "denied the revenue necessary to compensate unavoidable

Royston Morgan Collection

A 1975 Leyland National MK 1 in poppy red National Bus Company livery on the regular climb up to Townhill, South Wales Transport's toughest route, on a sunny afternoon in 1984.

One of three AEC Swifts that didn't stay long with SWT seen at Singleton Hospital in September 1969. They transferred to London Country in June 1971.

increases in costs," and he also pointed out that if the councils were so concerned about the effect on the travelling public they could use their powers under Transport Minister Barbara Castle's Transport Act of 1968 to subsidise rural bus services and arrange travel concessions for the old, blind and disabled.

The new powers given to local authorities as part of the Act were something they were reluctant to use, despite a warning from SWT chairman, Bernard Griffiths, in May 1970, that it was the councils who would ultimately have to decide whether to save uneconomic services.

"We have lost nearly half of our travelling passengers, 30 per cent of them in the last 10 years, but our mileage has not been reduced accordingly," said Mr Griffiths.

If local authorities wanted to retain routes making substantial losses, they would have to make a contribution on a social benefit basis: "We are called upon by the Government to pay our way. If we are to do that, and we are going to try to do it, then we have to take a different line with many uneconomic services," he warned.

An example of what could happen was not long in coming. In 1971 three local councils, Pontardawe,

Llandeilo and Cwmamman, agreed to jointly subsidise five SWT valley routes on a trial basis. But following a survey they concluded there was no reason why the services should be loss-making and stopped the subsidy. On August 14, SWT withdrew the services. It meant that people living in the village of Garnswllt faced a three mile walk to get to Ammanford, while children and commuters from Betws would have no bus service. The routes were taken over by small, private operators, something that would increasingly happen on other non-profitable SWT routes as the 1970s unfolded.

Cash-strapped local authorities remained reluctant to come up with cash to retain loss-making bus routes. In August 1973 Glamorgan County Council, which had become the authority responsible for transport, finally agreed to subsidise bus services, but only with matching cash from the Welsh Office. It gave £69,000 to SWT, Western Welsh and Red & White to keep 36 services running but the subsidies were only to last a year and the companies had asked for £268,000. In 1974 local government was reformed in Wales and the county council was replaced by West, Mid and South Glamorgan which began to subsidise loss-making routes on an annual basis. By 1981, SWT was receiving £1.3 million in revenue support from Dyfed and West Glamorgan county councils and by 1984 this had risen to £1.8 million by which time a new way of subsidising bus services was introduced.

Back in 1971 however, SWT's immediate priority was to halt its substantial losses. As well as higher fares and fewer services, the company announced that it was cancelling all orders for new buses in 1972.

"The bitter truth is that we cannot buy new vehicles without the money to pay for them," said Mr Woodworth. It meant SWT's engineering staff were being called upon to patch up buses that were 18 or even 20 years old. That summer Mr Woodworth warned of heavy losses and announced: "Staff redundancies, are on a distressing scale in most departments. The dramatic change indicates the serious plight of the company and, indeed, of the industry generally because our experience is by no means unique."

SWT's new chairman, John Robinson, warned at the company's annual meeting that year: "Empty bus seats tell their own story, the private car, the irregular and unlicensed operation of vans and even TV in the home all contribute to the decline in passenger traffic. Against this background, which is posing a threat to our very existence, we have to take every possible step to streamline our structure, cutting any dead wood that may be there and reshape it to meet the challenge."

It would mean another major shake-up. United Welsh's depot in Clydach closed in September 1971 and staff transferred to Pontardawe. Just a few weeks later it was announced that Western Welsh's Neath Abbey depot and its services would be transferred to SWT on January 1, 1972, and SWT's depot in Eastland Road, Neath, which had opened in 1933, would close. In March 1972 WW's Haverfordwest depot and 60 staff also joined SWT which meant the company, until the previous year largely restricted to an area from Porthcawl in the east to Carmarthen in the west and the valleys running down to Neath and Swansea, now ran buses across a wide area of South West Wales.

During the summer of 1972 Mr Woodworth described 1970-71 as disastrous years for SWT, but at last he was able to report a glimmer of light on what had been a long, dark road. Losses in July 1972 were down to £20,000 compared with £200,000 the same month the previous year. By December 1972 Mr Woodworth was able to report that SWT was in a much stronger position: "The heavy loss of passengers which has haunted us for so long is showing signs of easing considerably," he said.

But it had all come at a terrible price. Staff with many years loyal service to SWT had been forced to leave, routes had been ravaged and morale was at an all-time low. It is not difficult to imagine the effect on the workforce of such drastic cutbacks and the uncertainty of not knowing where the axe would next fall. It was not helped by the ragbag of vehicles SWT now had to use.

A convoy of Bristol VRTs heads along The Kingsway, Swansea, 1983.
Royston Morgan Collection

SOUTH WALES
Associated with the National Bus Company

OFFICIAL FARE TABLES.

INTRODUCED 17th JUNE, 1973

15p

Vehicles way past their best were still being run on frontline services and it showed. During the 1950s and 1960s SWT had ensured a high level of fleet replacement every year but at the beginning of the 1970s, due to its precarious financial position, this was on a very definite hold.

Back in 1961, every SWT vehicle was an AEC and pride was taken in the appearance of the fleet. By 1971 there was a mix of vehicles in the new, enlarged company, many of them elderly. Now running alongside SWT's Regents and Reliances were United Welsh's fleet of Lodekkas and MWs, dating from the late 1950s and early 1960s. Thomas Bros's mix of Leylands and AECs included vehicles that had been new in the mid-1950s.

It was not helped by the myriad of liveries in which they ran in service. There was SWT's traditional maroon livery and the lighter red and cream which it introduced in 1968; there were coaches still in N&C's chocolate brown and red colours; The turquoise and cream of Thomas Bros was still in evidence as was the Tilling red of UWS. Soon they were joined by Western Welsh vehicles in that company's traditional red livery and the blue and ivory it had adopted for its coaches and dual-purpose vehicles from 1965. Then from 1972 a new edict went out from National Bus Company that all buses were to be repainted into its poppy red livery.

It hardly presented the appearance of a united fleet and the lack of new vehicles also didn't help. Just 20 came in 1971 and of these 12, all AEC Swifts, a new single deck model for SWT, were quickly despatched to fellow NBC company, London Country, to help its chronic shortage of modern buses. Another 21 Swifts that SWT had ordered for 1971 delivery were diverted to London Country before delivery although the situation was helped by the

Former West Midlands MCW bodied VRT, NOB 424M departs from the Quadrant bus station, Swansea on service 20 to Blue Anchor, Penclawdd, July 1984. *Stephen Miles*

arrival of 15 1971 Bristol RELLs transferred from Western Welsh. Only eight new saloons entered the South Wales Transport fleet in 1972.

Some vehicles simply had to be withdrawn, they were too elderly to continue, but they were replaced by buses that were not much younger. In 1971 and 1972, 22 vehicles that had been new as coaches to Western

National were converted into 45-seat buses and put to work on a variety of SWT routes. Buses from the Red & White fleet and dating back to 1957 also saw service. The situation was not helped by the poor industrial relations of the 1970s which delayed new bus deliveries. SWT did not begin receiving substantial numbers of vehicles until 1973 when the first of what would eventually be a fleet of 121 Leyland National single deckers arrived. They were the kind of standardised bus that SWT chairman Bernard Griffiths had hoped he'd never see when he addressed Western Welsh's annual long-service awards dinner in 1969.

"The idea is that public service vehicles should be made more comfortable, warmer, well ventilated and built to a standard to ensure that they would be produced at a reasonable price," said Mr Griffiths.

"The idea is a good one as long as it does not mean in practice that the buses will be stereotyped, uninspiring types of vehicles that everyone will have whether they like them or not. I like to see some of the differences in vehicles we see today fulfilling local and special needs. I hope we will never see the day when we are told this is the bus you can have, take it or leave it."

In 1973 that day arrived for SWT with its first Leyland Nationals and it was eventually planned to have many more of these vehicles in service, according to general manager Frank Woodworth when he spoke to the South Wales Evening Post at the time. It was very much a case of 'take it or leave it,' These vehicles were the National Bus Company's standard single decker and entered the majority of the fleets of its subsidiaries during the 1970s. They represented the bland, corporate face of NBC, everything had to be the same, individuality was not tolerated. SWT's poppy red Leyland Nationals looked exactly like Red & White's or Western Welsh's, staff from the three companies wore the same blue uniforms, British Electric Traction's policy of allowing its subsidiaries latitude had gone and with it the loyalty felt by staff and passengers to individual companies like SWT, N&C and Thomas Bros. BET had seen the importance of fostering these relationships, NBC in its corporate drive did not.

As SWT struggled to cope with declining passengers and heavy financial losses, it was

On the Kingsway . . . and on service, a 1979 Bristol VRT heading for Morriston.
Royston Morgan Collection

One of the last Regents alongside one of the Bristol VRTs that replaced them, at Morriston Hospital, Swansea, 1982.
Stephen Miles

On its way to Rhossili, this packed vehicle seen leaving the Quadrant bus station, Swansea, was one of two former Alder Valley Bristol VRTs transferred to SWT. Unlike their SWT sisters they had Gardner engines and were three inches lower.

Royston Morgan Collection

being bombarded by NBC corporatism. In 1971 Sir Frederick Wood took over as chairman at NBC and concluded that, like the Greyhound coach network in America, its buses and coaches needed to be as high profile as possible. So the edict went out that buses should be poppy red and coaches all white. In the autumn of 1972 NBC's new livery was launched and SWT and the other subsidiaries had no choice, but to comply. There was even a corporate identity manual which SWT and other NBC companies were ordered to follow. It included a list of approved terminology for signs at bus stations. So buses pulled in at bays, not gates or stands. Passengers made reservations, not bookings, and if they needed assistance had to look for information, not enquiries. If they needed to spend a penny they did so at toilets, not lavatories and it was ladies and gentlemen who used them, not men and women.

This is not to say that NBC was the sole or even the main cause of the bus industry's problems in the 1970s and the first half of the 1980s. The issues were too deep seated for that. Whoever ran the services was bound to see passenger figures plummet as car ownership rose. But if NBC was not the root cause it was not the panacea, either. It failed to halt SWT's decline during the 1970s and early 1980s. It is interesting to speculate whether, if BET had survived and SWT had remained a private sector company, things may have turned out differently. The problems would have been the same, although the ways of tackling them might have been different. Indeed, if SWT had stayed in the private sector, the cutbacks in the 1970s might well have been even more drastic. A private company with

shareholders has to act swiftly to eliminate losses or it is doomed. BET might well have ordered even more wide-ranging economies than the ones implemented by SWT between 1970 and 1973. In the public sector SWT, as part of a large group, was somewhat protected. In fact, during the first half of the 1980s it was one of only three NBC subsidiary bus companies to lose money. The other two were Western National and what by then had become National Welsh following the merger of Red & White and Western Welsh in 1977.

As the 1970s slipped into the 1980s, SWT's problems continued to mount. In 1981 it carried 38.3 million passengers, by 1984 this was down to 29.9 million. Service cutbacks meant that by 1984 it owned just 304 vehicles compared to 539 in 1971. Between 1981 and 1984 it received £6.4 million in revenue support from the local authorities and after this was taken into account, over the same period made a profit of only £500,000. The cuts continued and in September 1984, SWT closed its Neath depot. Only 15 years earlier the town had four major bus depots, owned by SWT, Western Welsh, United Welsh and N&C. Many service withdrawals were announced, but even after these were implemented, the scale of services was still superior to those operated by SWT's successor, First Cymru. As SWT general manager, David Bending, said at the time: "The level of service run by the company will still be a good one, but obviously the

Rescue mission became seven hour nightmare

Clive Pewsey, who joined SWT's Llanelli depot maintenance team in 1979, remembers a seven-hour nightmare rescue operation, all because of a low bridge. Clive, who now lives in South Australia, was sent out with one of the fitters to bring back a coach that had broken down in Kilgetty, just outside Saundersfoot.

"We had an AEC Regent double decker that had been adapted as a tow bus," he recalls. "There was no Carmarthen by-pass then and the Regent wasn't the fastest of vehicles. We got to Kilgetty, but found we were on one side of a railway bridge and the coach was on the other. The Regent was too high to go under it, so we had to turn around and drive back to Red Roses and go on the Narberth road towards Saundersfoot.

Adapted as a tow bus Regent V 594, in Dillwyn Street, Swansea November 7, 1982. *Stephen Miles*

"This diversion alone took us two hours and by the time we found the coach and towed it back to Llanelli via Narberth the whole episode had taken about seven hours!"

Clive later transferred to SWT's Ravenhill garage as a fitter and machinist. "I worked alongside Gerry Kearn and Mike Hansford. Gerry had an identical twin brother who was a foreman at the depot, it took me quite a while to tell them apart. We had regular six a side football tournaments and I don't remember losing any of them."

One day Clive remembers taking a Leyland National for a test run and ended up at Joe's ice cream parlour with four colleagues. "I don't think there was too much supervision in the works that day!" he said.

Tow bus 594 rescues a failed VRT at Singleton Street, April 13, 1982.

A typical scene at Brunswick Street depot in the 1970s sunshine and, right, the building awash with floodwater after a sudden downpour in 1956. *Royston Morgan Collection*

effect on the individual will be very great indeed." That is certainly true: if a passenger relies on a bus to get them to work at a certain time and after cutbacks it no longer runs, then they might find themselves out of a job.

As the 1980s unfolded it became even more crucial for SWT to pull itself out of the financial morass it found itself in. There was now a very different Government in power to the one that had created the National Bus Company 15 years before and a Transport Secretary with a remarkably different agenda to that of Barbara Castle. He had thinning grey hair and was usually to be seen behind a haze of blue cigarette smoke.
His name was Nicholas Ridley and he was planning yet another transport revolution. At the end of it SWT would be transformed into a totally different company once again.

The first of the MK 1 Leyland Nationals delivered to SWT, undergoing a tow. *Royston Morgan Collection*

The original SWT offices in Russell Street, Swansea and alongside their replacement, under construction in the 1960s.

Chris Taylor Archive

Convertible VRT 932 carries the name John H Vivian while providing a Park 'n' Ride service at Margam Park Vehicle Rally on June 25, 1989. *Stephen Miles*

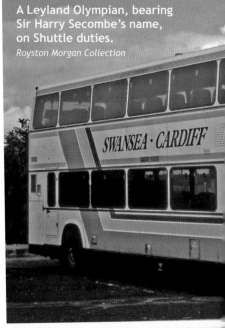

A Leyland Olympian, bearing Sir Harry Secombe's name, on Shuttle duties.
Royston Morgan Collection

Company played

Swansea born Harry Secombe was one of the country's most famous entertainers and best loved but less well known are his South Wales Transport links.

Anyone who has a bus named after them is being accorded a high honour and Sir Harry, as he became in 1981, uniquely had his name on three of the company's buses. This could be considered as particularly prestigious because SWT only named buses after five people in its entire 85-year history. Not even the magnificent coaches it ran on tours at home and abroad in the 1950s and 1960s were named.

In total, just eight vehicles received names, five open top double deckers, a single decker that was

specially adapted for disabled people, and two impressive double deck coaches that SWT bought for its Shuttle express service between Swansea and Cardiff.

Sir Harry's name appeared at different times on one of the open toppers, the single decker and one of the double deck coaches.

The second bus SWT named after the entertainer was a pioneering prototype that would set the standard for vehicles of the 1990s and beyond. It had been delivered new to the company's Brunswick depot in Swansea and later became one of the regular vehicles out stationed at Pilton Green in Gower. The vehicle was a Leyland National Mark 2 with a 680 engine. SWT had 115 Leyland National Mark 1s

delivered new between 1973 and 1979 but only had six Mark 2s and KEP 829X was a one-off that arrived in December 1981. It was the last Leyland National delivered new to SWT and initially had 52 seats before being upgraded to dual-purpose status with 48 coach-type seats and painted National Bus Company poppy red and white. In 1987 it became part of a Department of Transport backed project to make travel easier for disabled passengers. By the time it emerged from Ravenhill works in early winter that year, it had become a revolutionary new vehicle. Transformed at a cost of £1,500 worth of materials and 220 employee hours, it included major refinements to make travel safer and easier for both the able and disabled.

There were flat, non-slip floors, new handrails, vertical stanchions, extra leg-room for some seats, high intensity step lamps and a public address system. There were easy-to-read signs showing passengers where bell buttons to stop the vehicle had been placed and 'bus stopping' signs. There was also a compressed air

Driver Jeff Phillips and SWT's last ever conductor Johnnie Smith with 500 bearing its first name, Madam Adelina Patti, at Limeslade, Mumbles, August 5, 1987.
Stephen Miles

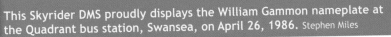

the name game

suspension system which allowed the bus to lower itself closer to the ground when picking up passengers. It was then reflated using battery-powered pumps.

These provisions, which became common-place, were revolutionary then and Sir Harry himself, accompanied by Virginia Bottomley, the Minister for the Disabled, came to Swansea to launch the vehicle, which was painted in SWT's new two-tone green livery. It then went on tour all over Britain as an example of the future of bus travel.

Swansea poet Dylan Thomas's name went on another open topper and later the second double deck coach, while the other personalities honoured were Madam Adelina Patti, John H Vivian and William Gammon.

Adelina Patti was a Spanish-born, highly acclaimed 19th Century opera singer who performed regularly for Royalty all over Europe, commanding high fees. She bought Craig-y-Nos Castle in the Swansea Valley in 1878 and lived there until her death in 1919 at the age of 76. She was a popular local benefactor.

William Gammon was the coxswain on the Mumbles lifeboat on the ill-fated night of April 23, 1947, when it went to the rescue of the SS Samtampa which had grounded on rocks in tempestuous seas near Sker Point, Porthcawl. He and the rest of the eight-man crew died in the disaster which claimed 47 lives.

John H Vivian was a Swansea industrialist involved in copper mining and copper smelting and was the town's MP from 1832 to 1855, the year of his death.

Sir Harry's links with SWT began as a small boy growing up in St Thomas, Swansea, in the 1920s. Every Saturday his mother would take him by tram to Swansea Market which he described as an Aladdin's cave. His father was a commercial traveller for a wholesale grocery firm, but three of his uncles worked for The Transport. They were Cyril Seacombe (they spelled their names differently) who was an accomplished entertainer himself. A well-known singer and compere, Cyril worked for SWT for 46 years, retiring as an inspector in 1972. Cyril started in

1925 and was the first conductor to work on the Mumbles Railway when it changed from steam power to electricity in 1929. Later he was often to be found on SWT's 77 bus service which replaced the train between Swansea and Mumbles Pier and passengers remember him as 'knowing everyone and having a friendly, smiling face which was a tonic for us all.'

His brother, another Harry, had started work on Swansea's trams as a conductor in 1921 and transferred to SWT's buses when the system closed in 1937. He was a regular on route 76 which ran from Brynmill to Port Tennant. He died tragically young in February 1956 and Ein Newyddion later said of him: "small in stature, he was a giant in cheeriness and tact and was as equally well respected by the passengers on his section as he was by all his colleagues."

Another brother was Stan Seacombe who was also a conductor for many years making for a real family tie with South Wales Transport.

Sadly, Sir Harry Secombe died in 2001 at the age of 79, but two of the buses named after him — the open top double decker, 931, and the revolutionary disabled single deck Leyland National, 829 survive in the custody of Swansea Bus Museum.

CHAPTER 11

Large scale revolution with small scale buses

The 1980s saw what was, in every sense, a transport revolution and SWT was in the eye of the changes. In 1980, it was a typical National Bus Company subsidiary. The mainstay of its fleet were 120 single deck Leyland Nationals and 91 double deck Bristol VRTs, the vast majority in poppy red livery. Coaches were usually Leyland Leopards, either in all-white or local coach NBC livery.

There were a dwindling number of AEC Regent Vs, AEC Reliances and Bristol RELLs and, more unusually for an NBC fleet, a large number of Ford buses with either Willowbrook or Duple bodies.

By 1990 the fleet consisted mainly of minibuses painted in a bright, two-tone green livery with yellow and red stripes. By then SWT was an independent company, but this too, was about to change.

David Bending arrived at SWT in 1980 as the new general manager and was followed two years later by Alan Kreppel as traffic manager. They would steer the company through the vast changes that followed. Sadly, Mr Bending died in 2013. Under his leadership a company that was losing money and passengers as well as being strapped with a high cost NBC fleet, was transformed into an operation that was profitable and importantly could boast rising passenger numbers.

But at the beginning of the 1980s SWT was in dire financial straits. A start had been made on revamping the network towards the end of the 1970s with major service revisions in the Neath, Port Talbot and Haverfordwest areas. It was obvious that much more needed to be done. In 1980 SWT was still running AEC Regents on daily service in Swansea. They could only operate with a driver and conductor and even some of the routes run by the more recent VRTs were crew operated. If costs were to be cut, it was essential that they became driver-only operated and the company took steps to speed this up. It put a strain on the driving school as conductors were trained to become drivers and extra instructor vehicles had to be brought in.

Service cuts were also needed. At the end of May, 1982, major reductions were made to Swansea services which saw some renumbered and more become driver only. It was estimated this would save £300,000 a year and most parts of the city were affected.

There were depot changes too. Gorseinon depot, which in United Welsh days in the 1950s had a fleet allocation of 52, was closed on November 1, 1980 and used as an outstation and a place to store redundant

A smartly turned out MCW MetroRider minibus in SWT's green and striped livery all set to operate the 24 service to Birchgrove shortly after its delivery in 1987.

Stephen Miles

A Bristol VRT picks up passengers in Princess Way, Swansea on the last day of double deck operation on the Port Tennant route, October 16, 1993.

vehicles. SWT's Neath depot also closed and in 1986 SWT's original garage, Brunswick Street in Swansea, followed suit and the company's head office, which had been in Russell Street right from the early years, moved to what had been The Magnet Club alongside Ravenhill depot. In the spring of 1985 SWT changed its management structure so that local depots handled secretarial, engineering and traffic responsibilities previously based at headquarters. Staff numbers were thinned down by around 100 to meet future anticipated needs and SWT was once again forced to say farewell to employees who had given exemplary service.

It was not all woe, however and there were innovations. In October 1980 two new unlimited travel tickets were introduced in Swansea. The City Rider gave a week's unlimited travel in the inner city area while City Rider Plus covered a wider area. Coaching was another sector which saw new developments. In 1979 Margaret Thatcher became Prime Minister and her Conservative Government brought in major changes which would finish off the National Bus Company. Initially, though, coaching was the target and the Transport Act 1980 resulted in the deregulation of express coach services. SWT was quick to take advantage and in September 1981 began a new motorway link from Haverfordwest to Bristol called ExpressWest which it ran jointly with sister NBC

companies, National Welsh and Bristol. Swansea was also one of the first places to get the new, faster and more luxurious, Rapide service to London, and SWT also introduced a faster link from Swansea to Birmingham.

But the Government had no intention of stopping at coaches, deregulation was intended to extend across the bus industry, and this is where Nicholas Ridley entered centre stage. Mr Ridley's bus Utopia was one of lots of small operators competing with each other to provide cheap and innovative public transport services for passengers. It did not turn out like that however, and 20 years later much of the industry was in the hands of a few major private companies. Mr Ridley insisted on continuing with his plans and in 1984 introduced a White Paper which detailed the break-up and privatisation of the National Bus Company. He also planned to change the licensing system to allow bus companies to run services as they liked if they believed they could be run profitably. The industry was appalled by this. Critics described it as a return to the 'cowboy' days before the Road Traffic Act of 1930.

Mr Ridley's ideas were not new, he did not wake up one morning with a 'Road to Damascus' revelation. His views on how the bus industry should be run had been around for a very long time. Back in 1964 SWT's chairman Raymond Birch hit out at claims being made by economists of the day that the right way to resolve the problem of loss-making bus services was to destroy the 1930 licensing system. While he agreed that "at first glance there were attractions in the idea of

125

A Bristol VRT heads into Prince of Wales Road on a cross-city route taking it to Limeslade, 1982.
Stephen Miles

A Bristol VRT caught on a rare duty on the No. 13 Townhill circular route involving one of the toughest climbs in SWT territory on November 16, 1993.
Stephen Miles

operators being able to run where they liked and charge what they liked." he warned that such a free-for-all would lead to too many vehicles of all kinds competing on the 'fat' routes with fewer than ever on the 'thin' routes.

"This could only end in the wholesale withdrawal of rural bus services and the creation of a bus-less countryside," Mr Birch told SWT's annual meeting in 1964. Of course, he was right. And what was true in 1964 was equally true in 1984 and all the problems he envisaged would come to pass before the industry reorganised itself again.

West Glamorgan County Council was horrified. It had been giving SWT revenue support each year to keep loss-making services running, but Mr Ridley's proposals meant bus companies would only run services they could make money on. It would be up to the local authorities to run those losing money by putting them out to tender. It was bound to be more costly for the

authorities and mean fewer services, warned the county council. Council leader Tom Jones said: "There is no way that we'll be able to afford to buy back the unprofitable services that the companies won't run."

The Transport Act 1985 was duly passed as envisaged by Mr Ridley, who probably didn't use buses very much himself. SWT had to sort out the consequences. It meant competitors could come onto any of its routes and SWT expected its most profitable ones to be the main targets. It had to strengthen its position to be able to deal with the opposition and that included ridding the fleet of high cost NBC vehicles, especially the fuel guzzling, unreliable Leyland Nationals. Major service revisions were introduced on September 15, 1985, and these saw off no fewer than 47 vehicles, including 28 Nationals. High frequency minibuses were introduced on routes where competition was expected, particularly on services from Swansea city centre to Mumbles and Morriston. They were in a bright, two-

A Leyland Olympian crosses the busy Dyffaty junction, Swansea, August 8, 1987. *Stephen Miles*

tone green livery and SWT made a start by painting its big bus fleet out of NBC poppy red into a similar livery to the minibuses.

Deregulation day was October 26, 1986, and SWT was as ready as it could be. Competitors included Morris Bros of Swansea, which registered two city services; Ferrytax registered an hourly all-day service between Neath and Port Talbot; Margam Cabs registered a seven-day minibus service in Port Talbot; and Ken Hopkins of Tonna in Neath registered a number of local services.

Meanwhile the county councils put non profit-making routes out to tender and independents won a number of these, including Hawkes Coaches of Waunarlwydd, which ran the little used Sunday service between Swansea city centre and Pennard. West Glamorgan had a horribly complicated tendering system which ranked tenders according to the type of service, population to be served, the number of people dependent on buses, problems in walking to destinations, the reasons for journeys and how many people used the service before deregulation, all calculated on a points system. It probably made sense to someone!

SWT unveiled its deregulation timetable just before what was nicknamed D-Day. 'No Bus Company Offers You More,' was its slogan, which was a bit of an exaggeration, but it was at least eye-catching.

The company had pulled out all the stops to make its services as attractive as possible. This was a new age for buses, the blandness of NBC was at an end. There were special bus and coach tickets to suit the needs of particular groups of travellers, such as commuters, shoppers, job seekers, children and pensioners. Money saving tickets gave unlimited travel in certain areas for up to four weeks. The company had negotiated discounts at Swansea stores for passengers travelling into the city by bus and there was a special SWT newspaper, delivered door to door, proclaiming the benefits of using the established operator with quality maintenance and long experience in running stage carriage services.

A Leyland Olympian crosses Princess Way, with Castle Gardens, behind, May 3, 1986. *Stephen Miles*

127

SWT still ran buses to less profitable places like Gower and the Afan Valley, but the historic X1 route, once operated by N&C Luxury Coaches between Swansea and Cardiff, was truncated at Bridgend. SWT also ceased to run to Brecon, a service it had operated for nearly 60 years. It was taken over by a newcomer, Silverline of Merthyr Tydfil. There was speculation that SWT would pull out of Haverfordwest, which was out on a limb, many miles from the nearest company depot, but the services were profitable and they continued, although in the tendering round that followed SWT did not get as many of the loss-making routes as it had hoped for. It did however cut back on its school contracts and stage carriage services in other parts of Dyfed blaming a poor school contract mileage rate and the council's cash limits on subsidies.

The effects of losses made during the 12-month long miners' strike in 1984-85 were still being felt and may have been partly responsible for the thinking behind some of the changes. SWT had a number of important National Coal Board contracts in the early 1980s and lost around £750,000 during strike. Towards the end of the dispute the NCB announced it planned to restart running buses to the pits for miners who wanted to return to work. In South West Wales that was barely a

trickle, but SWT was asked to provide buses and they were driven across picket lines by the managers, including traffic manager Alan Kreppel.

"The miners were warned to lie on the floor of the buses and we were told that when a gap appeared on the picket lines we were to aim for it as fast as possible," said Alan. "Despite the situation, relations between the miners and police were usually good, there wasn't the violence here that there was in some parts of the country. The most serious incident was when a stone was thrown through the window of one of our buses, but no-one was injured."

Gearing up for independence day

As the 1980s began to wane SWT's managers were gearing up for the next major change, the break-up and sale of the National Bus Company.

Although NBC pleaded to be sold as a whole to the private sector, Nicholas Ridley would have none of it and insisted on the companies being sold individually. He decreed that some were too large and ordered that they should be broken up. Crosville, for example, became two companies, Crosville and Crosville Cymru, Bristol Omnibus also split into two while the largest of them all, Midland Red, was divided into four. SWT, with 265 vehicles serving a compact area, was judged to be just right and was sold as a whole.

There were two bidders — one an SWT management team of four led by David Bending and the other a group of Swansea businessmen. David Bending became managing director, Alan Kreppel commercial director, Ivan Moore technical director and Gerard Turley who was brought in from outside finance director. The company secretary, Leslie

Leaving the Quadrant bus station, Swansea for Gorseinon in the mid-1980s this Mk 1 Leyland National was transferred to SWT from its sister operation, East Kent.

Leyland National's Mk 1, left, and 2, at Brunswick Street depot, August, 1980. The Mk 2 vehicle was later fitted with coach-style seats and painted poppy red and white, the company's dual purpose livery.
Royston Morgan Collection

A line up of green liveried Bristol VRT double deckers, all displaying advertisements celebrating SWT's 75th anniversary, 1989.

Royston Morgan Collection

Beynon, decided against becoming involved, but helped all he could with the management bid.

Alan Kreppel remembers: "As we were running the company, we had to meet the businessmen who were competing with us. It was a difficult encounter, to say the least, and it was made quite clear to us at that meeting that if they won the bid we wouldn't have jobs with the new company. David Bending and I decided immediately afterwards that if we lost, we would set up our own bus company in Swansea in opposition."

Then events took a sinister turn. SWT's Transport and General Workers Union branch decided to come out in support of the management bid and one evening Dai John, the fleet chairman, answered a knock on his door to be threatened by a man who told him to stop backing the management bid. Dai was understandably shaken but the man ran off. It has never been discovered who

he was or who he was acting for, if anyone. In the end it was the management bid that won the day. It had not been easy, the four directors had to put up £3 million and assets on the line included their own homes, but on May 8, 1987, SWT became the 35th National Bus Company subsidiary to enter the private sector. For the first time in its life, SWT was a truly independent company and its 950 staff were delighted. Alan Kreppel is full of praise for the way they supported the bid and says he wishes they could have been more closely involved, although 10 per cent of the shares did go to those who wanted them. "But we had to act at break-neck speed if our bid was to succeed, and with everything going on, the buy-out got pretty hairy," he said.

Blaenymaes-bound on the 25 route, and tailed by a Mini Link Mercedes 709D, Leyland Olympian C904 FCY heads along Oxford Street in the late 1980s.

Royston Morgan Collection

A Leyland National and one of the SWT's new MCW MetroRider minibuses in a close encounter at Sketty Park shopping centre, August 12, 1987. *Stephen Miles*

KILLAY SKETTY
THREE DUNVANT
CROSSES TYCOCH
the NEW LOOK for WEST SWANSEA
Commencing 16th August 1987
CITY MINI

But the cloud of uncertainty over SWT's future was lifted and it could now plan ahead. Alan Kreppel said the immediate plan of action was to ensure the company was financially stable and to grow the business. "We had to get rid of the high cost National Bus Company fleet as quickly as possible. NBC had allowed us to buy minibuses before the buy-out and there was no doubt that we could achieve the stability we needed with minibuses. When they replaced big buses on the Mumbles routes we saw a 131 per cent increase in passengers and we were looking for similar increases on other routes. Thanks to the minibus investment, by 1990 we were carrying more passengers than we had been in 1980."

Minibuses were cheap to operate and were proving popular with passengers who liked the fact that they ran more frequently and to places inaccessible to big buses. By the time of the buyout there were 53 in the fleet and by 1990 this had risen to 181. SWT had become a mainly minibus fleet with a declining number of larger buses. It meant more jobs for local people and finding drivers wasn't a problem in the late 1980s with a ready source of manpower following the job losses caused by post-strike pit closures.

More frequent minibuses also helped keep the competition at bay, but where it was encountered SWT took a zero tolerance stance. As David Bending said at the time: "We have to be firm with competition, if we allow it to continue unhindered it will grow and could become a threat to us."

It did not matter how small scale the opposition, SWT always reacted. Hawkes of Gorseinon ran an early morning service to the city centre through Sketty. It carried half-a-dozen passengers at most, but SWT responded by running a Leyland National a couple of minutes ahead, it even had a conductor, just in case the one or two users slowed it down and the Hawkes bus caught up. As the 1980s continued, SWT put the bad years of the 1970s firmly behind it. By 1989 it had 300 vehicles, mostly minibuses, operating 14 million miles every year and carrying 26 million passengers annually. The company celebrated its 75th anniversary with a huge transport extravaganza at Margam Park attended by thousands.

David Bending described the two years since the buy-out as a time of "vigorous expansion and improvement" with many services converted to high-frequency minibuses and the company maintaining a high profile in the community. "This is a policy which SWT will continue into the next decade and beyond. Complementing further minibus conversions, there will be a number of new and innovative schemes which will improve the lot of the company's customers and lead to a steady growth in business," he pledged.

But just a few months later it was announced that SWT had been sold to the expanding Badgerline group based in Weston-Super-Mare. SWT passengers and staff were looking at an uncertain future yet again.

Small buses that made a big impact

AT the beginning of 1986, nine minibuses in a bright green livery with headlights on moved in V-formation down the runway at Swansea Airport.

They heralded what was to become a transport revolution from the mid-1980s and once again SWT was at the forefront of the changes. Big buses were out, minibuses were the new order as National Bus Company fleets across the country started switching to smaller vehicles carrying as few as 16 passengers.

It had all begun in Exeter in 1984 when Devon General converted city routes from traditional double deckers to more frequent and more flexible Ford Transits. Passenger numbers shot up and other NBC fleets, including SWT, started taking a huge interest. In 1985 SWT asked NBC for permission to buy minibuses and the first arrived at the start of

the following year. SWT was the first major bus company in Wales to begin converting big bus routes into minibus operations but it was not the first time the company had run small vehicles.

Back in December 1978 SWT answered a plea from traders and residents of small villages between Mumbles and Bishopston in Gower for a bus service. It bought two, 16-seat Ford Transits "at advantageous terms" from City of Oxford Motor Services and put them to use on the route which it called Gower Pony. It proved more successful than expected and in 1980 SWT bought two new 17-seat Bedfords bodied by Reeve Burgess for the service, which was also popular with drivers. Trundling along quiet village lanes made a nice change from busy city centre routes but as so many drivers wanted to give it a try, rotas meant they could only do one week every nine months. Unfortunately passenger numbers were too low to keep it going and SWT withdrew it in the major service cutbacks of the mid-1980s.

The concept of the 1980s minibus craze was entirely different. Now the aim was to grow passenger levels by providing minibuses at

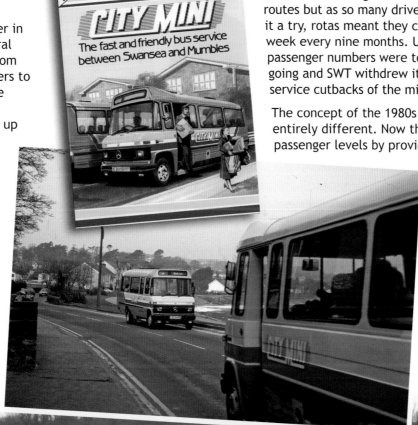

Two City Mini vehicles appear to sandwich a former London Transport Daimler Fleetline at Oystermouth bus station, February 14, 1986.
Stephen Miles

Two 20-seat City Minis pass on the first day of operation of SWT's new Mumbles service extension on February 17, 1986. Both vehicles are Robin Hood bodied Mercedes Benz L608Ds.
Stephen Miles

more frequent intervals than big buses and sending them to places where other buses were too big to go, such as through housing estates or along narrow country roads. More frequent minibuses were also seen as an important weapon to ward off competition, a major issue as the Government's Transport Act 1985 encouraged new bus firms to set up to compete against existing operators.

One of the two original Ford Transit Gower Pony vehicles negotiates Plunch Lane, Limeslade, May 17, 1977. *Stephen Miles*

simple, low cost and incredibly robust. Once one overturned on Mynydd Cadle Common but even though he was upside down, the driver was able to radio for help. We brought the bus back to Ravenhill and it was so little damaged that it was ready to return to service almost immediately. The driver was also back at work the same day."

SWT took 53 L608Ds in two batches. The first 201-215 (C201-215 HTH) were put to work in February 1986 between Swansea city centre and Mumbles, the second batch, 216-253 (D216-253 LCY) followed a few months later on the city centre to Morriston services. Ready When You Are was the slogan for the minibuses which carried City Mini fleet names and wore SWT's new two-tone green livery.

To herald the start of its first major minibus operation, SWT arranged the Swansea Airport publicity stunt, a nice idea. Unfortunately, the vehicles did not live up to the hype. They were Mercedes Benz L608Ds with seats for 20. You could just manage to squeeze through the entrance at the front but once on board the lack of space was obvious. There were single seats on the right behind the driver and they were so narrow that it was a case of one cheek on, the other off. It was pretty tight on the double seats opposite, as well, and you soon became friendly with the person next to you.

There was a small luggage pen and an overhead rack but space for packages and the like was at a premium. Yet SWT's publicity leaflets showed people coming off the vehicles with more parcels than Father Christmas. It was just not possible.

The L608Ds were slow, they lumbered along and were hopelessly under-powered. While that was not a problem shuttling between the city centre and Mumbles, it was when they found their way onto hilly routes such as Tycoch. But SWT loved them. Alan Kreppel, the traffic manager when they were introduced, said: "We wouldn't accept anything else. We insisted on the L608Ds because they were very

SWT was disappointed when the L608Ds were no longer available and switched in August 1987 to Metro-Cammell Weymann and its Metrorider. It took 25 in a deal worth around £625,000 for new minibus services to Uplands, Sketty, Tycoch and Dunvant which also meant recruiting 40 new drivers. They were a different type of vehicle altogether, more like a small bus and far more passenger friendly with 25 reasonably pitched seats. Yet SWT didn't like them.

"They were reliable but their problem was the manual gearbox and we had to carry out lots of work to make it suitable. They also suffered from internal rot which proved troublesome," said Alan Kreppel. SWT returned to Mercedes Benz for its next minibus order in 1987 and afterwards never took anything else. By the end of 1990 it had received 182 new minibuses, most of them Mercedes Benz with bodywork by Robin Hood, Reeve Burgess Beaver and Phoenix. There were 608Ds, 609Ds, 709Ds, 811Ds and the more powerful 814Ds. They became larger and the 1989-91 deliveries seated 31 passengers, which became SWT's maximum for minibuses. Most services were converted from big bus to minibus operations, all running at more frequent intervals and on a 'hail and ride' basis away from main roads. SWT stressed the convenience of the new vehicles and passengers were urged to 'Catch the bus from your own door.' All minibuses were non-smoking.

Each area had minibuses with a local fleet name but in the same two-tone green livery. They were City Mini in Swansea, Town Mini in Neath and Port Talbot, Sosban

Two City Minis head up Union Street, Swansea, during the 1990s. *Royston Morgan Collection*

Link in Llanelli, Mini Link in Gowerton and Gorseinon, Cleddau Mini in Haverfordwest, Myrddin Mini in the Carmarthen and Amman Valley areas. They achieved all that had been hoped of them back in 1985. Alan Kreppel had no doubts about that.

"Passenger numbers rose by 131 per cent on the Mumbles route after the minibuses were introduced," he said. "They rose on other routes, too, though not by as much. They also protected the company from competition, and reduced costs."

In 1987 SWT fleet chairman, Dai John questioned whether or not they were popular with passengers. He said that when a big bus and minibus on a common section of route turned up together, people would invariably jump on the bigger vehicle. He was also concerned about 'bunching'— two or even three minibuses on the same route turning up at once. This was perhaps inevitable when the service frequency was as high as every five minutes. But according to a survey carried out in the same year by Swansea University's department of geography, seven out of 10 passengers said they preferred to travel on a minibus. Convenience and frequency were cited as attributes and those questioned said minibuses made travel easier, especially into the city centre. By 1994 SWT was a mainly minibus fleet. There were just 12 full-size single deckers, two Leyland Nationals and 10 Dennis

The Swansea west minibus corridor was mainly operated by MCW MetroRiders such as fleet No. 266 seen in the city's Mansel Street, July 1989. *Stephen Miles*

Lances with Plaxton Verde bodies. SWT had only 19 double deckers running on just one regular service in Swansea. Minibuses ruled the roost but their day was coming to an end. For SWT had started taking a vehicle that would become its bus of the 1990s. It was the Dennis Dart.

A Robin Hood bodied Mercedes City Mini with a raised advertisement hoarding heads along West Way, Swansea towards the Quadrant bus station, 1987. *Royston Morgan Collection*

Ravenhill round-up

With the rapid growth of its fleet caused by the closure of the town's tramway system there came a point where South Wales Transport management realised the need for a much larger central depot and garage than that at Brunswick Street. Coupled with this was the economic benefit of having a base out of town and near the new housing estates. The decision was taken to build a completely new facility with offices and engineering facilities as well as extensive garaging space at Ravenhill. This was opened in 1937 and remained the company's central hub until its demise in 1999. Ravenhill boasted one of the largest span roofs of its type and accommodated the major proportion of the company's vehicles as well as offering state of the art conditions for their maintenance and upkeep.

Construction work underway at Ravenhill, 1936.
Gwilym Richards

Vehicles in the huge garage shortly after opening in 1937.
Chris Taylor Archive

This exterior of the garage in 1937 gives a clue to the fact that it was built on former farmland.
Gwilym Riohards

A mixed line-up of AEC Regent Vs and some of the Bristol VRTs that were to replace them at Ravenhill, 1980.
Royston Morgan Collection

Part of the engineering workshop in the 1970s.
Roy Kneath

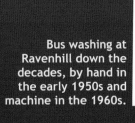

Bus washing at Ravenhill down the decades, by hand in the early 1950s and machine in the 1960s.

Route to be biggest was exciting, but ruthless

The prospects for SWT looked bright as the 1980s morphed into the 1990s, but behind the scenes, all was not well. Three of the four directors had become pessimistic about the future of the bus industry and decided they wanted out. Alan Kreppel, the commercial director, was the only one keen to stay.

So it was announced that David Bending, who had led the successful buyout in October 1987; Gerard Turley and Ivan Moore were leaving and in February 1990 SWT was sold to Badgerline with Alan Kreppel becoming the new managing director.

"I was more optimistic about the future of buses than the other three and we came to an amicable agreement that we would sell," said Alan. "It was a sad time, the four of us had gone through so much together during the buyout bid. We went with Badgerline because it seemed to offer the best for SWT." The company had been an independent firm for less than three years, now it was part of a major, private group again, but this time things were very different to what they had been in BET days.

Badgerline was a former National Bus Company constituent which had been sold to its management in the late summer of 1986. It aimed to become one of the industry's big players and had already taken over Bristol Cityline and Midland Red West and involved itself in various joint ventures. SWT was its first, and only foray, into South Wales, and relations were good between the parent company and its new subsidiary.

"We were happy, we felt we were being left alone and allowed autonomy," said Alan Kreppel. It was a good marriage, there were lots of similarities between the two companies and similar outlooks on the best way to run buses. Like Badgerline, SWT had a declining number of former NBC vehicles in its fleet in 1990 and both companies were replacing them with high-frequency minibuses. SWT liked being able to do its own thing, the only outward appearance that it belonged to Badgerline was the black and white badger cartoon character that appeared on the side of its buses. Some found it cute, others irritating, but at least SWT was allowed to keep its two-tone green livery and separate identity.

In 1990 it had around 300 vehicles and six depots. Swansea had two, one at Clarence Terrace for coaching, the other at Ravenhill which was the company's largest and where the central works were based. There were others at Llanelli, Port Talbot, Pontardawe and Haverfordwest, which also

Stephen Miles

A Plaxton Verde bodied Dennis Lance at Alfred Street, Neath on the fast, Saturdays only, service 458 between Banwen and Swansea, December 21, 1996.

Royston Morgan Collection

A mixed line-up of post privatisation, green liveried, single and double deck SWT vehicles at the Quadrant bus station, Swansea, 1995.

stationed vehicles overnight at Milford Haven, Pembroke Dock and Tenby. Port Talbot and Pontardawe shared an outstation at Millands Road, Neath. Pontardawe was responsible for routes run by one double decker and six saloons while Port Talbot was responsible for minibus operations run by nine vehicles. Pontardawe also outstationed a double decker, two saloons and two minibuses for routes in Ammanford.

SWT was by now the largest operator in what was then West Glamorgan and Dyfed. But to get there, it had to act ruthlessly at times. That was the case with the takeover of Brewers in January 1988. This was a family concern that ran services in Maesteg and when SWT found out that it was negotiating to sell to Daryl Davies of D Coaches in Swansea, it moved in quickly.

"We did the deal and took it over, Daryl was furious," said Alan Kreppel. Brewers became a sister company to SWT and later that same year it also set up United Welsh Coaches (UWC) which ran private hire and school contracts from the old United Welsh depot in Gorseinon. There were lots of transfers between the three fleets, with SWT Leyland Nationals and older coaches finding themselves with Brewers or UWC.

SWT also eliminated other competition by taking over Morris Bros, which had become part of the Capitol bus

group of Cwmbran, and in 1996 bought D Coaches with routes in Ammanford and down to Swansea. But it was with the demise of National Welsh (NW) that the company saw major expansion.

National Welsh was another former NBC company that had been sold to its management, but by 1990 it was clear the company was in trouble. In January 1991 it sold off the eastern area of its operations to Western Travel of Gloucester and for the next few months tried to soldier on from its Barry, Bridgend, Rhondda and Aberdare depots. It was fighting a losing battle however and the vultures soon began to circle, including SWT, which started to run competing services in the Bridgend area. It pulled out of the joint X5 service it had run with NW between Swansea and Hirwaun and started to run the route itself, a few minutes in front of NW buses.

The end was not long in coming and in January 1992 National Welsh called in the receivers. SWT initially bid to take over the Aberdare, Rhondda and Bridgend depots, but because of other operators' interest it later dropped the Aberdare and Rhondda plan, although it took over the Bridgend routes. Alan Kreppel makes no apologies for SWT's action. "We had to move the way we did because we didn't want another operator coming in. We had to have a strategy," he said.

But it was an expanded Brewers, not SWT, that eventually ran the Bridgend operations. "There were lots of operators who were prepared to give bus services a go and we needed a strategy to deal with

A Leyland Olympian with ECW bodywork squeezes down Oxford Street, Swansea in 1993. This vehicle was the last double decker delivered new to SWT.
Royston Morgan Collection

Leyland Olympian 903 on the X5 Swansea bound service loading passengers at Victoria Gardens, Neath, 1992.
Stephen Miles

this," said Alan Kreppel. "Port Talbot was experiencing more competition and we grew Brewers as a low cost operation to run services in Bridgend, Maesteg and Port Talbot to deal with it." It meant that SWT pulled out of Port Talbot and transferred the operations to Brewers, which painted its vehicles in a new, bright red and white livery. It grew to around 130 vehicles and became an autonomous operation within the Badgerline group, although operations were still overseen by Alan Kreppel.

So by May 1994, SWT was a company with around 235 vehicles. There were 18 coaches, used on National Express work, 172 minibuses, 20 double deckers, including two magnificent Leyland Olympian coaches which it used on its Shuttle motorway express link between Swansea and Cardiff, 10 single deck Dennis Lances bodied by Plaxton Verde which worked limited stop services branded Timecutter, 24 Dennis Dart midi-buses which was soon to become the company's standard bus, and the heritage Bristol K, the open-top bus which it had bought from Eastern National in 1974.

Clarence Terrace garage in Swansea had closed by now and SWT had depots at Ravenhill in Swansea, Haverfordwest, Llanelli, Pontardawe and in Johnstown, Carmarthen, after it won a number of Dyfed County Council bus tenders. Swansea was the main area of operations, around 100 vehicles were

used on city routes, many of them running on 10 minute frequencies or less. No new double deckers was the decree at the time, and that held fast. SWT never bought any new double deckers after the seven Leyland Olympians of 1985 and the policy continued into First Cymru days.

But by 1994, more changes were afoot and these would have a major impact on SWT during the last five years of its existence. Badgerline was by now listed on the Stock Exchange and was seeking a new partner to help it become one of the UK's big bus players. Another bus company called GRT, based in Aberdeen, had similar intentions and so in 1995 the two united and became First Bus. Badgerline had around 5,000 vehicles and GRT about 1,600, but it was soon clear who was boss.

Alan Kreppel said: "It was supposed to be a merger but GRT became dominant. Badgerline had been a group of bus people not interested in making mega bucks but the management style was different at GRT. SWT had been allowed a lot of autonomy but under First Bus we started receiving more and more decisions and instructions from Aberdeen. It was a case of we know best and you will do it. SWT had the best first-time MoT pass rate of any of the First companies with 98 per cent of our vehicles passing first time. But then we

Sandwiched between two Alexander bodied Dennis Darts in corporate First Bus livery is one of SWT's first batch of low floor vehicles, a Plaxton bodied Dennis Dart SLF in SWT post-privatisation livery, but with First logo.

Royston Morgan Collection

were ordered to make changes to vehicle maintenance procedures. First began expecting better and better financial returns. Things eventually came to a head and I was effectively sacked."

That happened just a few months before SWT became First Cymru and SWT's last managing director was Piers Marlow, who had been managing director at First's Provincial bus company based in Portsmouth. In April

What might have been! This Optare demonstrator was on hire to SWT in July 1992, but the company decided not to buy any, favouring Dennis Darts instead. *Stephen Miles*

1998 First, by now newly renamed First Group because it had also started running trains, decided to change the way it ran its Brewers and SWT operations and merged the companies into an enlarged SWT. It did not stay this way for long. First decided a change of image was required and started running the buses with First Cymru branding. Then it decided to change the company's name as well.

On March 28, 1999, the South Wales Transport Company passed into history. It had been in existence for exactly 85 years, one month and 18 days. At the end it had 350 vehicles and employed 1,000 staff. The policy was for a new, unified image that would be used by all First Group's bus subsidiaries. First's name and logo would appear on all the vehicles together with the appropriate company name, so the companies became First Midland Red West, First Western National and so on. There was no reason why SWT could not have become First SWT, or First South Wales, or why the company name should have had to change. But go it did and with it 85 years of rich history ended. In 2013, with

Three City Minis in Oxford Street, Swansea,1989, led by one of the 1989 batch of 31 seat Robin Hood bodied Mercedes 814Ds.

Royston Morgan Collection

Company's uniform approach

Some of the uniforms issued to South Wales Transport crews throughout the company's 85-year history.

Peter Nedin Collection

new First directors, there was another change. First Cymru buses began appearing with South Wales or the Welsh equivalent, De Cymru, name on their sides. Unlike in 1999, the value of having a local brand name to create customer loyalty had struck home.

Unfortunately, it was too late for SWT. The company known to generations as simply The Transport was no more. In 1964, when it celebrated its golden anniversary, SWT published a commemorative booklet looking back at its first 50 years. It also looked ahead to the next 50. "What of tomorrow?" one article asked, before continuing: "It should be remembered that The South Wales Transport Company is not just an inanimate body incorporated under the Companies Act; it represents a boundless reservoir of human energy and endeavour. Progress it will, progress it must."

The booklet highlighted what it described as the exciting times of the past, and promised that there would be equally as exciting times in the future. Those who produced that booklet couldn't have foretold that one day SWT would be no more.

Darts really hit the bullseye

At the start of the 1990s, SWT, like other operators, had been looking for a rather more sophisticated kind of bus than the minibuses that were then being used.

Step forward bus builder Dennis who, just at the right time, unveiled its Dart. It was to become SWT's bus of the decade and within six years the company had taken more than 130 of the type. Dennis had failed to hit the big time for the first 80 years or so of its existence. The end of the 1980s changed that. Dennis spotted the potential of buses that were a little larger than the 25 or 31 seat vehicles that were in use but which had more passenger appeal while still providing the benefits of minibuses.

The Dennis Dart was unveiled and SWT fell in love with it, although its first examples did not arrive until 1993. The Dart had all the attributes of a single deck bus with wide entrance and decent size gangway. It had excellent manoeuvrability and was as much at home on rural routes as it was in town and city centres. SWT was as pleased with its performance on the Gower and valley routes as it was on urban, stop-start services.

The Darts, when they arrived in Swansea, posed this interesting question: When does a minibus cease to become a minibus? The answer, as far as SWT was concerned, was when it seated more than 31 passengers. The Darts were little smaller than SWT's single deckers of the 1950s yet like the minibuses, were branded City Mini. They seated only 31 passengers although when the same sized vehicles entered other fleets they had 35 seats. SWT had a union agreement that meant drivers of vehicles with 31 seats or less were paid cheaper, minibus rates, hence the low seating capacity of its Darts. It raises an equally interesting follow-up question: if a 75-seat

Sisters often made tea for Townhill crews

Denzil Jones, of West Cross, Swansea, remembers the first buses to climb the notorious route to Townhill where he lived as a young boy.

"They were Swiss Saurer buses and they caused a lot of excitement," said Denzil, aged 92. "I can even remember the registration numbers on two of them, one was CY 9541, another was CY 9542.

From Switzerland to Swansea — a Saurer bus solves the Townhill problem.
Chris Taylor Archive

"There was a corner shop at the bus terminus and the two sisters who ran it used to make tea for the bus drivers and conductors when they arrived. I was only eight or nine at the time but I clearly remember going on the buses. It was 2d to come up the hill and a halfpenny to go down.

"I can also remember the summer service from Townhill to Caswell Bay, route 40. It was called married man's bay because it was where all the local families went."

A low floor Dennis Dart climbs Penygraig Road towards Townhill, Swansea, late 1990s. *Roy Kneath*

Heavy snowfall that brought unexpected call

Getting an unexpected call after heavy snowfall is among the memories of Alan West who worked as a driver and conductor for more than five years in the late 1960s and early 1970s.

"It was early one morning in the winter of 1968-69 and I wasn't expecting to go in because of the weather. I was still in bed when suddenly my mother was waking me to get up saying there was a bus waiting for me outside. It was being driven by Jimmy Hutin, a tremendous character, who had gone to Ravenhill garage and collected the double decker. He wanted to make sure he was paid for the shift!

"There were lots of characters among the drivers and conductors when I worked for The Transport but they were all good, tidy people. I remember one conductress actually booting one of the regular passengers who was causing trouble, off her bus. There were no hard feelings, he went back the next day and apologised."

Alan said the toughest route was undoubtedly the 79 from Swansea to Gors Avenue. "It was called Flagon Alley and no inspector ever dared board the late night service which we called the Last Gors, the passengers would have simply thrown him off. I remember on one occasion the conductor being warned by the passengers not to collect fares but as they got off the bus they gave him a tip."

Leyland Olympian double decker had 44 of its seats removed, would it become a minibus in SWT's eyes? As the question was never asked, it didn't become an issue and SWT continued to take 31-seat Darts. There were three batches of identical Plaxton Pointer bodied vehicles followed by two batches of the new low-floor version. The next Darts, and the last vehicles taken new by SWT, were larger 38-seaters bodied by Alexander. By the time SWT went out of existence it had more than 100 Darts in use on a wide variety of services.

Low floor vehicles made history

The 'low floor' revolution hit Wales in the mid-1990s and, as ever, SWT was at the forefront of events. It changed bus travel forever and made it easier for disabled and elderly people to use public transport.

The company invested £1 million in 12 low floor Dennis Darts that were introduced in Swansea in October 1996. They were the first for the company, which afterwards never took anything else, and also the first of their type in Wales. With step-free entrances and a low, flat floor along two-thirds of the length of the bus, they also

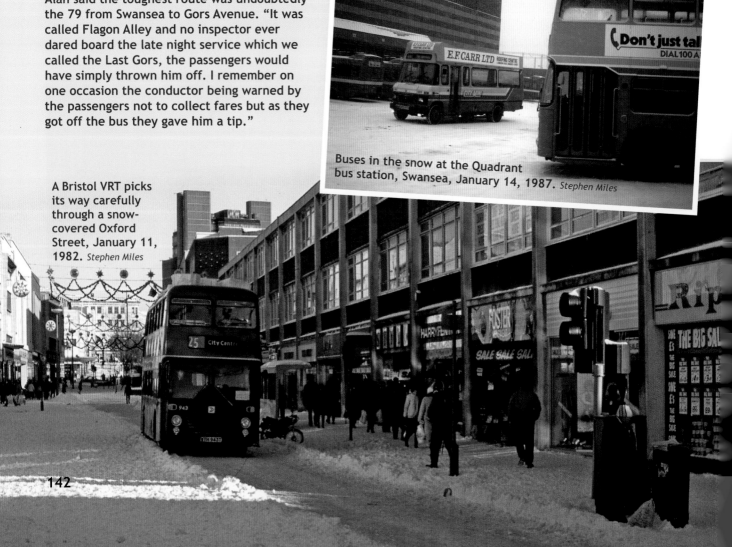

Buses in the snow at the Quadrant bus station, Swansea, January 14, 1987. *Stephen Miles*

A Bristol VRT picks its way carefully through a snow-covered Oxford Street, January 11, 1982. *Stephen Miles*

One of the first of SWT's low floor Dennis Darts on
display at Castle Gardens, Swansea, November 1996.

helped mothers with pushchairs or disabled people in
wheelchairs who could be wheeled straight from the
pavement on to the bus.

The new Dennis Darts had a specially designed chassis
frame and front axle which provided an entrance step
of only 325mm. This could be reduced still further to
245mm through the use of air suspension that
incorporated a 'kneeling'
mechanism. All the driver had to do
was press a button, and down the
bus went. There were even more
benefits. Pollution on the roads was
becoming an issue and the new
Dart SLFs were cleaner than their
predecessors. They had the latest
Cummins B engine to meet tight
new exhaust emission legislation
and ran on low sulphur diesel.

SWT put them to work on its
Swansea Eastside and Morriston
services, 30-33, and up to Townhill
on the 12 and 13 routes. Swansea
Council complemented the buses by

modifying all the bus stops in Townhill and a selected
number of stops on the Eastside routes. Kerb levels
at the stops were raised to 220mm across an average
of three metres so that there would be level access
from the pavement on to the bus entrance. To work,
the bus had to be able to pull up close to the
footway, which it could not do if there were cars
parked in the way so SWT appealed to motorists to
stay off the stops. With the passage of time, the
vast majority of buses are low floor, the concept has
also been extended to double deckers, and that makes
those first SWT vehicles historically important. One of
them, P580 BTH, the last in the batch, was passed to
Swansea Bus Museum in 2013 for restoration.

The batch, P569-580 BTH, fleet numbers 569-580, were
the last new vehicles to arrive in SWT's two tone green
colours. They had long lives, some of them were still
running for First Cymru in late 2013, at the age of 17!

A step entrance Dennis Dart winds its way out of
Port Eynon, Gower in August 2000. *Stephen Miles*

Sales

At times South Wales Transport painted its buses in special advertising liveries and although it happened more often in the 1980s, it was never common. Usually, it was double deckers which benefitted from the artistic talents of a painter's brush or the transfer artist's skills and there was a range of colour schemes which, while they might have brightened up the street scene, did render the bus anonymous

force

which may have made the lives of passengers more difficult. But it was a useful source of additional income as well as a way of publicising SWT's own services and special offers. Bristol VRTs that received all-over advertisements in the 1980s included 921, Asda; 934, South Wales Evening Post; 938, Swansea Sound; 940 SWT coach tours and minibreaks; 995, Top Rank; and one that seemed to cause widespread amusement at the time, 983, for Y-fronts!

Images from Royston Morgan Collection

145

CHAPTER 13

Buses that became a part of daily life for many

For 50 years a distinctive sound resonated through the towns of Swansea, Llanelli, Ammanford, Neath and Port Talbot. It was the growl of the AEC Regent double deck buses that served most of SWT's web-like route network. In their maroon livery they were a familiar and friendly presence on the streets. So much so, that for generations, they epitomised South Wales Transport.

The company thought the Regents were brilliant. It received more than 500 of the vehicles from 1932 until 1967 before finally saying farewell to them in 1982. SWT took all four production models — the early ones with rear entrances, the later ones with doors at the front — and put them to work on a variety of routes. Whether it was stop and start work in town centres, climbing Swansea's notorious hills or rolling along on rural routes, the Regents were ideal for the job.

There was never a closer transport relationship than the one SWT developed with the Associated Equipment Company and it was a remarkably faithful one. SWT started taking AEC engines in the 1920s and by 1960 had no other type in its fleet. Most were Regents but SWT also had single deck Regals and later, lighter weight Reliances. There were also batches of low-height Bridgemasters and Renowns and SWT was such a valued customer that it was often entrusted with trialling new vehicle types for AEC.

AEC was established in 1912 but it was not until 1929 that its Regents first went into production. SWT was slow to respond, and didn't receive its first until 1932, but the company soon put that right with a massive order for 50. They were much needed to replace out-of-date double deckers taken by the company in the 1920s. Before the Regents arrived SWT's newest double deck buses were 13 AEC 507s dating from 1926.

Bus designs had moved forward in that time and SWT's first Regents were to a design that basically would not change for 25 years. They arrived in two batches, with minor body style differences, seated 51 passengers and were registered WN 4749-4768 (fleet numbers 249-268) and WN 4869-4898 (fleet numbers 269-298). Few would deny that they displayed a resemblance to the 13 electric cars that had been introduced on the Mumbles Railway three years previously. That is because both were bodied by Brush with which SWT's parent company, British Electric Traction, had a close relationship at the time, particularly so because Emile Garcke, BET's founder, was also a Brush director. These modern looking vehicles transformed SWT's ageing bus fleet, but even they were eclipsed by the next batch of

Royston Morgan Collection

AEC Regent Vs carried millions of passengers during their long association with SWT. This 1965 Willowbrook-bodied version had a few of those on board as it headed into Swansea on route 14 from Pennard.

A driver climbs into the cab of the last AEC Regent V delivered new to South Wales Transport, at its Brunswick Street depot, 1969.

Regents. In 1937 Swansea's trams were phased out and to replace them SWT ordered 62 Regents. This time they had 56 seats and were bodied by Weymann, a company which for the following 25 years became SWT's favoured body builder. Again there were two batches, registered ACY 1-50 (1-50) and AWN 551-562 (51-62). Surprisingly they are recorded as having given some engineering problems initially but these must have been resolved for, despite the battering they suffered in the war years, most had long lives and the last, ACY 29, wasn't withdrawn until 1959, lasting another year as a learner vehicle.

SWT received no new buses during the Second World War and when it started taking new ones again in 1946 they were exclusively AEC. Previously the company had taken vehicles from a mix of manufacturers and the immediate post war fleet included Leylands and Dennis Lancets. From then on it bought only AEC and what splendid vehicles they proved to be.

The 10 years following the end of the Second World War have been described as SWT's golden age and that certainly extended to its vehicles. Those that arrived in 1946 were also bodied by Weymann but had even finer lines and curves. They were Regent IIs, although the actual differences between them and their 1937 sisters were minor. SWT took 41 between 1946 and 1948, 16 of

them were highbridge with 56 seats, the rest were low height vehicles that seated 53 passengers.

Then in 1949 the first of SWT's Regent IIIs arrived, again bodied by Weymann. Engineers loved the Regent III as it was so easy to overhaul, while drivers liked its large 9.6 litre engine, air-operated gearbox and brakes to ease their lot. There were 24 high bridge buses with 56 seats and six low height vehicles seating 53. These were followed by 23 similar low bridge buses in 1950. Two batches of highbridge Regent IIIs arrived in 1951 and the second batch looked squatter and more rounded than the first. This was because they were the first 8ft wide double deckers in the fleet, registered GWN 85-95, with fleet numbers 373-383. Vehicles of this width had been allowed since 1946, but approval had to be given for the routes they were to operate on, so SWT had stuck to 7ft 6ins. Then in 1950 the requirement was withdrawn and SWT started taking the wider vehicles which looked even better than their narrower sisters. From around the same time permitted vehicle lengths were also increased to 27ft.

More Regent IIIs arrived in 1952, including 11 that had been ordered by Llanelly District Traction as trolley bus replacements before SWT took over the company that year, and another 15 in 1953. The 1954 intake was different, JWN 901-915 (425-439) were lowbridge Weymanns once again but all 15 were SWT's first with the new look, enclosed radiator grilles and some had platform doors. Unlike their lowbridge sisters they seated 56 passengers.

Then in 1954 AEC exhibited its new Regent V double decker at the Commercial Motor Show. With its lighter chassis it cost less to run and was just what SWT had been looking for. It took the first production batch, MCY 400-419 (440-459), of which the first 10 were normal height, the second 10 lowbridge and some were later fitted with platform doors. This batch, and the ones that followed in 1955, 1956 and 1957 had rear entrances but in 1958 SWT's first Regents with front entrance platform doors arrived. There were 26 that year, all bodied by Weymann and were the largest yet, 30ft long with seats for 71 passengers. Similar vehicles came in 1959 and 1960 and the intake for 1960 also included six Willowbrook models which were the first to have rounded corners to the front wings. SWT asked for the change because wings on the earlier buses were catching in the bus washers. Willowbrook supplied the Regent Vs in 1961, 1962 and 1963 while the following year there was a mix from the two body builders plus a small batch, 429-433 (HCY 596-600) from Park Royal.

The final Regents which came in 1965, 1966 and 1967 were all Willowbrooks, but SWT reverted to 27ft 6 ins long bodies with seating for 64.

The Regents saw service right through the 1970s; they were in all-day service in Swansea as late as 1980, but by now their numbers were falling fast. One of their problems was that they couldn't be used for one person operation, although SWT did convert two, VWN 951 (535) and VWN 962 (546), for 'One Person Operation' experiments in 1972, but they were never used.

Upstairs...

Looking along the upper deck of a Willowbrook bodied, AEC Regent V April 5, 1981. . .

Royston Morgan Collection

. . . and looking forward along its lower deck. **...** downstairs

By 1982 just five Regent Vs remained in the fleet and they had been retained for the Swansea to Pennard route 14 which included a tight corner near the Plough and Harrow pub in Murton which only the Regents, because of their shorter length, could negotiate. At the beginning of February that year new Bedford YMQs were introduced on the route and the Regents went into well-earned retirement. The final five were CCY 981/9C, of 1965, GWN 859/64D of 1966 and GWN 867E

of 1967 and after being ousted from the 14 route on February 7 they continued on Swansea city services until February 26. They made special journeys the following day with commemorative tickets on sale for enthusiasts and went on show at the Quadrant bus station. It was GWN 867E, fleet number 889, which made the final journey on the day, from Craig-Cefn-Parc arriving back at the bus station at 11.20 pm. For the first time in half a century, SWT had no Regents in service. They were the last to be used on regular services in the whole of the National Bus Company. Sister company East Kent kept its Regent Vs later but they were only for schools services, although at times of vehicle shortages they did occasionally stray onto stage carriage services.

The last job 889 did for SWT was to help stop private cars parking on the forecourt of Gorseinon depot, which despite its closure SWT continued to use as a store for withdrawn vehicles. The bus was parked on the forecourt with a 'no parking' sign tied to its radiator cap — a sad end, if it had been the end, but both it and sister GWN 864D (886) were then sold to Pembrokeshire Agricultural Society for use as mobile judges offices and commentary boxes at Withybush showground near Haverfordwest. In 2010 the vehicles found a new home at Swansea Bus Museum.

Italian job was revolutionary

One type of single decker dominated SWT's fleet during the 1970s — the Leyland National. When the first arrived in 1973, it was nothing less than revolutionary.

General manager Frank Woodworth anticipated hundreds joining the fleet, indicating that the company would eventually be dominated by the model. It was certainly different from anything that had gone before. The Leyland National was developed as a joint project between SWT's parent, the National Bus Company, and Leyland. Styling for the new bus was carried out by Italian vehicle stylist Giovanni Michelotti and it was very different from the single deckers SWT was operating at the time. It had a box-like body with a distinctive roof-mounted pod at the rear that housed a sophisticated heating and ventilation system. Between 1973 and 1979, SWT took 115 of the type, all very similar 11.3 metre (37ft) long machines with 8.3 litre Leyland 510 engines and seats for 52, although a handful were modified with 50 seats. They could carry another 23 standing passengers and their 75 person capacity meant they were able to accommodate more people than the AEC Regent V double deckers that SWT operated at the time.

Unlike the Regents, the Leyland Nationals were fully equipped for pay on entry and SWT soon put them to work on its growing network of one-person operated routes. They quickly became a common sight across most of the company's operating area during the second half of the 1970s but were not without

SWT's first ever Leyland National climbs Mount Pleasant in its original livery, January 11, 1975. Stephen Miles

problems. One of these was the high fuel consumption which made them expensive to operate while another was the heavy smoking exhaust. When a driver started up the engine it sounded like a large petrol lawnmower, then there was a puff of smoke from the exhaust as the bus moved off.

Leyland Nationals were not popular. SWT's commercial director in the 1980s, Alan Kreppel, said one of the first tasks when the company was bought out by its managers in 1987 was to get rid of all the Leyland Nationals because of their high upkeep cost. To many people these vehicles represent all that was seen as being wrong with buses in the 1970s.

In 1980 SWT took five of the 11.6 metre Leyland National 2 model with Leyland 680 engines and followed this up with a solitary similar bus in 1982. Again, they had 52 seats but later SWT converted them all to dual-purpose machines with 48 coach seats. The company also received some Leyland National Mk 1s from sister NBC companies, East Kent and Maidstone and District. They were a mixture of 10.3 metre and 11.3 metre models.

Most were ousted during the minibus revolution in the second half of the 1980s, although some were still operating in the early 1990s. The Mk 1s were numbered from 701-815, while the Mk 2s were 816-820 and 829. Four of SWT's are now in preservation at Swansea Bus Museum: they are 756 and the last of the Mk 1s, 815, and Mk 2s 820 and 829.

Newcomers rolled out single manning

SWT continued to operate large numbers of the trusted and much-loved AEC Regent Vs until 1977, but early that year the streets of South West Wales began to witness a very different looking double deck bus. The first Bristol VRTs had arrived.

These buses dated back to 1968, so SWT was very late in receiving them. In fact its first VRTs were the series 3 model which had been introduced in 1974 and unlike the Regents all could be used for pay as you enter services. The first batch arrived to convert the long established Swansea-Gorseinon-Llanelli route to one person operation although many of the subsequent arrivals were crew operated, especially in Swansea. They were Eastern Coachworks (ECW) bodied and had Leyland 0.501 engines, were 9.3 metres (30ft 7 ins) long, 4.16 metres (13ft 8 ins) high, had a single front entrance and seats for 74 — 43 upstairs and 31 on the lower deck.

Crews were not impressed, and from the passenger's point of view they lacked style, charisma and comfort. But SWT put them to work on a wide variety of operations, from stop-start town centre services to fast, inter-urban routes such as the X1, Swansea-Bridgend-Cardiff. The VRTs certainly had a good turn of speed however and even found their way onto the Swansea-Cardiff motorway service. Sitting on plastic bus seats on the top deck of a VRT at speed on the M4 was, as many would agree, quite an experience.

SWT's fleet of VRTs was numbered from 905 to 995 and it continued to take the make until 1980. Three of them, 930-2, had convertible open-tops for use on summer services to Mumbles, Langland and Caswell bays. In 1983 SWT bought some used VRTs to cope with a reorganisation of school transport in what was then the county of West Glamorgan and these included the first series model, in addition to some unusual MCW bodied versions from the West Midlands.

Four former SWT, VRTs are in preservation at Swansea Bus Museum, they are 931, 942, 961 and 978.

Other vehicles played a part

SWT's bus fleet was dominated, at different times, by Regents, Leyland Nationals, Bristol VRTs and minibuses but the company also took small numbers of many other types of vehicle, particularly during the 1930s.

Back in 1934 it received eight, magnificent six-wheel AEC Renowns which were the largest double deckers of the day with seats for 64 passengers. They had 8.8 litre oil engines, pre-selective gear boxes and were found on SWT's number two route between Swansea and Llanelli. SWT also bought 19 single deck versions, also called Renowns, in 1933 and 1939 and deployed them on a number of

Weightwatcher Reliances were a fuel saver

Lighter weight buses to help save on rising fuel costs was the plea from SWT's engineers at the start of the 1950s and AEC responded to the plea with the single deck Reliance.

It was just what the company had been looking for. The fleet would continue to be dominated by double deck Regents, but alongside, it built up a sizeable contingent of Reliances which served it admirably for more than 30 years.

AEC developed the underfloor-engined Reliance in 1953 and SWT's first eight appeared two years later. They were 30ft long buses seating 44 passengers and bodied by Park Royal, which would continue to build the company's examples throughout the 1950s. Their BET-style bodies were not the most attractive, unlike SWT's AEC Reliance coaches with bodywork by Weymann and Harrington which were among the finest of the 1950s and early 1960s.

SWT took 144 Reliances new between 1955 and 1975, 42 of them coaches. The bus version improved in 1963 when SWT took its first 36ft long examples with seats for 53 passengers, again to BET design, but now bodied by Marshall. They had what at the time was called 'the new look' which gave much improved all-round visibility for the driver and passengers. SWT continued to receive this style of bus until the last went into service in 1972, five with high-backed seats which were put to use on the fast Llanelli-Swansea-Cardiff service taken over from N&C Luxury Coaches. SWT's last Reliances arrived in 1975 in the form of five Duple bodied coaches in poppy red and white livery.

The company gained other examples with the takeover of N&C and Thomas Bros of Port Talbot in 1971. SWT received 26

A newly delivered Willowbrook bodied AEC Reliance at Orchard Street, Swansea, August 1968. These were always known as the Townhill Reliances. *Royston Morgan Collection*

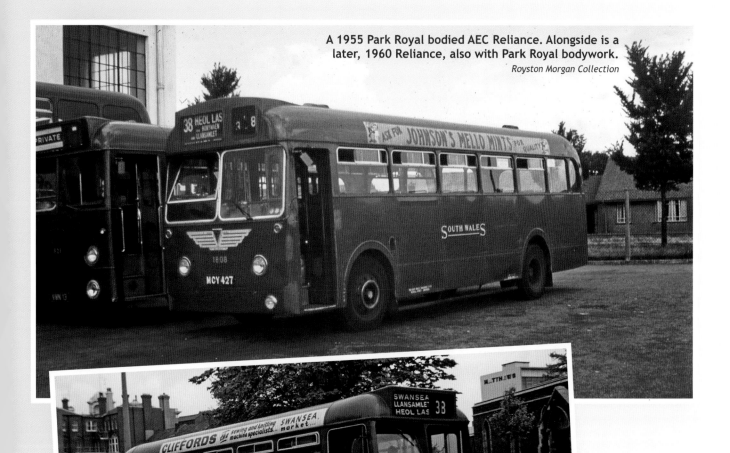

A 1955 Park Royal bodied AEC Reliance. Alongside is a later, 1960 Reliance, also with Park Royal bodywork.

Royston Morgan Collection

A 1962 Marshall bodied AEC Reliance at St Mary's Church, Swansea.

Royston Morgan Collection

AEC Reliance coaches from N&C, with bodywork by a range of companies including Plaxton, Duple Northern and Harrington, and 22 more from Thomas Bros, seven coaches and 15 buses with similar bodywork to SWT's own.

Another 20 Reliances entered the fleet with the takeover of the Western Welsh depots in Haverfordwest and Neath Abbey in 1972. They included 15 Marshall bodied examples with 41 high-backed seats that WW had used on express routes in West Wales.

The last Reliances in the SWT fleet were three 1974 Duple coaches which had been operated on Continental tour duties and National Express work.

They were withdrawn at around the same time SWT was bought by its management team in 1987 as part of the break-up of the National Bus Company instigated by the Conservative government of the day.

Willowbrook bodied dual purpose, AEC Reliance PWN 975G, delivered new in 1969.

Youngster kept an eye on the six-wheelers

Born in wartime Swansea, Royston Morgan lived in Gwynedd Avenue until he was eight, and vividly remembers the six-wheel AEC Renown saloons that ran on the 12 Route from Dynevor Place on the 11 minute climb to the terminus near where he lived.

"My father would take me to see these magnificent Brush bodied buses turning ready for the return journey — a minute shorter because it was downhill!

"My grandparents lived near the church at the top of Townhill Road and there was a bus stop outside their front window at which the Gwynedd Avenue 12 and Mayhill 12 buses stopped. I spent hours in that window watching the Renowns every 11 minutes or so.

"In 1949 my grandmother told me that the Townhill route was having new buses and took me on one on their first day in sevice. The new paint and hot brake smell after decending Townhill remains with me 64 years on! These buses were AEC 34-seat, Willowbrook bodied Regals with pre-selector gearboxes and blue seats and a special tapered rear end to avoid damage on kerbs when drivers reversed.

"My other grandad lived near Russell Street and I'd walk to the Brunswick Street garage and peer through the crack in the huge red wooden sliding doors at the array of red and cream buses inside.

"I remember having a lucky escape when the brakes failed on an AEC Regent double decker No 271 DWN (648) on the 40 route from Townhill towards Sketty Cross. The driver managed to stop using the handbrake, but not before demolishing a keep left sign and part of a wall."

Royston's family moved from Swansea in 1950, but he maintained his interest in SWT keeping up with developments thanks to Ernest Charles Hill, the newly appointed traffic manager at SWT and a friend of his dad. His parents retired back to Swansea in 1970, a time when he forged friendships with people such as Peter Wood the chief engineer and Gareth Davies the signwriter and foreman of the paintshop at Ravenhill.

Having lived in the Midlands since 1958 Royston also used to visit the Willowbrook factory in Loughborough to watch many SWT buses being built.

A lifetime's knowledge of SWT has seen him involved in most of the scale models of the company's buses produced by Corgi and EFE sometimes even producing a hand decorated sample for them to copy.

services, including that up and down Mount Pleasant hill to Townhill.

In contrast, in 1935 SWT took six of what were described as the revolutionary, side-engine AEC Q type bus, five new with bodywork by Brush and one ex-demonstrator bodied by Weymann. They could seat 39 passengers and were also used on the Townhill service. They lasted until 1949, but perhaps were just too revolutionary for SWT which did not buy any more.

The company was dominated by AEC Regents and AEC Reliances from the 1940s through to 1970, but in 1969 it bought three examples of the AEC Swift which were unusual in that they had front and centre exits. The engine was at the rear and this enabled the front portion of the bus to be at a lower level.

The Swifts were the first SWT single deck vehicles to have the new-style bright red livery with cream flashes below the front and rear windows. More were to have followed, but in the financial crisis that hit the company around 1970 all went instead to London Country, including the 1969 buses.

Many different types of vehicle entered the fleet from 1971 when SWT took over N&C, Thomas Bros and United Welsh. These included Leyland Tiger Cubs from Thomas Bros and Bristol Lodekkas, LSs, MWs and RELLs from United Welsh. SWT took over the Haverfordwest and Neath Abbey depots of Western Welsh in 1972 and this introduced more Leyland Tiger Cubs to the fleet. There were also four Leyland Atlanteans bodied by Northern Counties used on the Haverfordwest to Milford Haven route, SWT's first double deck vehicles to be used on one-person-operated services. They were not SWT's first Atlanteans, in 1970 the company had swapped 13 of them, bodied by MCW or Weymann, for nine Willowbrook bodied AEC Regent Vs with the City of Oxford bus company. The Atlanteans had been acquired in the takeover of the J James fleet in 1962.

The 1970s was a time of uniformity with Leyland Nationals and Bristol VRTs dominating the fleet, but in 1985 SWT took some Leyland Olympian double deckers.

This Bedford YRQ was delivered new to SWT in 1973 and used on the service from Haverfordwest to Swansea.
Royston Morgan Collection

A gathering of AEC Regents at the Quadrant bus station Swansea the day after they ended service breaking a link that had endured for more than half a century. The last ever SWT Regent journey in revenue earning service was made on February 27, 1982. It was the 10.25pm Craig-Cefn-Parc to Quadrant bus station service 5 worked by driver Hugh Jones and conductor Paul Leharne. Their rostered evening shift VRT failed and was replaced by Regent 889 GWN 867E. *Stephen Miles*

Driver Peter Nedin and conductor Mike Dunby at Pennard Cliffs, Gower, with the Regent V they crewed on a special running day to salute the end of the Regent era. *Stephen Miles*

Many National Bus Company subsidiaries had similar machines but SWT's were unusual in that they had Cummins engines and were bought by West Glamorgan County Council as part of its transport grant budget. There were only seven, but it seemed as if there were more as SWT used them on a variety of routes, including the X5 from Swansea to Neath and Min-yr-Awel or Hirwaun. One of them deputised on the Shuttle motorway service between Swansea and Cardiff which was served by two magnificent Leyland Olympian coaches bought by SWT from sister company, Thamesway, in 1991. The 1985 Olympians were the last double deckers to enter service from new with SWT.

Minibuses were to the fore in the second half of the 1980s and Dennis Darts started to become the standard bus from 1994. But that year SWT also bought 10 Dennis Lances with Plaxton Verde single deck bodies. The company was part of Badgerline at the time and the Lances were that group's standard vehicle. SWT's were used on fast inter-urban routes branded Timecutter, running from Swansea to Neath.

Rival Leylands gave sterling service

SWT may be best remembered for the large number of Regents it acquired between 1932 and 1967, but in the late 1930s it also amassed a large number of double deck buses engined by AEC's great rival, Leyland.

They would give sterling service during the war years and many lasted into the 1950s. The first six, Leyland TD4s with low height bodywork seating 59 passengers, arrived in 1936, but the main bulk came in 1938 with more following in 1939. They were all Leyland TD5s which, with their Weymann bodies, looked similar to the TD4s. There were 36 in the first 1938 batch and 25 more in the second. Another 25 identical buses arrived in 1939 and the last of this batch would not be withdrawn until 1955. They also had low height bodies but with seats for 53 passengers. SWT made them work hard, the TD5s were sent on the Swansea to Brecon

A single deck Bedford Lex Maxeta alongside the former Oxford Street School, Swansea, 1983. These short vehicles were bought to replace AEC Regent Vs on the Swansea to Pennard service with its tight Plough Corner turn at Murton.
Royston Morgan Collection

route, a two-and-a-half hour marathon journey over the Brecon Beacons, and on the company's routes in Gower. They also saw service on the tough Carmarthen to Llanelli semi-rural route and were familiar performers on Swansea's town journeys. Despite this, SWT switched its allegiance to AEC after the Second World War and took no more new Leylands until three single deck Leyland Leopards joined the fleet in 1963. These had been ordered by J James of Ammanford which SWT absorbed in 1962.

Regals were quiet and smoother

Most of SWT's buses were double deckers but the company also took a fair number of single deck buses for more lightly used services or on routes better suited to smaller vehicles.

There was a variety of types in the 1930s but after the war SWT settled on the AEC Regal, both for bus and coach work.

The first Regals joined the fleet in 1933. They were 10 luxury saloons with bodywork by Weymann and coach seats for 28 passengers. They had petrol engines which aided quieter and smoother running, and all of them were called up for service with the Royal Air Force in July 1940 with no fewer than six being destroyed by enemy action.

In 1936, SWT took eight Regal IIs with Brush bodywork and seats for 39 passengers and these were the last until a large number of the Regal III model arrived in 1949. There were 48, 34-seat buses, most with bodywork by Willowbrook, and three coaches with 30 seats and Windover bodies. SWT took another nine Regal IIIs with bodywork by Willowbrook in 1950 and 17 coaches, three of them for use on Continental tours. Some of the buses were specially adapted for the Townhill route and the last were withdrawn in 1961.

The final Regals for SWT were four coaches which joined the fleet in 1953 and 1954. They were Regal IVs with bodies by Windover. They had luxury seating for 35 passengers and were SWT's first underfloor-engined models. One was exhibited at the 1952 Commercial Motor Show, but its bodywork was controversial, either loved or hated. They lasted until 1961-2 but in the meantime AEC had produced the Reliance, a lighter-weight model, and SWT had the bus of its dreams.

Trade union officials who represented SWT staff at a presentation evening. Among them are Bob Ley, fleet chairman; Lyn James and Frank Watts.

Problems caused delivery delays

Industrial problems, economic difficulties and the effect of the three-day week caused severe delays in the delivery of new buses to SWT in the first half of the 1970s.

But it had an ageing fleet that desperately needed renewing and, like only a small number of other National Bus companies, it turned to Bedford and Ford to help out.

While there were long delays with VRT and Leyland National orders, new Bedfords and Fords could generally be delivered within six months. So in 1973 SWT ordered 35 Ford R1014s with Willowbrook 001 bodies and these arrived over the course of the first eight months or so of 1974. They had 45 seats and were intended for more lightly used services, such as the Gower and West Wales rural routes. Their expected lifespan was seven years. In the meantime SWT also ordered nine Bedford YRQ and three Bedford YRT coaches with Willowbrook 002 Expressway bodywork for use on the fast Swansea to Cardiff and Carmarthen to Cardiff services. They were the first Bedfords ever ordered by SWT and would be the only 002s delivered to the National Bus Company. They had box-like bodies with huge windows. When they started off it sounded as if their wheels were skidding on grease.

Heavy delays to vehicle deliveries continued into 1976 so SWT ordered 17 more Ford R1014s with 43-seat Duple Dominant bodies in 1976. Many of these ended up in the Port Talbot area where they were used on routes around the Afan Valley. In 1980, by which time the early Willowbrook buses were being withdrawn, SWT ordered 18 Bedford YRQ vehicles, again with Duple Dominant bodies. Some had coach seats for 45 passengers, the others were 43-seat buses.

The last Bedfords ordered came in 1982 and were strange looking machines with Lex Maxeta bodies to seat 37. The five were specially shortened YMQ buses which replaced the company's last AEC Regent Vs on the Swansea to Pennard service. This involved a sharp turn near the Plough and Harrow pub in Murton. The YMQs had short lives with SWT once the corner was widened.

The company built up a fleet of 106 Ford and Bedford vehicles. One has returned to Swansea. It is Lex Maxeta, LCY 299X, pictured on the opposite page, which has found a new home at Swansea Bus Museum.

Many roles in long serving buses career

Lyn James wasn't only an SWT driver, he was also branch secretary for the Transport and General Workers'Union for 17 years, was SWT welfare fund treasurer, and chaired the employee committee that ran the staff canteen in Swansea's Quadrant bus station. Lyn had originally joined United Welsh in 1947 as an apprentice fitter at the age of 15.

"The company was still independent then and ran Albions," he said. "It became part of the state-owned Tilling group in 1950 and after I returned from National Service UWS took over the Swan bus company. I went to their garage in Bishopston to work because it ran Daimlers with pre-select gear boxes which I had been taught to work on while in the army. Unfortunately, I suffered dermatitis because of the oil and I switched to driving, initially temporarily, but continued until I finished in 1992." Lyn's regular route was the 17 from Swansea to Llanmadoc in North Gower, but he also drove the 252 between Swansea and Cardiff. "It used to pass a rehabilitation centre for down and outs in Stormy Down and one day one of them missed the stop. We got to Pyle and he demanded to be taken back to Stormy Down. One of the other passengers came to my aid and simply booted him off the bus so we could continue on our way."

In the early days he remembers on one occasion getting a surprise passenger. "It was in Gowerton and a mother handed my conductor, Howell Morgan, her small baby to hold, saying she had to return home because she had forgotten to change out of her slippers," said Lyn.

Regent Register

South Wales Transport took delivery of a total of 515 Regents. There were 112 of the first model, 38 Regent IIs, 132 Regent IIIs and 216 Regent Vs. Most had bodies by Weymann, but towards the end Willowbrook became popular while a few had Park Royal bodies. SWT also received nine Willowbrook Regent Vs in 1970 from City of Oxford Motor Services. The company also had eight unique, specially built, ultra low, single deck Roe bodied Regent Vs for low bridge routes in the Llanelli area.

A 1963 Willowbrook bodied AEC Renown waits for passengers alongside St Mary's Church, Swansea, late 1960s.

A 1961 Park Royal bodied AEC Bridgemaster at Oystermouth bus station. In the background, a Regent V. *Royston Morgan Collection*

Low buses that

Banging your head was a hazard for passengers on SWT buses for many years. The problem was the number of low bridges in its operating area which meant it had to use low-height double deckers on some routes.

A little under a foot lower than conventional height vehicles, these buses were known as lowbridge vehicles while those of normal height were highbridge.

The lowbridge buses had design problems. To prevent the upper platform encroaching too much on the lower, the buses had a right-hand side gangway upstairs with raised, bench-style seats on the left. This caused difficulties for passengers, who often had to clamber over other people to get off the bus, and for the conductor, who had to lean across passengers to collect the fares. The raised position of the seats meant passengers' heads all too often came into contact with the bus roof. Downstairs, the upper gangway dropped down above the right-hand seats and the result was often more sore heads.

It was also crucially important that highbridge buses did not stray accidentally onto lowbridge routes. To help prevent this, in 1958 SWT renumbered its 198 lowbridge buses into a separate series but by then

A Crossley bodied AEC Bridgemaster demonstrator at Windsor Road, Neath alongside the town's railway station forecourt, late 1950s.

an alternative had been found. In 1949, the Bristol manufacturer had come up with the Lodekka. It had a drop-centre rear axle allowing a low gangway on the lower deck which meant the floor of the upper deck could be lowered without penalising the height downstairs. When SWT took over United Welsh Services in 1971 it inherited 74 of these vehicles but in the mid-1950s Bristol models could only be supplied to bus firms in the state sector.

SWT's supplier, AEC, devised its solution in the mid-1950s and came up with an equally clever name, the Bridgemaster. The concept was similar to the Lodekka and the first was exhibited at the 1956 Motor Show.

SWT's first Bridgemasters arrived in 1959, two batches totalling nine rear-entrance buses seating 72 passengers with bodywork by Park Royal. They were followed by six more the following year, this time with forward entrances, and by the third prototype, quite unlike SWT's other examples, a rear entrance Crossley model that was demonstrated to other bus

SWT's first Bridgemaster with strip lighting on the ceiling, in Station Road, Port Talbot, mid-1960s.

caused a headache!

operators around the country before arriving at SWT in 1960. The company took 23 Bridgemasters in total and used them on routes where there were low bridges, including Tycoch and Brynmill to Port Tennant, and from Swansea to Neath or Aberavon Beach. But they were not a success, SWT's parent, British Electric Traction, was not happy with them and only 179 were built between 1957 and 1962.

AEC decided to have another go and produced the Renown, based on a design using a separate chassis. SWT was the first to receive them in 1963, all forward entrance buses to seat 71 passengers with bodywork by Willowbrook or Park Royal. These 19 vehicles were the only Renowns purchased new although SWT inherited another four when it took over Western Welsh's Neath Abbey depot in 1972.

These attractive, and most comfortable 1965 buses, were bodied by Northern Counties and had seats for 67. They were usually found on the Swansea-Morriston-Neath-Porthcawl route and were the last Renowns in SWT service, the 1963 batches all having left the fleet by 1975.

The upstairs of a Lowbridge double decker . . .

. . . and the downstairs

CHAPTER 14

Serving the surrounding towns and countryside

Much of its life may have been centred on the urban hub of Swansea, but South Wales Transport began with a valley route and never forgot that there were passengers to carry out of town. Serving surrounding towns and countryside brought fresh challenges, but, more importantly the company expanded its network of routes and further established a presence throughout south west Wales.

Such expansion was never easy. Llanelli, for example, became one of SWT's most important operating areas — second only to Swansea — but it took nearly 40 years to achieve. The company was running buses to the town soon after its formation in 1914, but the main provider there was Llanelly District Traction which operated trams, then trolleybuses and buses. That was how things stayed until 1952 when SWT bought it out. The move caused a huge row, but it meant that SWT became the most important bus company in Llanelli and remained so until its own demise in 1999.

Back in 1914, things were very different. SWT's second only service, which began in June that year, was from the tram terminus at Cwmbwrla in Swansea to Loughor Bridge. The following month it was extended to Llanelli. The buses used were based in Swansea and SWT used a plot of waste ground in Llanelli to park up vehicles. Any expansion thoughts were put on hold during the First World War, but when hostilities ceased the company turned its attention to the town once more, albeit on a small scale.

In 1921 it opened its first Llanelli garage in Spring Gardens with just three buses, a Leyland, a Belsize and an AEC. There was a staff of three drivers, three conductors, a mechanic and a part-time driver/conductor. They operated just two local routes, one from Llanelli to Pontarddulais, the other to Carmarthen and there were two work shifts for which the conductor received the equivalent of 6p an hour, the driver 7.5p an hour. The first bus left the garage at 4.20 am and the only way the crews get could there by that time was to walk or cycle.

One of the first Llanelli drivers was David Evans, who had completed 45 years with SWT when he retired at the beginning of 1962. David spent his first eight years on the Llanelli to Pontarddulais service and for 10 years was a regular driver on the No. 2 route from Llanelli to Swansea. He recalled that weight restrictions on the old Loughor bridge meant passengers had to get off at one side of the bridge, walk across, and get back on at the other side. The state of the roads was another problem.

G Lumb

Just six inches clearance, but it was enough. This 1963 Roe bodied AEC Regent V was one of just eight built specially for use in Llanelli to cope with the town's low bridges.

A Leyland National on one of the picturesque routes operated by the company's Port Talbot depot in the Afan Valley, June 20, 1982.

"There were many which had ruts so deep that the bus was anchored like an engine to a railway line," said David. "There was no alternative but to drive straight on and hope for the best."

By the mid-1920s Llanelli was growing in importance and bus firms like SWT were playing a major part in that. The town clerk told guests at the annual dinner of Llanelly Chamber of Commerce in April 1925 that on Saturdays alone, 566 bus journeys were being made to and from the town and as many as 60,000 people were being brought by bus to the town every week. It was something that tradespeople had to appreciate and be thankful for, he said.

However SWT was far from being Llanelli's only bus operator, or even its main one. In 1929 there were no fewer than 22 companies running buses around the town and they were providing the company with fierce competition. At this time, SWT had major expansion plans into West Wales from its Llanelli base and if these were to be achieved then it had to tackle the opposition. It was slow to do so, although in the end it was its financial problems and the history and growth of its fellow BET subsidiary, Western Welsh, in West Wales which was the reason that vehicles from the Llanelli garage eventually travelled no further west than Carmarthen.

But SWT still had aspirations for the area and in May 1935 took over JM Bacus of Burry Port and the Gwendraeth Transport Company of Pontyates. This gave it new services between Llanelli, Bryn and Carmarthen. The three-vehicle business of Treharne Brothers of Ponthenri and its route to Llanelli was bought out in July 1936 and the same month saw the more important acquisition of John Brothers of Grovesend in Gorseinon which ran from Llanelli to Neath and Porthcawl.

As the company's growth continued in the second half of the 1930s, Spring Gardens was no longer large enough so in 1938 the company moved to larger premises in Copperworks Road and after the war it opened new offices in Stepney Street. It still remained in the shadow of Llanelly District Traction however, although that was about to change.

Back in 1910, the Electric Light and Traction Company, part of the Balfour Beatty power group, took over Llanelli's trams and the following year converted them from horse-drawn to electricity. The first routes ran from the town centre to Bynea, Felinfoel and Pwll and in 1932 the trams were replaced by trolleybuses and routes extended, including the town centre to Bynea service which ran to the Carmarthenshire boundary at Loughor Bridge. Local transport historian, Geoff Griffiths, recalled the changeover: "The trolleys were a vast improvement on the trams, being quiet, smooth, comfortably upholstered in hide, well lit, frequent and cheap, so quiet in fact that workers on early shifts complained that the loss of the rattle of the

159

trams caused them to oversleep. I well remember them being loaded to bursting point, sometimes the conductor was unable to get round to collect the fares, or see when people were boarding or alighting. The hub of the system was the railway station where many people interchanged between road and rail and also served many who worked south of the railway where low bridges precluded the running of trolleybuses. Regular passengers were known, often personally, and looked out for at their stops, and in those days they were virtually at every street corner."

Trolleybuses, of course, are less flexible than buses because they have to follow overhead electric lines and in 1936 single deck motor buses were added to the fleet to get to places not accessible by the trolleys. Major changes followed the Second World

1952 Regent III Weymann HWN 846 fleet No 423 was ordered by Llanelly District Traction, but delivered direct to SWT and withdrawn in 1965.

War when the Government nationalised the electricity industry and created the British Electric Authority whose subsidiary, the South Wales Electricity Board, saw its function as providing electricity, not running public transport. On March 22, 1952, it sold Llanelly District Traction Company to SWT. When the announcement of this was made it was greeted with anger by many in the town. Llanelli's mayor claimed that the £50,000 price tag meant SWT had purchased the undertaking 'for a song' and hit out at the BEA for not offering it to the council which, he said, would gladly have paid the price to run its own transport service. "Yet the BEA, which operates under nationalisation, has allowed it to go to private enterprise," he stormed.

It was a highly unusual move at the time, for while many transport concerns were being nationalised this was probably the only example of one being de-nationalised, that is sold by the nationalised area electricity board to SWT, part of a private bus group. More controversy followed for SWT lost no time in announcing that it wanted to abandon the 27 trolleybuses and replace them with motor buses. But this needed an Act of Parliament which was objected to by Llanelly Corporation and also Carmarthen County Council which wanted to retain its right to take over the system if it chose. In the end Parliament agreed to extinguish the county council's power, but gave the corporation the option to purchase the bus services in 1972, although that was never taken up.

Just eight months after taking over Llanelly District Traction, in November 1952, buses replaced the trolleybuses and again many townspeople were not happy because the fares went up. The traction company had based its

A trolleybus typical of those used by Llanelly District Traction until SWT took it over. *Chris Taylor Archive*

Chris Taylor Archive

Llanelli's Robinson Street depot at the very end of its trolley bus days, 1952.

South Wales Transport's depot at Inkerman Street, Llanelli, 1966. It formerly housed the town's long-serving trolley buses.

fares on 1907 scales and were ridiculously low, ranging from a halfpenny single to a maximum 3d single. But SWT's move did not affect patronage. Passenger totals rose as the company increased the level of services provided by its buses compared to that of the trolleybuses. The number of vehicles it needed to run the town's routes rose and it now had two Llanelli garages. It still had Copperworks Road, from where it ran rural routes, and it also took over Llanelly District Traction's larger depot in Robinson Street which provided buses for the town services. By 1959 SWT had 70 buses in Llanelli running more than two-and-a-half million miles a year. Staff numbers had risen to just over 300 by this time.

Having two garages in the same town was not a satisfactory arrangement. So in 1965 when South Wales Electricity announced it was moving from the offices it had kept alongside Robinson Street garage, a £50,000 project was put into motion to enlarge SWT's Robinson Street depot so that Copperworks Road garage could close. In future vehicles could be housed in one depot and staff would have better working conditions and canteen facilities.

It might have been expected that people living around Copperworks Road garage would have been glad to see the back of it. The noise of bus engines and smell of exhaust fumes from early morning until late at night in a residential area can hardly have been ideal. But that was not the case. Mrs E David of nearby George Street wrote to SWT in the summer of 1966 saying how sorry she was to see the company leaving Copperworks Road.

"I am sure that I speak for the majority of the neighbours when I say how we have appreciated the kindness of the personnel of the garage," she wrote. "They have always been ready to help anyone in trouble and have always been most courteous and friendly at all times. Our loss, I am sure, will be the gain of the new neighbourhood. Good luck to them all!"

The changes went ahead and in 1966 SWT had a vastly improved Llanelli base. It meant buses entered the depot in Robinson Street and exited in Inkerman Street where new offices were located, so the garage's postal address changed to Inkerman Street. New canteen facilities included a billiard table, draughts, dominoes and darts for staff on work breaks.

The buses running on town routes during the 1950s and 1960s included the SWT staple vehicles for the time, AEC Regent III and Regent V double deckers and single deck AEC Reliances in the traditional maroon livery. In the 1970s they gave way to Leyland Nationals, Bristol VRTs and Fords in poppy red National Bus Company livery. Llanelli was not immune to the decline in passenger numbers and the company's financial woes of the 1970s and vehicle totals and services were reduced during this time. The depot was hard hit by the closure of local pits at the end of the 1984-85 miners' strike. Not only were National Coal Board colliery contracts

One of Llanelli's successful Sosban Link minibuses.
Stephen Miles

A unique mix of diesel, dirt and disinfectant

It seems that women on the buses weren't part of the plan when designs were drawn up for the South Wales Transport company's depot at Eastland Road, Neath.

John Southard remembers that when he was a youngster in the 1950s both his mother and aunt worked there, mother as an office cleaner and aunt Vi in the canteen.

"We lived in London Road at the time. At the back of our house stood the busy South Wales garage. There was no women's toilet there so often the conductresses would use our outside toilet," he recalled.

"In front of the house was a bus stop with a shelter and I clearly remember men waiting here for the double deckers that would carry them to the night shift at the Abbey works, Port Talbot and also late night revellers singing at the top of their voices as they waited for the last bus.

"Sometimes I would be allowed to go into the garage, often picking up used tickets or ringing the bell on the double deckers. The building had a smell all of its own, a strange mix of cigarettes, diesel, dirt and disinfectant. But unforgettable all the same.

"There was always something going on there. Buses would be cleaned at the end of their daily duties; there were maintenance pits where mechanics would attend to repairs, particularly on a Sunday when there were fewer buses on the roads.

"At Christmas my mother, along with many of the wives of staff, would prepare food for the children's party. It was held in the nearby British Legion club. One of the drivers would play Father Christmas and be hauled along on a large wooden sleigh. We'd all have a photo taken with him after being presented with a brown paper Brooke Bond tea carrier bag containing a gift.

ended, but there was less money in the local economy and fewer passengers.

Then in 1985 salvation appeared to dawn in the shape of the minibus. SWT was hooked and started to replace big buses in its fleet with 20 seaters running at more frequent intervals in a bright, two-tone green livery with yellow and red stripes. More convenient services and more friendly minibuses would bring people back to public transport, the company hoped. The age of the minibus dawned in Llanelli on September 1, 1986, when the first services were converted. There was a major publicity drive and a competition was held in conjunction with local schools to come up with a new name for the minibuses. It materialised as Sosban Link and all small vehicles based in Llanelli carried this name.

By 1989, when SWT celebrated its 75th anniversary, there were just five large SWT buses based in Llanelli, four coaches and one Leyland National. The rest of the depot's allocation, 37 vehicles, were minibuses seating between 19 and 25 passengers. They ran on local town routes and on the Swansea-Gorseinon-Llanelli service, SWT's original route in Llanelli. As the 1990s dawned, SWT, like other operators, was looking for rather more sophisticated vehicles and the Dennis Dart came along just at the right time. The company still called them minibuses although they were not that much smaller than the full size AEC Reliance single deckers it had taken in the 1950s.

Sliced up buses solved a problem

Two of the oddest looking buses ever operated by South Wales Transport made their appearance in Llanelli during the summer of 1959.

They looked like the standard AEC Regent V double decker that the company was taking at the time but they seemed to have been sliced in half!

Eastland Road depot, Neath, mid-1950s.

A line up of ultra low build Regents at the Inkerman Street depot, Llanelli, March 30, 1972. SWT had eight of these vehicles and was the only company in the UK operating single deck Regents. *Stephen Miles*

The two newcomers were followed four years later by six almost identical buses and the eight were destined to be unique. SWT bought them to solve a low bridge problem in the New Dock area of Llanelli. Some of these bridges were just 9ft high and this meant that traditional single deckers could not get under. What was needed was something even lower.

So SWT got together with AEC to see if a solution could be found. They came up with the idea of putting together a traditional standard Regent V double deck chassis with a specially designed low-height single deck body produced by bodybuilder Roe of Leeds.

In July 1959 the first two, TCY 101 and TCY 102, with fleet numbers 33 and 34, entered service on the L7 and L8 routes from Penyfan to Morfa and Machynys. They replaced two low-height single deck AEC Regals that Llanelly District Traction had been using on the routes since 1947 and in 1963 were followed by six more, 279-284 DWN, with fleet numbers 35-40. They succeeded six 1950 AEC Regal III's that Llanelly District Traction had also been using on the L7 and L8.

Low they might have been but they only made it under the dock bridges with inches to spare. They also had a light body weight which meant they could achieve some speed, although passengers were unlikely to have appreciated this as their chassis was designed to take the weight of a double deck body but being single deck would have given an uncomfortable ride over rough roads and level crossings.

Another problem was that they were traditional half-cabs, which meant the driver sat in isolation in his cab with a conductor collecting the fares. With only 37 seats, this was not economical and in 1967, number 37 was converted to one person operation as an experiment. The trade unions were not happy however and the idea was eventually abandoned. SWT had tried

to find a solution to the capacity problem on the New Dock routes many years earlier when it experimented with two buses carrying a large number of standing passengers. Two Regals, dating from 1938, with seating for 35, were adapted in 1952 to carry 22 or 23 standing passengers by the removal of six of the seats. It can hardly have been a pleasant ride and both buses were withdrawn in 1956. In the end the problem resolved itself when the services were re-routed or the low bridges removed and this saw the demise of the eight Roe vehicles in Llanelli with some transferred to SWT's other depots, but all had been withdrawn by 1972.

Of the eight, only one has survived, 282 DWN, fleet number 38, and this made a return to Swansea in time for SWT's 75th anniversary celebrations in 1989. It was stored by the National Museum of Wales for a number of years, but found a new home at Swansea Bus Museum where it has been restored.

Neath depot solved a growing problem

SWT ran buses in Neath and Port Talbot from its earliest days. The company's third service started on August 25, 1914, operating from Morriston to Neath, Port Talbot and Taibach.

Once again however, as with Llanelli, it would be many years before SWT became the principal operator in either town. In Port Talbot after the First World War there was a myriad of small operators, all engaged in cut throat competition, while in Neath the town's passenger services were in the none too reliable hands of unique gas trams.

Only three tramway systems in Britain chose to use gas power and of these, Lytham St Anne's and Trafford Park

A driver and his 1954 Weymann bodied AEC Regent III with its new look, enclosed radiator grill, outside the Eastland Road, Neath garage, 1958.

in Manchester had given up the struggle by 1903. This left three unwanted gas trams and Neath Corporation snatched them for the system it had built in 1899. It ran for about four miles from Villiers Street in Briton Ferry, through Neath town centre, to Skewen, and the fare was 1d a mile. It would not be an exaggeration to say it was a bit of a farce. The rails were in such poor condition that there were frequent derailments and the system was totally overcrowded, sometimes as many as 100 people crammed onto a single tram. It was hopelessly slow and underpowered, often the passengers were asked to push the tram up inclines.

Gavin Henry retired as an SWT inspector in 1957 after 38 years with the company and recalled some of the problems: "The trams had no weather protection for the driver. During the winter it was nothing to see the tram trundling along on its own with the driver walking alongside to keep warm and keep his circulation going." From 1902 the system had been run by the Provincial Gas Company which, to no-one's surprise, went bankrupt in 1916. The corporation persevered on

its own until 1920 when it finally admitted defeat and the system was abandoned in favour of SWT's buses.

But running Neath and other eastern area services from its Brunswick Street depot in Swansea was causing the company reliability and administrative problems. So in 1923 SWT arranged to garage vehicles at the former tram depot in London Road, Neath, for which it paid Neath Corporation £200 annual rent. As the number of routes the company operated rose, the depot became too small and in 1933 SWT opened a new one in Eastland Road. However, it was not the only company with its eyes on Neath. The Great Western Railway had been developing local bus routes to act as feeders to its trains while Red & White had been buying up local independent operators. The GWR buses became Western Welsh in 1929 while the Red & White companies were amalgamated as United Welsh Services in 1938. These two companies also opened depots in Neath and SWT had to share the passengers. The number of buses it kept at Eastland Road rose to just over 30 and this is how it remained for many years.

There was expansion however. By 1951 SWT was running buses from Neath to Banwen, Clydach, up the Neath Valley to Pontneathvaughan, and to Llanelli. There were also a number of town services but United Welsh was the larger operator with around 56 vehicles at its Neath depot at this time. Western Welsh and Red & White were also running services from Neath to Aberdare, Merthyr and Porthcawl. SWT had even less of a toe-hold in Port Talbot where services were operated mostly by Thomas Bros and Western Welsh. SWT continued its service to Taibach, which was extended to Swansea and Margam, and had a joint service with Llynfi Motors between Aberavon Beach and Maesteg.

All that changed in 1971 when SWT took over N&C Luxury Coaches, Thomas Bros, and United Welsh. The following year it also took over services run by Western Welsh from its Neath Abbey depot. SWT became the dominant operator in Neath and Port Talbot and its operating area expanded widely. It gained the Thomas Bros. depot in Sandfields and 50 buses but now

A line up of buses at the SWT's Neath Abbey depot, 1982, shortly before its closure.
Colin Scott

Engineering and traffic staff of the Eastland Road, Neath depot with the last vehicle to leave before it closed, February 28, 1971. Inset: Driver Dai Richards and conductor Glyn Jones ready to take the the last bus out.

its Eastland Road garage in Neath was no longer large enough and this closed in early 1971. Bus companies are generally very busy operations, but with SWT it seems there was occasionally room for sentiment such as on the last operational day of the depot. When it opened in 1933 the first vehicle in was driven by a young Dai Richards. Dai was still working there as a shunter in February 1971 when the depot closed. So who better than him to drive the last vehicle out, which is exactly what he did. The honour of accompanying Dai as his conductor was Glyn Jones, at the time the only remaining conductor from the company's previous depot on the site of the town's tram depot in London Road. Initially SWT transferred to the UWS depot but the whole operation in Neath went to Western Welsh's Neath Abbey depot in 1972 which then housed 85 vehicles.

But as elsewhere, the 1970s were tough times for SWT in Neath and Port Talbot. Passenger numbers and revenue fell and action had to be taken to redress the situation. In June 1980, there was a major upheaval of services in both towns with routes in Port Talbot branded as Afanway. Some services were improved, others went and there was a major publicity campaign to promote the new routes. All buses and bus stops in Port Talbot were branded with the Afanway logo, a free newspaper detailing the changes was published, and there was a special display mounted in the Aberafan

Shopping Centre when badges, carrier bags and balloons were given away. Unfortunately the decline continued and in February 1983 there were further cutbacks, although they meant that Port Talbot depot now had an allocation of two Bristol VRTs, the first double deckers at the garage since Thomas Bros's open-top Bristol was withdrawn in 1969.

SWT also closed its Neath depot. Just 15 years previously there had been four main bus depots run by the different companies in the town, but now routes were run from Port Talbot or Pontardawe garages with vehicles kept overnight in Neath's Milland Road. By 1989 the Neath allocation was just one double decker, six single deckers and nine minibuses. Most of SWT's bus services in Neath and Port Talbot were now operated by minibuses and in September 1992 the Port Talbot depot was handed over to SWT's sister company, Brewers, a family-run company that had been taken over in 1988. In April 1998, it was decided to merge Brewers and SWT and Port Talbot depot was back with SWT once more. But this was to be a short-lived reunion, for just 12 months later, SWT was replaced by First Cymru.

Colourful celebrations

Special events and anniversaries offered opportunities for SWT to adorn its vehicles in various liveries. The designation of Swansea as a city was one example where signwriter Gareth Davies was able to show his handiwork. To celebrate the Silver Jubilee of Queen Elizabeth II in 1977, open top Bristol KSW 500 was painted silver while in 1989, to mark the company's 75th anniversary, Bristol VRT open-topper, 931, was painted in former SWT Maroon with a cream band. Some years earlier, in 1984, VRT 939 had assumed a mainly yellow scheme to represent Vanguard Motor

Services, a pioneer of buses in Gower, to celebrate 75 years of bus operation on the peninsula. In 1982, 984 was painted in red and cream livery and re-numbered 4 to mark the 175th anniversary of the Mumbles Railway. This commemoration may puzzle some as SWT celebrated the 150th anniversary of the railway in 1954, so how could it celebrate the 175th in 1982? The answer is that some celebrate the anniversary of the founding of the railway, 1804, while others the year the first passenger service ran, which was 1807. So in 1982, SWT was commemorating the first passenger train.

Royston Morgan Collection

Royston Morgan Collection

A crowd of hikers prepares to board
a Bristol VRT 984, liveried to
celebrate the 175th anniversary of
the Mumbles Railway in 1982.
Royston Morgan Collection

Chapter 15

Motorway meant faster and further express trips

It had been a long time coming, but finally the M4 between Swansea and Cardiff was complete. The so-called 'missing link' between Pencoed and Pyle opened on Friday, September 18, 1981, and the following day in heavy rain South Wales Transport started a marathon express coach service from Haverfordwest right through to Bristol.

Branded ExpressWest, it provided the fastest ever journey times by bus between West Wales and Bristol. East from Swansea, the route took in Port Talbot, Cardiff, Newport and Bristol; west it split into three sections, one to Llanelli, which was numbered the X10, a second to Carmarthen and Haverfordwest, the X11, and the third to Carmarthen and Haverfordwest via Tenby and Pembroke which was the X12. They were later renumbered 610, 611 and 612 to fit in with the National Express system.

The service was jointly operated by SWT, National Welsh and Bristol Omnibus, which at the time were all subsidiaries of the National Bus Company.

ExpressWest was extensively advertised, a jingle was devised and played on Swansea Sound, the local radio station, and a new livery devised with ExpressWest lettering along the sides with red and blue stripes tapering towards the back of the vehicle. The drivers wore National Bus Company uniform with a special ExpressWest tie and a badge with the service logo and their name on it.

Services along the M4 in South Wales had started the previous year when SWT and National Welsh began a joint motorway express service between Llanelli, Swansea and Cardiff.

A shortage of coaches meant Llanelli depot sometimes sent Leyland National buses out for the service, much to the consternation of the National Welsh drivers who took over the service at Swansea.

There was at least one occasion when a service didn't run simply because a National Welsh driver had refused to take out the Leyland National vehicle.

ExpressWest came complete with new coaches, although the Willowbrook bodies used were not considered to be the best. But at least they looked the part and were a boost to bus services in West Wales. SWT's service 301 had previously only provided three journeys on weekdays from Haverfordwest to Carmarthen and passengers from there had to travel to Swansea via Llanelli, the faster motorway wasn't served, unlike

Stephen Miles

A 1982 Willowbrook bodied Leyland Leopard coach in original white ExpressWest livery at Cardiff that year. It was one of a number which South Wales Transport operated.

One of three 71-seat Plaxton Paramount 4000 double deck coaches used on SWT's Swansea to London National Express Rapide services.

ExpressWest which now ran a two-hourly direct service from Swansea to Carmarthen in just 55 minutes. Between Cardiff and Bristol, ExpressWest replaced another X10 which had been jointly run by National Welsh — from its Aberdare depot — and Bristol Omnibus, every two hours. It had previously been another 301 and was started as a fast new link between the two cities in 1966 when the Severn Bridge was opened. As an ExpressWest route it became a more convenient hourly service.

Convenience was not the only bonus however. The service was also remarkably cheap. A single fare for the five-and-a-half hour journey from Haverfordwest to Bristol cost just £2.90 while the single from Cardiff to Bristol, a 75-minute journey, was only £1.50 and £1.75 day return. There was no doubt that the company was providing value for money.

There was an even better bargain though. National Bus Company partners at the time offered Wanderbus day out tickets at just £2.95 and these were valid on the entire ExpressWest route. So you could get on a coach in Swansea, go to Bristol and then even further afield, perhaps Bath, Weston-Super-Mare or Wells, all on the one ticket. Later, the Crosville bus company joined the service when it was extended from Carmarthen to Cardigan and between Aberystwyth and Swansea.

ExpressWest was a boon for commuters looking for cheaper fares and comparable journey times to those offered by British Rail.

Summer was busy on routes to the coastal holiday towns of West Wales, although in winter passenger numbers dwindled. This was one of the problems with ExpressWest as South Wales Transport's former commercial director, Alan Kreppel, recalled:

"When the sun shone in the summer we would need two or three duplicate coaches, but on rainy days in the winter there were very few passengers using the services.

"Another nightmare was that with four operators it was complicated to run with our coaches ending up in different places which we had to retrieve. We ended it finally because the railways improved their West Wales services and there were similar improvements between Cardiff and Bristol."

SWT eventually replaced the Swansea-Cardiff section with a new motorway service called Shuttle while National Express ran from Cardiff to Bristol. The Shuttle service became so popular that to cope with increased demand at peak times the company brought double deck vehicles into use to cope.

But there is no doubt that ExpressWest helped rejuvenate coach services across South and West Wales during the 1980s.

A double deck Leyland Olympian coach named Sir Harry Secombe takes on passengers for Swansea at Cardiff bus station while operating the high speed Shuttle service, **May, 1991.** *Stephen Miles*

End of the coach route monopoly

In October 1980, the Government introduced what it called the most important reform of the bus licensing system for 50 years.

The Transport Act of that year saw the removal of road service licensing requirements from express services, excursions and tours.

National Express no longer had a monopoly on coach routes and a new consortium known as British Coachways was created to run rival services. It included Morris Bros of Swansea which started a competing Swansea to London service with Volvo B58 coaches which were superior vehicles to the Leyland Leopards National Express was running. If it was to compete effectively National Express would have to buck up its ideas and this became SWT's problem. In May 1981, the company took over the Swansea-based operations of National Travel (South West) and 25 coaches, all Leyland Leopards. The move meant that the previous decision to close Brunswick Street garage was shelved and SWT closed Swansea's smaller Clarence Terrace depot instead and transferred its 25-vehicle allocation and the National Travel coaches to Brunswick Street.

The system was that National Express sold the tickets, drew up the timetables and set the service standards while SWT provided the vehicles. Fares were slashed to compete with British Coachways, but it was clear that standards also needed to be raised and the Leopards were simply not good enough. SWT took delivery of the last of them in 1982 and although by then the search had begun for a superior coach, prompt action was needed to see off the British Coachways challenge.

It came in the shape of the Rapide concept which involved faster, more luxurious express services with hostesses or stewards serving food and

A 1979 Duple-Dominant bodied Leyland Leopard in ExpressWest livery shortly after arrival at its Bristol coach station destination, 1987. These vehicles were originally delivered in NBC poppy red and white livery.

drinks on board. Swansea was one of the first to get Rapide and the go-ahead was given to start the London service in May 1982. The problem was that there were no suitable coaches available so two were hired from Trathens of Plymouth, both MAN SR280s. By the standards of the time, they were exemplary. Both had 44 reclining seats, were equipped with videos and had toilets and a luxurious interior with full sound insulation. Styling was continental with an angular outline and bonded glazing. It was hoped the new service would appeal to both business people and leisure travellers. A period return costing just £11.50 and valid for three months was introduced while the single fare from Swansea to London was only £6.50. The route, which also served Port Talbot and Bridgend, took just three hours and 35 minutes. It became an instant success and in May 1983 the first new vehicles arrived in the shape of five Leyland Tigers with high-floor Duple Caribbean bodies, seating 46 passengers with similar facilities to the SR280s. Another five identical coaches followed in 1984 and four Duple Caribbean 2 vehicless in 1985.

In plain National livery, 1967 Harrington C37F bodied AEC Reliance YCY296 is seen in 1970 after fleet re-numbering from 1046 to 115.

Days out to London at reasonably priced fares were now possible. In the meantime, British Coachways hit difficulties and its partners started to pull out of the consortium. Morris Bros. withdrew in the summer of 1982 and the whole operation ended the following October. One of the British Coachways B58s has been restored and can be seen at Swansea Bus Museum, together with its Ride the Flag slogan, a blatant rip-off of British Airways' Fly the Flag phrase.

Rapide, which set higher standards than other National Express services, continued until the end of the 1990s when it was re-branded, the name finally disappearing in 2000 and replaced by GoByCoach.com.

A 1982 Willowbrook bodied Leyland Leopard in later ExpressWest livery 1987.
Royston Morgan Collection

Holiday trip led to a summer as a bus conductor

In the summer of 1952 Geoff Clifford had an unexpected, albeit brief, opportunity to discover exactly what the role of a bus conductor with South Wales Transport involved.

"We were living in Liverpool and I was a student in Manchester," recalled Geoff. "My parents, brother Peter and I had enjoyed a couple of weeks staying with Jack and Theresa Hodge in Mumbles, which we knew well having lived there from 1930 to 1938. Jack worked for SWT and just before we were due to return home, I mentioned that I would have to find a job for the remainder of the summer. He said that South Wales were taking on students, suggested I apply and invited me to stay on with him and his wife which I did.

"After 10 days training I joined the ranks of students disguised as bus conductors. Being turned loose on unfamiliar routes tested my shaky mathematics — and the patience of some passengers. It was quite an ordeal to begin with, but even if practice didn't make exactly perfect, it made the job enjoyable. Working days started at varying times from the bus garage at Brunswick Street. An early start meant catching the 4.15am 'convoy' from The Square in Mumbles. I had to do this on several occasions in order to take the 5.00am bus to Port Talbot steelworks. At least I didn't have to sprain my brain on this trip as all the workers had passes which, most of them assumed I wouldn't even bother to look at. They were surprised when I yelled 'Passes please' prompting them to scrabble hastily through their pockets.

"Trips up to Townhill and Mayhill were brief and I did many. Buses crawled up these hills and cascaded down again. The experience was not unlike being a conductor on a funfair helter skelter. My 'conductoring' in Swansea was not intended as work experience, but simply as a way of earning cash. Along the way though, I met many interesting and friendly people and thoroughly enjoyed myself."

A coach bodied Bristol RELL on National Express duties.

Shuttling along to effortless success

One of SWT's success stories of the late 1980s and early 1990s was its Shuttle express service which quickly and effortlessly connected Swansea and Cardiff along the M4.

Demand was so high that there were capacity problems at peak times so in 1991 the company cast around for a solution.

Around this time SWT's sister company in the Badgerline group, Thamesway, was using double deck Leyland Olympian coaches on its busy London to Southend services and SWT borrowed one for evaluation on its Shuttle route.

The 1985 coach with seats for 45 upstairs and 28 on the lower deck proved up to the task and so two of these impressive six-year-old vehicles were bought from Thamesway. They were described at the time as being temperamental vehicles, but SWT engineers once more showed their skills and transformed them into dependable coaches. They certainly gave a comfortable, smooth ride, even at speed on the M4, and in their eye-catching white with red and green striped livery were a good advertisement for fast coach travel. SWT numbered them 908 and 909. They were also named Dylan Thomas and Sir Harry Secombe respectively. They gave fine service for five years.

Busy day brought a real challenge

Summer days at Swansea's Quadrant bus station were always busy which could sometimes present a challenge like the day the ExpressWest service to Bristol had left full with another 32 passengers on board a duplicate coach.

But there was a major problem — the second vehicle had no driver. It was handy, then, that SWT's traffic manager

A Duple bodied Bedford YMQ in the South Wales NBC local coach livery passes the site of St Thomas station, Swansea and heads east on May 3, 1986. *Stephen Miles*

at the time, Alan Kreppel, was shopping in the city centre and had called round to see how things were going. "I was met by the coaching inspector who told me of the problem and I asked if I could help," Alan recalled.

"It was either drive the coach to Bristol myself or do the inspector's job, I chose to drive."

So to the relief of the waiting passengers it was off to Bristol, although when they arrived there safely they might not have been aware that one of SWT's top managers had been at the wheel. Alan deposited his passengers in Bristol and even picked up a few on the way back, but the day wasn't yet over.

"When I arrived back at the Quadrant bus station in Swansea, I saw the previous ExpressWest service was only just pulling out, so I asked the inspector why it was late," said Alan. "He told me the service had left on time, but just before it got to Loughor Bridge on its way to Llanelli one of the passengers had told the driver those on board could hear a knocking at the back."

Stephen Miles

A 1980 Willowbrook bodied Leyland Leopard negotiates York Street roundabout, Swansea on the 252 service to Llanelli.

Nothing was showing up on the driver's dashboard to indicate a fault, but he stopped the bus, got out and went round the back of the vehicle. He opened the luggage boot and to his horror a man staggered out! Apparently, back at the Quadrant bus station, he had been trying to grab a suitcase right at the back of the boot. Drivers have long handles with hooks to deal with such problems, but this passenger had to get inside the boot to reach the case. As he did so the driver had walked round to the back of the vehicle and seeing no-one there had slammed the

luggage boot door closed with the gentleman still inside! The driver had to bring the coach back to the bus station, but in the meantime the police had been called because it was a complete mystery where the passenger had gone. He was reunited with his anxious wife and two very relieved children.

One of the last three AEC Reliances in SWT service, UCY 182N, in 1986.

This Duple Northern bodied former N&C coach, delivered new in 1966, was in SWT's dual purpose livery and operating the Treorchy to Cymmer route on August 27, 1974. *Stephen Miles*

SWT's high-level route linking two valleys was one of the most spectacular in the country but suffered a significant problem — it attracted very few passengers.

The route that no one wanted

The 246 service linked the Afan Valley north of Port Talbot with the Rhondda Valley on the other side of the Bwlch mountain and those who used it were rewarded with incredible scenic views. It wasn't a traditional bus route. Buses had replaced the railway which once connected the two valleys via the Blaenrhondda tunnel, the longest solely in Wales at 3,443 yards.

The tunnel, which opened in 1890, was costly to maintain and it closed in 1968 on safety grounds, initially temporarily, but it never re-opened and the buses became permanent.

Originally N&C Luxury Coaches ran this replacement service from Cymmer over the Bwlch Mountain to Blaenrhondda. Railway guards became conductors on the buses, though they probably had an easy life given the limited number of passengers.

The railway service that the buses were linked to closed on June 20,

1970 and with it went the replacement service. It was at this point that SWT began a five return journey a day service funded by Glamorgan County Council that became its only route into the Rhondda Valley.

Astonishingly, given the demand, a two-hourly Monday to Saturday service was provided from Cymmer to Treorchy. The 1971 timetable shows the first journey at 6.45 am from Cymmer and the last at 9.15pm. Buses left Treorchy at 7.25am until 10pm.

The journey through the tunnel by train took six minutes, the bus route over the mountain to Treorchy took 30 minutes.

It soon became clear that this level of service was far too high. Buses were often running almost empty over the mountain, so by 1973 the timetable had been reduced to just three journeys each day on weekdays. These left Treorchy at

9.45am, 11.45 am and 6.45pm and Cymmer at 8.45am, 10.45am and 6pm. In a bid to increase passenger numbers, connecting services to Port Talbot and Maesteg were timetabled which also had a timing point at the top of the Bwlch Mountain. It is highly unlikely though, that many passengers were either set down or picked up at this spot. It is miles from anywhere although there is often an ice cream van there in summer as motorists stop to take in the dramatic views.

Even this level of service was too high, and by the end of the 1970s it was down to just two journeys on Saturdays only, extended to Port Talbot and Swansea and renumbered 226.

The first of these left Port Talbot at 9.05am and reached Treorchy at 10.10am and left at 10.20am for Swansea. The return from Swansea was at 4.50pm and this arrived at Treorchy at 6.20pm with the return

Driver John Hughes turns NCY 885 at Cymmer station in 1968 while on British Rail service, Cymmer to Treherbert.

John Hughes, right, with a railway guard at Treherbert station, having just arrived on the route from Cymmer.

to Port Talbot at 6.35pm. All four journeys had connections at Treorchy for rail services to Cardiff.

"Some Saturday afternoons saw me catching the 4.50 pm service from Swansea over to the Rhondda," recalls Return Ticket author Jonathan Isaacs.

"I was regularly the only Swansea passenger on the bus, one of the Ford Duple 43-seaters based at Port Talbot.

"The drivers would look at me in astonishment as if I was an endangered species, which on this route I suppose I was. Yet 52-seater Leyland Nationals heading from Swansea for Port Talbot at the same time were packed, so perhaps lack of publicity might have been one of the problems with the 226.

"A dozen or so passengers would join me at Port Talbot and from there we'd enjoy a ride through one of the most delightful of the South Wales valleys. The Afan Valley thoroughly deserves its nickname of Little Switzerland.

"From Blaengwynfi I would be the sole passenger once more. The driver would often turn around in his cab and with a smile say: 'It's just you and me then.' To which I

would answer: 'Looks like. I'll stay on if you will!' Then we were off, climbing the steep streets of Abergwynfi and then up the long, winding road to the top of the Bwlch, the Ford's engine making such a clamour I wondered if we would make it. We always did and as we completed the final bend on the journey up, there was just time to take a last look at the Afan Valley and then we were on the highest point with views all round. To the north east, the Brecon Beacons; to the east, the lower hills that shelter the South Wales valleys; to the south, the Vale of Glamorgan, the giant chimney at Aberthaw power station a prominent landmark.

"If the day was particularly clear, the Bristol Channel and the coast of Devon could also be seen. This was in summer, of course!

"The winter was very different and I remember returning home to the Rhondda on the 226 after a heavy

snowfall. As the bus climbed the Bwlch in the dark, it seemed as if we were travelling through a tunnel of snow and ice.

"At the junction for Nantymoel we would begin our long descent into the Rhondda, with the long ribbons of terraced houses that make up Cwmparc, visible on the left and soon we'd cross the bridge into the village and pass the first buildings since we left Abergwynfi 25 minutes earlier.

"From here it was just a minute's ride to our destination, the Parc and Dare Hall in Treorchy, home to one of the most famous male voice choirs in the world.

"There would be around half-a-dozen people waiting for the return trip. They had probably come over on that morning's journey, perhaps to visit friends or relatives. The service ended in the mid-1980s and with it, the only direct link between the two valleys."

CHAPTER 16

Liveries, crashes and keeping the legend alive

South Wales Transport had a range of liveries during its 85 year history and while some were more successful than others, all were memorable. For people of a certain age, it will be of buses painted in a distinguished maroon livery that will strike a nostalgic chord. The slightly younger will remember the brighter poppy red vehicles of the 1970s, while for those younger still it will surely be the two-tone green minibuses of the 1980s.

At the very beginning SWT buses were green, although some of the older employees remembered them as green and cream. As little is known about these early vehicles, perhaps they appeared with different applications but in 1920 the company fitted in with general British Electric Traction policy and started to paint its buses in a mainly red livery. This was to become known as the BET livery, although it appeared in different shades. The livery of SWT's sister company, Rhondda Transport, for example, always seemed a little brighter than SWT's rather sombre maroon with ivory stripes, while Western Welsh's seemed brighter again.

In 1920 SWT's official livery was red below a black waist band, black mudguards, cream windows and roof, all with detailed lining out. A large underlined, South Wales fleet name, was carried on both sides.

When SWT's first Regents were delivered in 1932, they carried a much darker red livery with two cream bands — one below the top deck windows, the other below the lower deck windows — and had cream roofs. The fleet name carried on the sides became smaller but with the words Transport Co Ltd. inserted between the line and South Wales. When the 1937 Weymann Regents arrived to replace Swansea's trams, they were in similar livery but as they were owned by SWT's sister company, the Swansea and Improvements Tramway Company, they only had South Wales fleet names, also underlined. After the war, the band around the top deck was dropped and all buses carried South Wales underlined fleet names. Saloons carried the band around the sides under the windows.

Then in 1958, SWT's first forward entrance Regent Vs arrived and they came without any bands and single deckers lost theirs as well, which didn't help their appearance. Now the fleet livery was a rather dull all-over maroon, although the company plastered its double deckers with advertisements which brightened them up. Beer advertisements seem to have been popular, particularly for the local brewers, Felinfoel and Buckleys. One Regent V, 11 BWN, fleet number 571,

A 1953 Weymann bodied AEC Regent III alongside St Mary's Church, late 1950s. The colour differs from the usual maroon. The paint company advert is coincidental!

A 1962 Willowbrook bodied AEC Regent V at Ravenhill, September 1970 in the company's traditional maroon livery without a cream band.

a Willowbrook example of 1962, was repainted 10 years later to resemble a country pub as an overall advertisement for Truman's Beers. It was most unusual for SWT Regents to receive non-standard liveries, unlike the later Bristol VRTs which started replacing them in the fleet from 1977.

One other Regent V to receive a notable non-standard livery was another Willowbrook, 434 HCY, fleet number 601, which SWT painted green and white embellished with red dragons in December 1969 to commemorate Swansea being accorded city status. Wales Gas at this time was painting its service fleet in similar colours and they carried the Welsh word for gas on their sides, Nwy. So 601 became known as Newey. It stayed in this livery until July 1970 and interestingly the colours were also similar to Swansea City Council's dustcarts and other vehicles. If the council had gone ahead with its proposal to take over SWT's Swansea fleet in 1957, all the city's buses might have been in a similar livery.

The 1960s were a time of pastel colours and SWT began to experiment with brighter liveries. One double decker, 437 HCY, fleet number 604, received white window surrounds on its BET livery; CCY 985C, fleet number 615, was repainted cherry red with a white band, red wings and old style fleet name, while GWN 858D, fleet number 630, got a bright red scheme with

a white band between the decks and black wings with the fleet name South Wales in upper and lower case letters in blue appearing in the band towards the front sides of the vehicle.

But it was 439 HCY, fleet number 606, another Willowbrook example of 1964, which became the first double decker to be repainted in the livery that was eventually adopted as standard. It appeared in September 1968 in bright red and cream with a South Wales fleet name in sloping capital letters lined in blue. It was to be short-lived for in 1972, SWT's new parent, the National Bus Company, ruled that all buses should be in poppy red or leaf green livery while coaches had to be in all-over white.

This decision meant it was farewell to SWT's local coach livery, which was a splendid ivory and red with Gothic-style fleet names during the 1950s and 1960s until in 1968 when SWT took control of United Welsh Services and changed it to cream and light red with an SWT fleet name on an all-red arrow.

From 1971, SWT buses were on the road in a myriad of colours. The company took over N&C Luxury Coaches with their unusual chocolate brown and deep red livery, UWS with orangey-red, not unlike NBC colours, the turquoise and cream fleet of Thomas Bros, and in 1972, the red bus, and blue and ivory coach fleet of Western Welsh with its depots at Haverfordwest and Neath Abbey. With SWT's old maroon colours and its newer bright red and cream livery, the fleet was a hotch potch of colour until everything could be repainted poppy red. From 1972, SWT buses were repainted all-over poppy red with a white stripe, the single deckers with coach seats were red below the waist, white on top, while coaches were all-over white with large National fleet names in blue and red on the sides with small South Wales fleet names above the wheel arches on the front. It was all about shouting out NBC's identity, although the South Wales fleet name continued to appear on the sides of SWT's buses and in 1978, when the campaign for a Welsh language TV channel was at its height, the Welsh equivalent De Cymru began to appear on the offside. Poppy red didn't prove to be a good livery because it started to fade quickly. When it did SWT's buses took on a distinctly orange tinge.

But everything comes to an end, and thankfully the NBC scheme started to disappear by the mid-1980s when Margaret Thatcher's government decreed that the end of NBC was nigh. SWT started painting some of its coaches in a retro white and maroon livery with grey stripes, it was not an eye-catching scheme, to say the least, and happily was also short lived because now NBC was being privatised and SWT was sold to its managers who adopted a new bright livery of lime green (upper) and leaf green (lower) separated by a broad white band

with poppy red and canary yellow stripes.

It first appeared on SWT's earliest mini buses which started to arrive in February 1986 but it was actually designed for conventional buses. SWT invited local design agencies to submit liveries and the winner was Plum Design of Fforestfach which went on to design all SWT's corporate material after the company was bought by the managers. Initially it had been intended to have local fleet names on the sides of vehicles. There was to be a Swansea & District with a Swan logo, Llanelli & District with a rugby player in the appropriate red shirt logo, Milford Haven District with a puffin logo, and Neath, Port Talbot and the Swansea Valley with their individual identities. But as the fleet started to receive huge influxes of mini buses, the names were dropped in favour of City Mini for Swansea, Sosban Link for Llanelli, Mini Link for Gorseinon and Gowerton, Valley Link for the Swansea Valley, Town Mini for Neath and Port Talbot, and Cleddau Mini for Haverfordwest and Milford Haven. Big buses simply received the SWT logo on their sides.

SWT put the new livery on display with the slogan 'Go for Green' and while it may not have been to everyone's taste, it was a vast improvement on what had gone before. The coach version which first

appeared on Duple bodied NCY 476R, fleet number 168, was less effective however, and several alternative schemes were to follow. It certainly suited SWT's Bristol VRTs. The first to receive it was TPE 152S, fleet number 996. It also looked fine on the Leyland Nationals, although the company's habit of placing paper advertisements on the vehicles' sides ruined the effect. The first Leyland National to receive it was JTH 773P, fleet number 773. The livery also looked good on the mini buses and on the Dennis Darts as well when they started to arrive in 1994.

A 1962 Willowbrook bodied Regent V at Gorseinon depot, looking a little weary towards the end of its working life with SWT.
Royston Morgan Collection

Weymann bodied 1952 AEC Regent III HCY 829 in original SWT maroon waits at St Mary's Church, Swansea in the mid-1950s.
Colin Scott

Ordered by Thomas Bros. of Port Talbot, this Willowbrook bodied AEC Reliance is on schools duties shortly after delivery in June 1971. The vehicle is painted in SWT's interim livery before the arrival of poppy red.
Royston Morgan Collection

In 1995, SWT found itself part of First Bus with a new policy as regards liveries. It was decreed that older buses would retain their existing company colours but new buses would appear in a livery for the whole group.

The idea was that passengers seeing one of the new vehicles coming would know they were getting a low-floor bus with plush, corporate interior. Conversely, of course, if they saw a bus in SWT colours pull up at their stop, it would highlight the fact that they were getting an old bus, so the policy did not seem to make an awful lot of sense to anybody outside First.

Then there was that livery. There may have been a few worse liveries than the one chosen by First, but it is perhaps no surprise that it became universally nicknamed Barbie, after the popular toy doll, and was a strange pink and magenta which looked jaded even when newly applied. It was also ruled that the First name would take precedence over the local company fleet name on the sides of buses and later the local name was dropped entirely.

The mistakes of the 1970s, when National Bus Company corporatism saw off familiar, well-loved local liveries, were being repeated, but while 25 years earlier SWT had been allowed to keep its identity, even this was now lost.

In 2013 however, a turnaround in policy saw SWT's successor, First Cymru, put South Wales, or the De Cymru Welsh language equivalent, on the sides of its buses once more. The 'Barbie' livery was also being phased out too and though the replacement may be an improvement, there will still be many who mourn the passing of SWT's maroon and ivory stripe.

Routemaster gave travellers a rare treat

More than a few passengers must have wondered what was going on in the heady summer of 1989 when instead of their usual South Wales Transport vehicle they were greeted by the sight of an AEC Routemaster double decker pulling up at the kerb.

Not only that, but the vehicle, usually only part of the London scene, and generally in a shade of red was liveried in bright blue and orange.

The bus had in fact come a lot further than London to ply its trade in SWT territory for a week. It was one of 22 on the payroll of Strathtay Scottish in Dundee, Scotland and made the trip to South Wales after a brief bus rally stop-over at North Weald.

At the wheel was Sholto Thomas, formerly from Swansea and at the time commercial manager of Strathtay Scottish, part of the Scottish bus group.

"I'm a Swansea boy and had remained in touch with some enthusiasts and former schoolmates from Dynevor School, during my career in Scotland ," said Sholto.

"I was contacted by SWT to see whether we could hire them a Routemaster for their 75th anniversary celebrations. This was agreed and we arranged to meet at the North Weald bus rally near London on June 18, as a party was bringing SWT Olympian 906 to the rally.

"Both buses journeyed to Swansea in convoy the evening after the rally. I had brought the RM down from Dundee with another enthusiast the previous day. It was then used by SWT on various routes in the Swansea and Neath areas during the following week, at the end of which the main anniversary celebrations were held in Margam Park on June 25."

The next day Sholto and his trusty Routemaster headed North back to Dundee and local passengers settled back into their normal routine.

Open toppers had reverse colours

SWT's fleet was a sea of poppy red in the 1970s and almost nothing was allowed to break the mould. But three double deckers arrived in 1977 which were later repainted into what could be called a reverse livery.

They were three Bristol VRTs which were identical to others SWT was taking at the time, apart from one important detail — they had convertible open tops for use on the company's summer services to Mumbles, Langland Bay and Caswell Bay. They were painted white with a red stripe between the decks and while they carried the standard South Wales fleet name, they also carried a brand name — Skyrider. The three were RTH 930S-932S, fleet numbers 930-932, and they joined the only other open-topper in the fleet, the former Eastern National Bristol K, WNO 484, registered 500. Unlike the K, which was a permanent open-top bus, in winter the VRTs had their roofs put back on and were used on normal services. The four were joined in 1984 by an ex-London DMS, KUC 220P, fleet number 864, which received the same Skyrider livery, although only the roof above the upstairs windows was detachable. It was also used on normal services out of the summer season.

Controversy of the Big Red Bus

SWT turned the clock back in the summer of 1996 and the move caused controversy. The majority of its buses were in the two-tone post privatisation green livery but the company decided to paint three Bristol VRTs in old-style red livery with a white stripe between the decks.

It gave them the brand name Big Red Bus and operated them with cheaper fares to the Clase, Penlan and Blaenymaes districts of Swansea. SWT then started to proclaim the benefits of big buses in direct contradiction to its publicity about the benefits of mini buses. It seemed to be a case of having your cake and eating it. But what caused the controversy was the decision to allow passengers to smoke on the upper deck. Health campaigners were appalled by the move and called it a retrograde step.

The dazzlingly liveried Strathtay Scottish Routemaster in Alfred Street, Neath in the company of an SWT Leyland National, 1989.
Stephen Miles

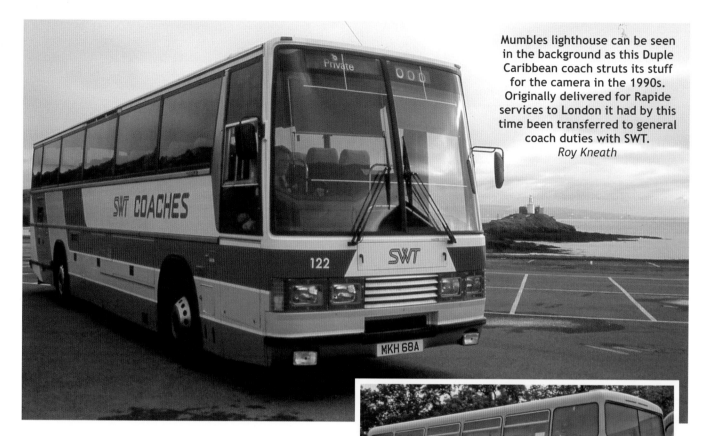

Mumbles lighthouse can be seen in the background as this Duple Caribbean coach struts its stuff for the camera in the 1990s. Originally delivered for Rapide services to London it had by this time been transferred to general coach duties with SWT.
Roy Kneath

Soon after privatisation, SWT had banned smoking entirely on all its buses, one of the first companies in the UK to do so. The Big Red Bus was later withdrawn and the company's no-smoking policy was vigorously enforced.

Accidents kept the bodybuilders busy

Repainting of vehicles is not something restricted to livery changes for any bus company. Periodically bus and coaches will be given a repaint to keep them looking fresh.

Sometimes however accidents, both major and minor can see vehicles hauled into the body and paintshops. Serious accidents involving buses are relatively uncommon, but when they do occur the results can appear spectacular. Fortunately, while the damage to vehicles can be severe, casualties among passengers and crews are rare.

Nearly 40 years separate two of the most serious accidents involving SWT vehicles, and both involved burst tyres. In 1943, a front tyre on a double decker burst causing the bus to career off the road and down a railway embankment

A 1985 Leyland Olympian liveried in SWT's post-privatisation colours. *Royston Morgan Collection*

at Pwll near Llanelli. Four passengers were killed and the widow of one of them received £2,025 damages against the company, which the courts ruled had been negligent in failing to maintain the tyre properly.

The controversial Big Red Bus, 1995.
Royston Morgan Collection

SWT commercial director, Alan Kreppel, remembered the second, which happened on the M4 near Swindon in 1982: "One of our London coaches was coming back to South Wales when the tyre burst on a lorry travelling in the opposite direction. It went out of control and hit the coach, taking out the whole side. Four of the passengers were killed. Some years later we had three incidents involving blow-outs at speed on our Duple Caribbean coaches which were used on the M4 Rapide service, the drivers managed to get on to the hard shoulder. Tyres aren't owned by bus companies, they rent them from the manufacturer, and these accidents resulted in a major investigation."

An SWT recovery team surveys the scene after this double decker on the No 42 route from Swansea to Margam came to grief and toppled sideways on the A48 at Baglan, near the former Pine Tree filling station on a wet day in 1953.

SWT always took the safety of passengers and its crews very seriously. From 1930 it presented drivers and conductors with road safety certificates at an annual awards ceremony attended by the chief constable and civic dignitaries. Staff frequently received pep talks on such issues. One of these appeared in the staff newsletter, Ein Newyddion, in January 1955. Apparently, accidents were more likely to happen between 1pm and 3pm, around the lunch hour, while the peak period was the rush hour between 5pm and 6pm when 'schools, factories, offices and shops release a flood of people, all homeward bound on foot, on cycles and in cars, lorries and buses. This is the time more than any other demanding the highest standard of care and attention.'

The article warned: 'Beware of relaxation, inattention and impatience, nurtured perhaps by boredom and fatigue that can overcome the most careful employee when a shift is drawing to a close.'

Accidents were not limited to SWT's buses, there were several involving the Mumbles Train in the 1950s. The railway was brought to a standstill in April 1954 when a two-carriage train collided with a car that was crossing the line opposite Sketty Lane while in 1957 a van leaving Swansea Bay station goods yard crashed into an approaching train. In July 1959, two double-car trains collided on the single track near Blackpill station.

Rear end damage after a tipper truck came into contact with this Regent V at Ynysforgan.

In 1956 there was concern about the rising number of accidents involving passengers getting on and off buses, particularly at traffic lights. Most of SWT's double deckers had open platforms at the rear and there was little to stop people jumping on and off as

This Regent V went topless after trying to pass under low bridge in 1970.
Royston Morgan Collection

This AEC Regent III toppled over onto cottages at Tyr Halen, Baglan, while negotiating a sharp turn from Old Road, on a wet autumn day in 1958. A relief service vehicle, it was driven by a driver new to the route. It was not seriously damaged and continued in the fleet until 1965.

they liked. The company urged conductors to do everything possible to discourage passengers from alighting at points other than official stopping places.

By 1960 it was becoming less of a problem for SWT. New buses had entrance doors at the front that were controlled by the driver or conductor. The 20 Regent Vs the company took that year showed the research being undertaken by manufacturers and operators to meet increasing demands for safety, as well as comfort and economy. The new buses had entrance/exit doors that were three inches wider for speedier boarding and alighting. There was better rear visibility and a mirror was placed above the doors so the driver in his cab could see the staircase. The lower deck had a bell, the upper a buzzer so the driver knew where the conductor was and he could watch passengers getting on and off if necessary.

But in September 1956, accidents were a worry and SWT's general manager, Mr H Weedy, urged crews to take extra care to avoid accidents with the approach of winter. "My eyes have been attracted lately to an increasing number of scratched, dented and torn panels of buses, the result of someone not taking reasonable care," he said.

In May 1958 SWT's chief engineer, Phil Wickens, said accident damage was still causing concern and by July that year it was becoming a major issue. There were 100 accidents that month compared to 62 in July 1957 which Mr Weedy said was deplorable. "Accidents cost money and this matter is a serious reflection on our staff and it is quite useless issuing Safety First certificates and holding dinners while the present state continues," he stormed. It was no better the following year and now Mr Weedy upped the rhetoric.

There were no fewer than 400 accidents involving passengers on board, or getting on and off buses in 1958 and there were more accidents generally that year than in 1957, which cost SWT £20,000.

Mr Weedy warned: "Drastic action will have to be taken if the position doesn't improve." He was particularly angry about 22 collisions between buses and lamp-posts. "Lamp-posts don't walk across the road, so I think it can be assumed that in most cases it was our fault," he said. "I would say that 50 per cent of the time in our body shop is spent in dealing with accidents and even then we are unable to cope with them, as you will see if you look at the state of the fleet."

The lecture seemed to have had an effect. By 1962, when SWT's buses were running 14 million miles a year, the number of accidents recorded was just under 1,000 and only a third of them involved staff in any measure of blame while most were minor in

A vehicle on its side after coming to grief on the 82 route to Bonymaen, in the 1930s.

nature. Then in the summer of 1963 Swansea was declared 'The Safety Town of Great Britain' and received The Firestone Trophy, which was presented to the town or city with the highest road safety rating. SWT was Swansea's biggest road user and the company told its drivers they could "deservedly bask in the reflected glory of the honour bestowed on the town."

Of course, accidents inevitably continued to happen, SWT had 922 in 1966 and 887 the following year, but they don't seem to have been the major issue that they were for the company in the late 1950s. Even so, there were seven accidents involving damage to bus roofs between July 1969 and September 1970. No-one was injured, but repair costs to buses were high and drivers were urged to take extra care.

Low bridge accidents involving buses remained a worry and Alan Kreppel remembered there were four shortly

after he joined the company in 1982. "I was very concerned and we took immediate steps to improve driver training and tighten controls on vehicle allocation to ensure double deck buses didn't go on to routes with low bridges," he said. "Depots had a mix of double deckers and single deckers and we had to have mandatory single deck workings on certain routes to make sure double deckers didn't stray on to them."

Where did SWT's old buses go?

Where do buses go when their years of faithful service are over? Sadly, the majority end up on the scrapheap and there are very few SWT buses surviving today that date back to the classic days of the 1950s and 1960s.

Bus preservation did not really begin to take off until the mid-1960s, too late for many vehicles, such as those graceful Weymann bodied Regent IIIs that were familiar sights in the towns of South West Wales for so many years.

Some buses did have lives after they were withdrawn by SWT, not always as public service vehicles. In the earliest days the life of a bus was about eight years and

An unusual incident in Swansea where a double decker toppled sideways, early 1950s.

Minor accident damage in the course of repair at Ravenhill, 1956.

These two Leyland Nationals came to grief and collided on Penygraig Road, Townhill, early 1980s.
Roy Kneath

later, as vehicles became more robust, this rose to 12 years, although in reality some did as many as 16 or even 18 years service by which time they were usually well and truly ready for transport heaven.

In the 1920s many SWT buses were converted for use as lorries while in the thirties some became caravans, the magnificent six-wheel AEC Renowns of 1934, for example, were converted to caravans for Coney Beach amusement park in Porthcawl. Other withdrawn SWT vehicles were snapped up by smaller, independent bus operators who put them on less onerous duties.

Work underway re-bodying 1937 AEC Regents at Ravenhill bodyshop, 1950.

Breakdowns & branches

South Wales Transport always retained a small number of withdrawn buses for itself and converted them to towing vehicles or for use as trainers or tree-lopping. As can be seen from the images here these vehicles took on many shapes and forms and even donned the odd livery of their own too!

This retired Park Royal bodied AEC Regent V was pressed into use as a temporary office and store at Gorseinon depot in the late 1970s following the closure of Llanelli depot. It provided a base for around 40 bus drivers and conductors and their inspector as well as offering them canteen facilities.
Royston Morgan Collection

Some saw more exotic use as promotional vehicles abroad. One of the Regal IV coaches of 1953 was exported to Spain while the AEC Bridgemaster demonstrator SWT was supplied with in 1960 ended up in San Fransisco.

SWT retained a small number of withdrawn buses for itself and converted them to towing vehicles or for use as trainers or tree-lopping. A handful were retained as mobile offices, but the eventual destination of all these was the scrap yard.

One vehicle, a Park Royal bodied AEC Regent V was even used by the company as an office and canteen at its Gorseinon depot and served admirably in the role for a number of years.

But while the buses may no longer be a familiar sight on the roads of Swansea and the surrounding area the South Wales name lives on, albeit in a slightly different guise. South Wales Transport (Neath) Ltd, is a family owned, independent bus and coach hire company based in Neath. It is not part of any large bus group and operates a mixed fleet of modern vehicles.

The rear platform and stairs of a 1939 SWT Leyland double decker with Weymann bodywork as it looked outside the former Swansea General Hospital on March 30, 1982. The section, from 580 (CCY 975) was donated to the hospital in 1954 after the bus was withdrawn and used to assist with the rehabilitation of patients with mobility problems.
Stephen Miles

Peter's 45 years of safe driving is proud record

Driving for 45 years and not a single accident, that's the proud record of SWT and First Cymru driver, Peter Nedin. He joined United Welsh in 1969 at its Clarence Terrace depot in Swansea, moving to SWT when it took over UWS in 1971. Peter still remembers the first bus he ever drove, a UWS Lodekka, fleet number 980, which he took on the !6 route from Swansea to South Gower.

"Clarence Terrace depot also took over some of the workings of the N&C service between Swansea and Cardiff, the route was renumbered 252 and I drove that as well, initially with a conductor and then one-man working," said Peter. "At the time the services went from the old UWS bus station in Singleton Street, the drivers and conductors had a small rest room and paying-in office under the stairs, it was very small. The bus station was a nightmare as passengers could walk where they liked. The health and safety people would never allow it now."

When the Quadrant bus station replaced Singleton Street in 1978, Peter and the other former UWS drivers were transferred to Brunswick Street and he found himself behind the wheel of the much easier to drive Regent Vs. He drove every type of bus, from Leyland Nationals and Bristol VRTs to the Ford single deckers SWT took in the 1970s and 80s. His most vivid memory is of August 3, 1981, when the pleasure boat, the Prince Ivanhoe, sank off Horton, Gower.

"SWT provided six VRT double deckers to ferry the 450 passengers back to Swansea," recalled Peter. "I drove the shuttle bus from the beach to the other buses which were waiting on the main road. What surprised me was how calm everyone was."

Peter's long, accident free record earned him the Road Operators Safety Council's Safe Driving Diploma. He was still driving two-days a week for First Cymru in 2014, on the 36 service between Swansea and Morriston. He is an active volunteer at Swansea Bus Museum and can be seen at all its rallies and special running days.

Peter Nedin, at the wheel of a Bristol Lodekka in his early driving days.

Bus museum keeps the legend alive

It was a lucky SWT bus indeed that avoided the ultimate fate of the scrapyard and the biggest collection of those that did can be found at Swansea Bus Museum.

"Very few withdrawn SWT buses survive today and we are fortunate to have in our custody the main collection," said museum treasurer Mal Hier.

"The museum is proud to have what is believed to be the oldest surviving AEC Regent V, MCY 407, dating from 1955; a Park Royal bodied Bridgemaster of 1959, UCY 837, one of only four rear-entrance Bridgemasters known to survive; a Weymann Fanfare coach from 1956, NCY 626, one of only two of its type still existing; a 1963 Roe bodied single deck Regent V, specially designed to pass under low bridges — one of only eight of its type ever made and the sole survivor. The museum has another five Regent Vs from the 1960s, including Willowbrook bodied GWN 867E, the last of its type in SWT service.

"We also have examples of SWT's more recent types, the Leyland National — two MkIs and two MkIIs — and the Bristol VRT, four of the series 3 type, one of them delivered to SWT with a detachable roof," said Mal.

"Although they only date back to the 1970s and early 1980s, their number is declining fast and very few remain."

Looking resplendant on its way back from a rally at Kidderminster, in October 1993 is MCY 407 — fleet number 447 — the earliest AEC Regent V in the collection of SWT vehicles at Swansea Bus Museum. *Stephen Miles*

The museum also has three SWT mini buses from the 1980s and volunteers are working on the first Dennis Dart delivered to the company in 1994, L501 HCY, and one Dennis Dart P580 BTH of 1996, the last vehicle delivered to SWT in two-tone green livery and one of the company's first batch of low floor vehicles. It is the sheer scarcity of the vehicles that makes the work of the bus museum so important in perpetuating SWT's memory.

Museum chairman Alan West said: "Withdrawn buses that were previously not known about do pop up from time to time, although whether the museum can save them depends on the vehicle's cost and condition.

"We have 25 volunteers here of all ages and it's a labour of love," he said. "We'd like more people to become involved with our work and we welcome anyone who would like to help. We keep the memory of SWT alive through the restoration work we do here and with our open days and running days in which there is a lot of general interest."

The seeds of Swansea Bus Museum were sown in 2005 when three local bus enthusiasts formed the South Wales Transport Preservation Group. Their small collection of vehicles were assembled into a 9,000 sq ft building in the city's Hafod area.

As the South Wales Transport Preservation Trust, the group became a registered charity in August 2005 and increased the collection of vehicles until the point was reached where a larger site was required. In 2008, a building of 12,500 sq ft. was found at the former AWCO works site which was being redeveloped as SA1 Business Park. The year 2010 saw a turning point. A 50,000 sq ft building, became available just off Fabian Way on one of the main approaches into Swansea.

Pulling power

When things went wrong and SWT buses broke down the team above and their recovery vehicles were brought into action and sent to the rescue. Like the company's buses, the vehicles certainly changed down the years, but the tasks they performed remained similar from start to finish throughout its history.

Stephen Miles

A volunteer engaged in restoration work on the body of one of the growing number of South Wales Transport vehicles at Swansea Bus Museum, which houses a selection of vehicles operated by the company during its history.

Stephen Miles

One of a pair of retired former SWT AEC Regent IIIs of 1951 vintage, used by Port Talbot Borough Council's housing maintenance section as mobile workshops and canteens. This one, tagged Bus 76 by the council, is seen in 1970 after being retired for the second time.

During the same year, the group acquired the assets, comprising seven buses and many spare parts, of the 447 Group who had operated within two former munitions tunnels at Pembrey Country Park, Llanelli. Included in that collection was the former South Wales Transport AEC Regent V 447 (MCY 407) which, as the 10th Regent V built, is the oldest surviving example of this model, and a 1950 Daimler bus, the sole surviving vehicle of Swan Motor Services of Bishopston, who were absorbed into United Welsh in December 1950.

Looking to the future, those responsible for the museum have determined aspirations to purchase a suitable building in which the vehicles can safely be stored in and worked upon. A building of around 30,000 sq ft would also allow for the opportunity to better display its growing collection.

The group's collection continues to expand, now numbering around 50 vehicles, with several originating from operators elsewhere in the UK.

The museum's profile has continued to increase nationally, due to its dynamism and comprehensive collection of historically important buses and coaches.

Unfortunately, it is too late for many of SWT's classic buses, we only have photographs to remember them

This sorry line-up of retired and redundant vehicles was awaiting its final fate at the former Thomas Bros. depot in Acacia Avenue, Sandfields, Port Talbot, mid-1970s.

Colin Scott

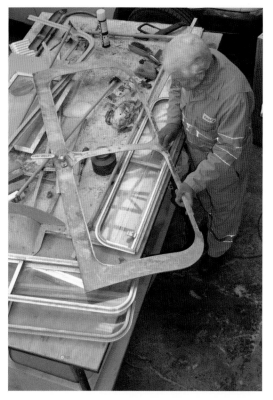

Work in progress on restoring AEC Bridgemaster 1203, one of a batch of five delivered new to South Wales Transport in October 1959. The vehicle is one of only four rear-entrance Bridgemasters known to survive in preservation and was scheduled for return to the road for the centenary of SWT's formation in 2014.

now. But a couple of years back a remarkable survivor was discovered. It is a 1923 AEC 403 type, CY 5981, a 54-seat open top double decker, which left SWT's fleet around 1932 and disappeared, only to be discovered more than 80 years later under a railway arch in London, still with its period adverts and gold leaf fleet name. It has been brought to the museum for eventual restoration. It gives hope that there may yet be one of those wonderful Weymann Regent III double deckers of the early 1950s still out there somewhere, perhaps standing unused and deteriorating in a barn or some other old building, which might be returned to Swansea as a wonderful example of South Wales Transport's glory days.

Some of the vehicles that can be seen at Swansea Bus Museum where a willing band of volunteers is helping to keep the memory of the city's buses alive.

Journey's end
— and a salute

This return journey, through 100 years with a fondly remembered bus company, has reached its final destination. But while this is the last page in the book, it can be considered the most important as it offers the opportunity to salute all those without whose help Return Ticket — the Story of South Wales Transport would not have been possible.

In many ways the book is the result of a team effort. Paramount among that is the passion of David Roberts at Bryngold Books for his determination and drive to turn our shared vision of a salute to South Wales Transport into reality. The result, published to coincide with the centenary of the formation of the company, is a timely and lasting tribute. David's design skills and assistance in bringing everything together proved invaluable. That said, he would also be the first to share my appreciation for the efforts of the rest of 'the team' — those who have contributed words and pictures to help rekindle memories of The Transport.

Particular thanks must go to Stephen Miles for allowing use of his unsurpassed images of many phases of the company's final 30 years and his enthusiastic guidance on technicalities. Royston Morgan is another whose encouragement, coupled with access to his picture collection, was a huge bonus, particularly in the early days. Alan Kreppel's insight into some interesting times in the life of the company also proved invaluable.

Others whose support was appreciated include: Michael Taylor for affording access to the Chris Taylor Archive; Swansea Reference Library, Swansea University, First Cymru, Colin Scott, David Beynon, Roy Kneath, Swansea Bus Museum, Peter Nedin, Ashley Lovering, Roy Wilcox, Cheryl Roberts and Neil Melbourne.

Generally I have acknowledged those whose photographic contributions have been included, but on occasions, particularly with collections, this has not always been possible. Hopefully anyone whose credit may have been omitted will be understanding and pleased to have played a part in helping to illustrate this history of a transport legend. Many photographs were sourced from the long running series of annual pictorial nostalgia books on Swansea, Neath and Port Talbot produced by Bryngold Books. We thank their donors too.

Last, but by no means least, we are indebted to Professor Garel Rhys, someone with more than simply a passing interest in South Wales Transport, for providing such an interesting and informed foreword.